10/97

COMING INTO BEING

Artifacts and Texts
in the Evolution of Consciousness

Also by William Irwin Thompson

The Imagination of an Insurrection: Dublin, Easter 1916

At the Edge of History

Passages about Earth

Evil and World Order

Darkness and Scattered Light

The Time Falling Bodies Take to Light

Blue Jade from the Morning Star (poetry)

Islands Out of Time (fiction)

Pacific Shift

Gaia, A Way of Knowing (Editor)

Selected Poems, 1959-1989

Imaginary Landscape: Making Worlds of Myth and Science

Gaia Two, Emergence, The New Science of Becoming (Editor)

Reimagination of the World (Coauthored with David Spangler)

The American Replacement of Nature

World Interpenetrating and Apart: Collected Poems, 1959-1995

COMING
INTO
BEING

Artifacts and Texts
in the Evolution of Consciousness

William Irwin Thompson

St. Martin's Press
New York

COMING INTO BEING:

ARTIFACTS AND TEXTS IN THE EVOLUTION OF CONSCIOUSNESS

Copyright © by William Irwin Thompson, 1996. All rights reserved. Printed in
the United States of America. No part of this book may be used or reproduced in
any manner whatsoever without written permission except in the case of brief
quotations embodied in critical articles or reviews. For information, address St.
Martin's Press, 175 Fifth Avenue, New York, N.Y. 10010.

ISBN 0-312-15834-3

Library of Congress Cataloging-in-Publication Data

Thompson, William Irwin.
    Coming into being : artifacts and texts in the evolution of
consciousness / by William Irwin Thompson.
       p. cm.
    ISBN 0-312-15834-3
    1. Consciousness—History. 2. Culture—Origin. 3. Evolution.
4. Mysticism. 5. Mythology. I. Title.
BF311.T484 1996
155.7—dc20   96-616
                                        CIP

Book design by Acme Art, Inc.

First edition: May 1996
10 9 8 7 6 5 4 3 2 1

Permissions

Grateful acknowledgment is hereby made to the following publishers for use of material under copyright:

Verses 1-5 of the Mandukya Upanishad, from *The Upanishads*, translated by Eknath Easwaran. Copyright © 1987, Nilgiri Press, Tomales, CA 94971. Reprinted by permission.

Quotations from *Lao-Tzu, Tao Te Ching* by Robert Henricks. Copyright © 1989 by Robert Henrick. Reprinted by permission of Ballantine Books, a Division of Random House, Inc.

"Poem 10" from *Tao Te Ching* by Stephen Mitchell. Translation copyright © 1988 by Stephen Mitchell. Reprinted by permission of HarperCollins Publishers, Inc.

"Ceaseless Flows that Beck" by Arthur Waley from *The Book of Songs*. Reprinted by permission of HarperCollins Publishers, Limited in the U. K.

I would also like to thank the laboratory of Dr. Lynn Margulis, Department of Botany, University of Massachusetts at Amherst for the drawings by Christie Lyons and Laszlo Meszoly used in chapter 2.; and Michelle Laporte for the drawings of the figurines and statuary pictured in chapter 5.

Contents

*For Laurance S. Rockefeller
in profound gratitude
for more than twenty-two years
of friendship and support
for the Lindisfarne Association*

Foreword

This book is addressed more to the imagination of culture than to the academic management of scholarly research. It would be impossible for any individual to have scholarly or scientific expertise in all the areas that I need to consider in examining the human evolution of consciousness; so, clearly, the only way to go from one end of history to the other, covering many different fields, is to shift from an academic to an aesthetic mode of cognition. Sometimes, I may know a little more about some subject than others, but my orientation is always that of a male heterosexual writer trying to understand his literary tradition at a time when neither one's traditional culture nor one's traditional sexual mode of being in a body is sufficient to understand the cultural transformation engulfing us on a global scale. My impulse was not to retreat defensively into a tight canon of masterpieces for a vanishing "Western civilization," but to try to expand imaginatively into a global canon of masterworks that expresses our new sense of identity in a planetary culture in which Enheduanna, Valmiki, and Lao Tzu speak to us as much as—and not in place of—Homer, Sappho, and Virgil.

As I encounter it, this new planetary culture is not simply a reaction to our new technologies—be they aerospace, atomic, genetic, or electronic— but an expression of a spiritual evolution that is actually pulling out these new technologies. From this perspective, I see the *Zeitgeist* as serving as midwife to the birth of a new humanity. The Indian philosopher and yogi Sri Aurobindo, in his evolutionary philosophy, calls this historical emergence "the Supramental Manifestation."[1] Well, when the Supramental manifests, the old mental realm is transformed or reconstructed into a work of art. This is what Marshall McLuhan meant when he miniaturized Hegel's dialectic into the aphorism of "The sloughed-off environment becomes a work of art in the new invisible environment."[2] When you have satellites in outer space you get environmental art on Earth. So, in much the same process of *aufheben*, when you have the Supramental manifestation, mentation becomes an artistic function and you get the new literary genre of *Wissenskunst*. First you get Jorge Luis Borges's parodies and satires of scholarship in his short works of metafiction, then you get Stanislaw Lem's witty reviews of nonexistent books in *A Perfect Vacuum,* and then lyrical poems of description and meditation turned into the scientific nonfiction essay, as in the case of Dr. Lewis Thomas.

Although my orientation to the texts is that of a writer and not a scholar, my way of living out loud with these ideas and visions is also that of a talker. In more than thirty years of public lecturing, I have probably given as many as a thousand public talks. And, for the most part, they were given as live talks without notes, not as texts read out loud before an academic audience. The first volume of *The Time Falling Bodies Take to Light* was originally presented as a series of talks at the opening of Lindisfarne-in-Manhattan in the fall of 1976. This book can be seen as a second volume addressed to the theme of literature and the evolution of consciousness, and, like the first effort, this work began as a series of talks given at the Lindisfarne Symposium at the Cathedral of St. John the Divine in New York from 1992 to 1994.[3] I began the literary reworking of the transcripts of these talks in Zurich, and this cold winter's activity deep in the heart of the self-controlled, Swiss-German-speaking world made me fondly aware of just how unusual and wonderful that expressive subculture of the Upper West Side of Manhattan is. My audience of forty to fifty individuals was a collection of writers, composers, artists, mystics, filmmakers, video artists, and, from time to time, a few graduate students from Columbia University, a few blocks away. I would talk for an hour, then we would take a twenty-minute break so that people in the group could get to know one another. After the break, we would have more than an hour of general discussion, and then we would walk over to the local Greek restaurant, the Symposium, to continue our discussion for another two hours over retsina or Greek beer. The group was an absolute delight, and when I tried to carry on with this series of talks on the theme of literature and the evolution of consciousness in San Francisco, where psychotherapy and psychedelic drugs have re-placed religion and art, I realized with a sharp sense of pain and loss just how extraordinarily rare that highly educated and literate culture of the Upper West Side is. It may well be the last habitat for the endangered species of the American intellectual.

Laurance Rockefeller was the patron who supported, over the years from 1974 to 1996, this and many other programs of Lindisfarne. As an expression of the great age of American philanthropy, Laurance Rocke-feller expressed a grand renaissance vision of culture and helped me to understand why New York had become the preeminent world city of the twentieth century. James Parks Morton, the dean of the Cathedral of St. John the Divine, was the cultural impresario who had turned a stone cold church into an electric cultural transformer and invited me in. Just as the medieval cathedral had served as the birthplace of European drama, its steps offering a space that was a crossing of sacred and secular, temple and marketplace, and providing just the right energy of opposites for the emergence of a new genre, so it was with Dean Morton's Cathedral of St. John the Divine, for the good Dean's juggling of ritual and irreverence provided me with just the right kind of cultural opening for a genre of mind-jazz—a genre that was not at home in the traditional church, the academic university, the New Age therapeutic workshop, or the practical political think tank.

With Laurance Rockefeller serving as my patron, and Dean James Parks Morton as my sponsor, I had, as the wife of Bath said, "the world in my time." To both of them I am deeply grateful for the experience of an era of New York that is passing away with our generation. I hope that they find this book to be an expression of the culture and time we all shared.

The collection of artists, writers, scientists, musicians, and composers who kept on coming over the years to hear me talk in New York were not interested in sitting still for an academic lecture about dates and sources; they understood at once that the relationship of the talk to the text was very much like the relationship of a familiar song to the unfamiliar explorations of a jazz soloist. As "My Funny Valentine" was to Miles Davis or Chet Baker, so the *Ramayana* or the *Rig Veda* was to me. Everyone there realized that I wasn't talking about the past; I was conjuring with ancient texts to imagine a metaindustrial horizon for our future.

COMING
INTO
BEING

Artifacts and Texts
in the Evolution of Consciousness

1

OUR CONTEMPORARY PREDICAMENT AND OUR PRESENT EVOLUTION OF CONSCIOUSNESS

The self-inflicted apocalypse of the Branch Davidian sect in Waco, Texas, the bombing of the federal building in Oklahoma City, and the nerve gas attack in the subways of Tokyo present us with images of a world transformed beyond belief by the process of belief itself. When we add to these perceptions, Mad Max images of technicals in trucks in Somalia, teenage gangs in South Central Los Angeles, tribal massacres in Rwanda, and religious genocide in Bosnia, we realize that the civility that is meant to be the foundation of civilization has become an antiquated thing of the past. Our new culture is not so much postmodern as postcivilized, and this cultural shift involves not a step forward but an electronic meltdown of civilization in which barbarism and savagery boil up to the surface once again. As James Joyce prophesied in *Finnegans Wake*: "Television kills telephony in brothers' broil."[1]

If we try to fall back within the mental walls of the city-state of the university, we find no defense of civilization there, for the lusty pioneers of thought there are busy undermining civilization and trying to find a way out into some smaller and more intimate form of ethnic or subcultural allegiance. For these academic post-Nietzschean and postmodern thinkers, civilization is simply a construct, a discourse of power projected onto an imaginal geography that was set up by an imperial elite for the aims of its own clubbish supracultural world. One can find no hope for "civilization" in reading Michel Foucault or Edward Said, and no security in retreating into the academic confines of the Blooms — Allan or Harold. Whether of the Left or Right, these reactive academic subcultures are like boutiques within a shopping mall: the different decorations only disguise the spiritual uniformity of the material.

As one turns from newspaper or book to watch the evening news, one feels as if the news were something like the Muzak one hears on boarding an airplane: it's there to lie about the frightening reality of our situation. Information has become our Second Nature, but in spite of our incredibly advanced electronic media, we can sense that television does not embody the truth, that it is a consensual delusion, a droning Muzak inside an electropop mediocrity. The citizen, informed or otherwise, no longer exists; there is only the pageantry of celebrities and the media's loyal subject.

Now perhaps we can appreciate the cults. Paranoia is one reaction to living in an informationally supersaturated solution in which the media never tell the truth and never really discuss the cultural options at stake. If NAFTA and GATT, the Gulf War, and the war in Bosnia are never to be discussed in such a way as to give "an informed citizen" the choices between different paths of cultural evolution, then one is compelled to imagine one's own pattern of connectiveness for the disparate matters never discussed by the media. Although the major arms sellers of the world are also the sitting members of the United Nations Security Council, they present invocations of peace and light that have nothing to do with the reality of their arms industries. France will sell arms to Iraq, Russia and China will sell arms to Iran, and the United States will sell arms to Israel, Turkey, and Saudi Arabia so that the world of business as we know it can continue. Free of the burden of reflecting on what we see, we are able to see what we believe in personal cosmologies that are epistemological caricatures of the unspoken reality.

The camera has been replaced by the video synthesizer; mimesis has been replaced by fabrication. Since CNN's reporting on the Gulf War turned the whole event into an infomercial for the U.S. arms industry, one that helped the United States sell billions of arms and make small beer of the lethal brews of its competitors, why should some not make up their own camcorder movies of world events? If Ted Turner's CNN is the rich white trash's network for the poor, why shouldn't the poor white trash come up with their own Aryan nation news with its reports that the United Nations is planning to invade northern Michigan and that the CIA blew up the federal building in Oklahoma City? If talk show hosts and radio commentators gain attention and become rich only to the degree that they are intellectually pornographic, why shouldn't the average subject of the mediocracy aspire to his or her own fabrications of cultural history: that the holocaust never happened, that NASA never went to the moon and that the moon landing was all done in a television studio, that the Rockefellers are planning to set off a thermonuclear war and shift their world headquarters from New York to Crestone, Colorado. Having lived in Canada, I have a personal paranoid conspiracy theory, which is that the real purpose of NAFTA was to use cheap Mexican labor to break down the social democracy of Canada so that real estate developers could get control of Canadian water supplies to develop dry but chic Santa Fe into the next L.A. The techniques used for hostile takeovers of corporations in the 1980s are now to be used for nation-states in the 1990s. Accordingly, the pieces of Canada are now worth more than the MacDonald/Laurier nineteenth-century railroad nation-state whole, so raid it, break it up, and sell off the pieces, and keep the water for Santa Fe and a spillover for a second Silicon Valley Star Wars development in Colorado Springs. Hey, what do you think President Bush and his kid were up to in that Silverado Savings and Loan scam anyway?

Marshall McLuhan died too soon. I'm glad that at least I had the chance to sit in on one of those Monday nights at the Coach House at St. Mike's College at the University of Toronto. We need Marshall now because this new world of the media certainly does prove his old adage that "every media extension of man is an amputation."[2] If we have cars we don't walk to the corner store anymore. If we have artificial intelligence extending the central nervous system into cyberspace networks, we all get dumber, and the best the World Wide Web can offer us is a color-degraded image of a postcard size Monet or a narrated tour through Elvis Presley's Graceland.

McLuhan's quips and aphorisms were not simply wisecracks about the media, they were expressions of a theory of the evolution of consciousness. At each stage in the cultural evolution of humanity, a new medium of communication comes forth, and that medium then effects a shift to a new form of polity. We begin with the origins of language in the African savanna, and we end up with the disintegration of literature on the Internet. For McLuhan, there were five evolutionary stages or quantum jumps:

1. Oral
2. Script
3. Alphabetic
4. Print
5. Electronic.

If we restrict ourselves to the evidence of the endocranial casts that show more highly developed language articulation centers for archaic Homo sapiens than for Homo erectus, then we can say that oral culture was roughly from 200,000 B.C.E. to 10,000 B.C.E., or basically the glacial epoch. Then the system of signs on the walls of caves such as Lascaux began to become a script. This script developed from the Old Europe of 6000 B.C.E.[3] to the Sumer of 3000 B.C.E. with the increase in the size of settlements, from Çatal Hüyük in Anatolia to Uruk in Mesopotamia. Priestcraft and writing reinforced one another to give us city-states that sometimes federated and at other times conglomerated to expand into empires. With the rise of middle-class capitalism, with its "Gutenberg galaxy" of printed books and printed money, these empires became replaced by industrial nation-states in a new global formation called the world economy.

1. Culture (200,000 to 10,000 B.C.E.)
2. Society (10,000 to 3500 B.C.E.)
3. Civilization (3500 B.C.E. to 1500 C.E.)
4. Industrialization (1500 to 1945)
5. Planetization (1945 to present)

Each of these forms generated a unique polity.

1. Band
2. Tribe
3. City-State to empire
4. Nation-State
5. Noetic Polity

And each of these generated its characteristic form of cohesive association.

1. Dominance
2. Authority

3. Justice
4. Representation
5. Participation

The band was based on dominance. In Bonobo chimpanzee bands, we see a system of female dominance; in other primate groupings we see forms of male dominance, often but not always in the form of a single dominant male. In the second level of the tribe, the characteristic form of cohesive association is one of authority in the figure of a matriarch or a patriarch. When tribes begin to cluster within more cosmopolitan cities—and this transformation is described in the Old Testament in the social developments from Saul to David to Solomon—literacy becomes critical, and a group of palace high priests works to create a canonical sacred text that can hold the warring tribes together within a literate and urban civilization. As an expanding trading class grows in numbers through world commerce, and as literacy becomes democratized through printed books so that it is no longer the prerogative of a class of high priests associated with a palace, then pamphleteering, philosophy, argument, and discourse become the political instruments for the shift from medievalism to modernism. The landed aristocratic warrior and the priest lose power to the scientist and artist who become the avatars of the new world of the mind. After the Depression and the Second World War, this nationalistic culture of the grand philosophies of the state went up in the smoke of the battle of the great ideologies: Fascism, Communism, and Democracy. With the rise of the new postwar forms of electronic communication, philosophy and reasoned discourse could no longer hold together in the supersaturated solution of the global media. Democracy was replaced by mediocracy; citizen was replaced by media subject. Vast electronic latifundia took control of sports, entertainment, politics, journalism, and education; in fact, all forms of culture simply became variants of the entertainment industry. In the hands of a few giants of industry—Ted Turner, John Malone, Michael Eisner, or Bill Gates— new mergers, such as those of CNN and Time Warner or Disney and the American Broadcasting Company, created new global streams of techno-swill in which the believing subject was fed like cattle in feedlots. Neither the scientist, the philosopher, nor the artist can counter this huge social transformation. The scientist is dependent on the funding systems of late capitalism for his or her costly research, and the solitary artist, in order to communicate with this electronic society, must become a celebrity—a personality managed by a publicist, a public figure constrained to turn ideas into sound bites and sell them to the public on talk shows—and this packaging automatically makes him or her an expression of the dominant culture. As McLuhan said, "The medium is the message."

But it is a paradox of complex dynamical systems that every shift to a higher level of organization also energizes the lower level to return in compressed and novel variations of the older form. In the hominid band, the system of association is based on dominance. Today, this form of association has returned as a nativistic reaction to the cultural entropy of the megalopolis and has become the teenage gang. In society, the form of human association is the tribe and is based on authority, matristic or patriarchal.[4] This form of association also has its nativistic return today in the form of a cult or sect headed by a guru or mediumistic prophet. Civilization represents an effort through written laws, literature, and philosophy to achieve a balance between the conflicting powers of military dominance and religious authority through the form of a system of justice for the city-state. Plato's *Republic* and Sophocles's *Antigone* are cultural documents that capture the conflict of this cultural shift from society to civilization. The nativistic return of literate civilization within our electronic postcivilization is expressed in the miniaturized city-state of the university surrounded by the cultural entropic zone of the ghetto. Think of Columbia and the University of Chicago. Within these fortresses of higher learning, academics such as Allan Bloom speak out as nativistic Platos. In national politics, the system of association is based on representation, but in the informational overload of the electronic media, this system breaks down and can no longer be based on pamphleteering, philosophical books, and reasoned discourse. It becomes a crossing of entertainment, televised sports, and celebrity management in cultures of the shared consensual delusion we know of as a presidential campaign. The citizen who is "morphing" into the loyal subject of the media demands participation in the pageantry. He or she too wishes to become a celebrity and go on television. People will do anything or say anything to go on afternoon talk shows. Good taste and decorum are expressions of the vanished civilization. Television becomes, in fact, a new kind of human sacrifice. Rather than an Aztec ripping out of the heart from a living body and a tumbling of the bloody corpse down the pyramid steps before an awe-inspired multitude, we have a form of evisceration in which the heart of the individual's life is ripped out. Nicole Simpson loses her life, but so, in another way, does Marcia Clark in trying to seek justice for her. Lonely stalkers haunt their favorite celebrities, and anyone who goes on television has need of a private security force. This system of celebrity association contributes to the generalized state of cultural entropy as each spectator of the pageantry of the media tries to become his or her own spectacle. Fast-fame takeouts litter the information superhighway strips of the new electronic America. The media acolytes seek to attack the White House to gain attention, verbally expose themselves sexually on afternoon talk shows, or form a congregation around their personal obsessions. Think of Lyndon Larouche or David Koresh.

The new departure expressed by the AUM movement in Japan or the Aryan nation and Right Wing militias in the United States is that the nativistic movement has now moved up from the level of the tribe nativistic-ally reacting to a cosmopolitan city-state—the biblical pattern of the patri-arch Abraham leaving Ur of the Chaldees—to that of an imaginary nation nativistically reacting to electronic planetization. Cult is trying to become culture. Terrorism is amateur government. Sometimes, as in the cases of the Mafia in Sicily, the Medellín cartel in Colombia, the IRA in Ireland or the PLO in Israel, terrorist organizations can successfully challenge the nation-state's claim to a monopoly on legitimized violence. As the nation-state melts down in the global economy of GATT and NAFTA, the cult is actually declaring war on the nation-state and declaring its own statehood. Ulster, Palestine, Quebec, Chiapas, and Bosnia are not the only versions of this shift; now we have AUM and Aryan nation. Not surprising, the United Nations is hated as a new Catholic Church with a new Inquisition fighting the forces of this new protestant reformation. As local wildcat oil developers once hated John D. Rockefeller and the world's first multinational corpo-ration, so now their rural populist grandchildren hate the elitist Trilateral Commission, the Council on Foreign Relations, the United Nations, the Rockefellers, and the New World Order. Just as the United Nations makes its move to become a global police force and to usurp from the nation-state the right to legitimacy in the application of military violence, so the subnatio-nal group in a disunited nation makes its move to form regional militias that demand to have weapons as good as those of the national soldiers they intend to fight.

Thus the representational government of the traditional literate nation-state undergoes an electronic meltdown in which archaic forms surface in new formations. Reasoned discourse in parliaments and sen-ates is replaced by celebrity management for the new masses of the electronic mediocracy. As politics and sports create the Superbowl of the permanent presidential campaign, civilized discourse is displaced to the academy, but as reason is now powerless to counter either the economy of late capitalism or electronic media's power to swamp literacy, "discourse" becomes an object of academic analysis, and violence becomes the virtual mode of discourse. As McLuhan said, "the sloughed-off environment becomes a work of art in the new and invisible environment." The new and invisible environment is the shift from natural selection through the vehicle of the human animal body to evolution by cultural intrusion. As sperm counts begin to drop from industrial pollution, reproduction shifts from the family to medibusiness. Just as agribusiness once appropriated the family farm, so now medibusiness is appropriating the family body. Small wonder that the members of the radical Right shout in the streets for "family values." In suburban culture, with rifles and family values, we have the ghost dance of the rednecks. In urban postmodern culture, however, the body is the sloughed-off environment, so it is being painted, sculpted, pierced, lifted, and tucked. This is what tattooing and body piercing are all about in our retribalized global village in which sex as a reproductive way of life has been replaced by sexuality as a lifestyle: straight, gay, bi, or kinky. Since sex is no longer the agency of natural selection, sexual words become the punctuation marks in the new discourse of violence in gangsta rap. "Fuck" and "bitch" are not tropes in the traditional sense of poetic discourse; they are cries in a sociobiological agon and part of the male display of conflict.

For the epoch of biological evolution, the human body had its own forms of signaling when to start and when to stop violent conflict. As Conrad Lorenz demonstrated in his classic study, *On Aggression,* when the wolf bares its throat to the fangs of its opponent wolf, it is a signal to the attacker that it has achieved dominance and can now back off. Similarly, the moose's great rack of antlers is not so much a weapon for stabbing and slicing, but a display meant only for those Twyla Tharp times "when push comes to shove." Inevitably, in a conflict between bulls, one of them retreats and violence and death are unnecessary. But because of what McLuhan termed "the media extensions of man," the evolutionary system of inhibition expressed in the body and its forms of body language is short-circuited. Consider the fact that if we bump into someone around the corner, we back off and courteously excuse ourselves. But if someone cuts in front of us on the highway in an automobile, we shout out our obscenities in a steel-encased rage. We lose the system of checks and balances expressed in the physical body with its biological systems for dealing with and containing aggression. Consider again how people on talk radio will become enraged over the day's news, or how people who live in the cyberspace of electronic bulletin boards will "go up in flames." There are no bodies in these modes of communication, so as we shift to "out-of-body forms of projection" into cyberspace networks, it is not surprising that the astral plane takes us over as we become possessed by those noetic parasites that older cultures liked to call demons. (I will have more to say about this when I discuss the demonology of the *Ramayana* in chapter 10.) Notice how much of the imagery of the electronic world of computer games and cyberpunk fiction is devoted to demons and dragons, voodoo, and heavy-metal comic book cartoons of beasts, monsters, and great-breasted Amazon warriors. William Gibson's cyberpunk fiction is not about electronics and data, for his data processing is far too grossly corporeal and materialistic for the true world of fiber optics and satellites. Gibson is a literary artist, the dharma-heir of Raymond Chandler and the 1930s, and his popular books are about the disintegration of the body in the new electronic world of the 1980s.

Now the wonderful thing about McLuhan was that he had not only a gift for capturing complex transformations in an aphoristic phrase, but also a general theory of the evolution of consciousness that he enlivened by pointing to fads and fetishes that only he could explain. When I was a young instructor at MIT in the 1960s, McLuhan spoke to a small faculty meeting. His manner of speech incensed the engineers. McLuhan said "The bomb is information." And the engineers went up in smoke. No doubt, because they had probably worked on building the cursed thing. But McLuhan was right. The bomb as information was the whole foundation for the Cold War world. McLuhan not only commented on fads and trends, he also made a prophesy on the future evolution of humanity. Ironically, good Catholic that he was, in his *Playboy* interview in the 1960s, McLuhan went back to Dante and prophesied a time when the broken fragments of a retribalized humanity would be gathered up into the mystical body of Christ.

What McLuhan recognized, but did not explicitly state, was that our new highly advanced electronic media if used by evolutionarily unadvanced mortals will lead to cultural annihilation. These new media that work with the speed of light require a new spiritual consciousness of Light. They are so fantastically efficient that they cannot work to the good unless we are good; they only can be safely used if we tell the truth and live in the Truth. If we try to check and control them for lesser purposes, such as power, gain, misrepresentation, and the accumulation of wealth for private property in cyberspace, then blockages in the flow will generate distortions, noise, and a generalized cultural entropy in which no human relationships are possible. We end up in caricatures of religion in the form of demonic states of possession or William Gibson's dystopian nightmares of corporate dis-incarnation. Only now, thanks to cyberspace, these states of possession are not simply psychic states, they have become virtual states that are not restricted to virtual reality. Nothing less than truth, goodness, and a Bud-dhist universal compassion are going to get us through this transition from industrialization to planetization. Our level of consciousness has now be-come the biggest obstruction to the continuity of human existence. We have made normalcy nonviable, so we have opted for an "up or out" scenario in cultural evolution. We either shift upward to a new culture of a higher spirituality to turn our electronic technologies into cathedrals of light, or we slide downward to darkness and entropy in a war of each against all.

What the news should be reporting is the way in which three cultural transformations are so interlocking that the feedback of each on all is creating a condition that is not easily responsive to government control. The first transformation is the disintegration of our atmosphere. Because of massive industrial production of new gases, we are experienc-ing an increase in global warming and a thinning of the ozone layer. The increase in heat affects the currents in the ocean and the virulence of storms, and so hundred-year floods become annual events. The increased frequency of tornadoes, hurricanes, floods, and earthquakes means that government emergency funds and insurance companies become ex-hausted right at the time that industrial deforestation is kicking up new airborne viruses and causing an increase in plagues that also draw down on medical insurance funds.

The invisible polity is really the atmosphere, and its globally chaotic system sweeps over all the boundaries of the territorial industrial nation-states. So American acid rain destroys the Canadian forests on which the New York Times depends for its paper stock. To the south, in Mexico, the exported television images of wealth stimulate a repatriation as armies of the poor try to take back the land the United States took with armies of wealth. Meanwhile, in offshore strongholds and Monaco penthouses, currency traders shift dollars back and forth into yen and deutsche marks, making money only from "the difference that makes a difference" in seconds of time. These traders are beyond the control of any president, and so the fluctua-tions of dollars and pesos are as unstable and chaotic as the weather. As the industrial marketplace expands to planetary dimensions, and as the time of a transaction contracts to microseconds, a singularity is created in which the global marketplace, like a black hole sucking up a star, devours entire nation-states. As the currents of the biosphere interact with the currencies of the world economy, we get not an international politique, but a Gaia Politique in which an enantiomorphic polity emerges. Enantiomorphic means the shape of opposites, so this polity is like the atmosphere that emerges in the opposing but coupled systems of the ocean and the continent. The result is a shifting, chaotic, complex dynamical system that we call the weather. Climate may be predictable, but the weather is not. The state of the weather is much more than a territorial state of land: as a chaotic system, it is more of an archetypal image of our contemporary condition than the fixed earth of farmland and pastoral landscape. No longer is it a question of identity through *Blut und Boden*, the blood and soil of the Fascist's patriotic state, it has become the archetypal image of light and air. Political states are now much more like clouds than clods of dirt, for we have so sped up time with our nano-second electronic technologies that nations can now come and go in decades rather than centuries. Psychotics and paranoids sense this destabilizing shift and see their chance to make a state of being out of their obsession, and so cult tries to become culture in organizations like the Aryan nation. Since the Bible is the book of choice for these political extremists, the Bible provides the imagery through which they can think of themselves as the new Hebrews who will be led out of another mighty Egypt into their own promised land.

The third transformation that is interlocking with the disintegration of the atmosphere and the disintegration of the territorial nation-state is the disintegration of the body, especially the immune system's ability to identify the body in the chaotic flux of blood and air. We live in an invisible ocean of electromagnetic and chemical noise. With industrial gases everywhere, television transmission towers, microwave ovens, electronic watches, and cellular phones, the old evolutionary body has become chunks of meat floating in a planetary Mulligan stew of radiation and noise. Allergies abound, autoimmune diseases proliferate, and plague viruses take red-eye rides on jumbo jets. Now, as these three systems of meltdown interact with one another, they have a bootstrapping effect that enables them to magnify their influence in a runaway or positive feedback fashion. No American president can simply go on television to give a speech to tell reality in no uncertain terms to stop and return to normal.

So now we can see why this shift from industrialization to planetization involves a meltdown and disintegration of the literate, civilized, middle-class culture of the past. In the shift from the territorial nation-state to the noetic polity, there is a breakdown of bourgeois society that results in a shift to a new variant of medievalism. The rich get richer, the poor get poorer. The citizen-soldier is gone, replaced by SWAT antiterrorist professionals. Noetic polities are not territorial; they are nonlocal. So the increase in omnipresent environments of noise indicates a shift from mental solitude and reflection to gnostic lattices of network connectiveness. Inevitably, in any transition to a new level of organization, there is loss. Indeed, the fertility crisis within the populace of the technological world may signal just such a shift to larger forms of organization. As the biologist John Maynard Smith has pointed out about the major transitions of evolution: "Entities that were capable of independent replication before the transition can only replicate as parts of a larger unit after it."[5] The disintegration of the body is, therefore, one signal that evolution is no longer taking place at the level of the single organism. Evolution is now multiorganismic just as once it was multicellular. Once the cell enclosed molecules, then organisms enclosed cells, and now something else is enclosing us in distributive lattices of light. Christian mystics would call it the mystical body of Christ, Buddhists would call it the jeweled net of Indra, and fundamentalists would call it Satanic possession. Clearly, some new kind of religious knowledge and discrimination is called for, one not easily gained in our materialistic, technologically focused society.

There is another genius who wrote on the evolution of consciousness who can be of use here to help us understand our contemporary predicament as a choice between evolution and dissolution: the German turned Swiss cultural historian Jean Gebser. A refugee from Franco's Spain and Hitler's Germany, Gebser was a brilliantly intuitive intellectual mystic with a profound understanding of poetry and art. Right in the middle of the rise of Fascism in the 1930s and the descent of Europe into the Second World War, he had an intellectual vision of the evolution of consciousness that anticipated and excelled the whole New Age and the new paradigm thinking of the 1970s. Gebser was a friend of Frederico García Lorca and Pablo Picasso, and his understanding of culture is based upon a deep feeling for specific works of poetry and art. But his high cultural European approach to the evolution of consciousness makes it difficult for Americans to appreciate his work. We have so replaced culture with psychology, psychotherapy, and simplistic workshops on how to fix the depressive flats of our lives that we prefer the compulsive mappings and textbook categorizations of Ken Wilber to the poetic insights of Jean Gebser. Wilber seeks to control the universe through mapping, and the dominant masculinist purpose of his abstract system is to shift power from the described to the describer. As an autodidact from the Midwest, Wilber wants to promote himself as "the Einstein of the consciousness movement" and so he is announcing a trilogy of thousand-page tomes that will explain everything once and for all.[6] This form of scholarship is really a mode of psychic inflation and self-magnification; it is a grand pyramid of systems of abstract thought, piled on other systems of abstract thought, with Wilber's kept for the top. Never does one come upon a feeling for the concrete, a new look at an individual poem, a painting, or a work of architecture. Gebser, in contrast to Wilber, is the genuine article, a grand European thinker with a grand vision, but one who comes upon his general insights through a loving attention for particulars: through an understanding of the role of adjectives in the poetry of Rilke, the resurgence of a prehistoric matriarchy in the surrealistic line drawings of García Lorca, the meaning of an ancient Chinese mask that has no mouth, or the social significance of the lack of perspective in the paintings of Picasso. It was a Sisyphean labor to get my San Francisco students to read Gebser, for they all preferred the undergraduate textbook generalizations of Wilber, but characteristically the members of my New York Lindisfarne Symposium loved Gebser's masterwork and felt that his *Ever-Present Origin*[7] was the kind of book that changed one's life. Precisely because Gebser's rich high European culture takes for granted not just a knowledge of poetry and painting but an instant recall of famous poems and canvases, New Yorkers, who live in a museum-rich culture, can recall the pictures and understand the argument. The "New Edge" Californians think that a color-degraded image of a Monet on CD-ROM or the World Wide Web is better than the real thing.

Gebser can help us to steer wide of the California substitution in which the integral is a theme park simulacrum of electronics and psychedelics. Gebser is not a Disney animatron of the thinker; he is the real thing, a true European philosopher of art and culture who prophesied in the 1940s the shift to the new chaos dynamical mathematical understanding of nature, the new appreciation of matristic values in a dissolving of patriarchy, and the new spirituality beyond reactionary religions and deficient magical cults. Amazingly, Gebser seemed to be able to avoid the mistakes of other prewar thinkers, from the flirtations with Fascism that captured Mircea Eliade, Martin Heidegger, and Paul De Man, to the facile Communism that captured Louis Althuser and Jean-Paul Sartre, or the nihilism that destroyed Michel Foucault. Spiritual without being occult, Gebser also managed to avoid the psychic inflation of the self-elected guru that caught George Gurdjieff, so Gebser's work on the evolution of consciousness is well worth the effort, and now that it is available in an English translation, I hope that at least enough people will read him so that *Ever-Present Origin* does not go out of print.

Gebser's narrative is one of structural transformations of conscious-ness, a *Bewußtwerdungs prozeß*. These turnings and transformations (in Ger-man, *Wandlung*) are fivefold, and interestingly, Gebser's model is isomorphic to McLuhan's.

McLuhan	Gebser
1. Oral	1. Archaic
2. Script	2. Magical
3. Alphabetic	3. Mythical
4. Print	4. Mental
5. Electronic	5. Integral

Gebser's five structural mutations of consciousness should not be read as static stages or levels in a linear progression; they are processual trans-formations. His Eurocentrism derives not from any imperial contempt for other cultures, but from the fact that he was a political refugee with severely limited funds trying to flesh out his intuitive insights with the books that were at hand as he worked in the center of Europe, in Bern. Like McLuhan, Gebser holds out a visionary possibility for a transformation of conscious-ness in which the degenerative returns to the magical and the deficient efforts to recover the mythical are overcome in the quantum leap to the integral. In trying to understand this new level of global consciousness, Gebser became interested in the Zen philosophy articulated by D. T. Suzuki and the integral yoga of the Indian evolutionary philosopher Sri Aurobindo.

Although Gebser did not elaborate the point, I noticed in reading his works that a dark age is characteristic of the transition from one structure of consciousness to another. Before agriculture, there was a loss of culture in the Mesolithic; gone was the high culture of Paleolithic Lascaux, but not yet come was the high culture of the Neolithic. So in the Eocene weather change, with its 300-foot rise of the seacoast level there was an Atlantean inundation that engulfed the old glacial world. Agricultural society stabilized itself from 9500 to 4500 B.C.E., and then came the Kurgan invasions and the destruction of the undefended agri-cultural villages of the great goddess. So before civilization, there was a second dark age transition. By 2500 B.C.E., civilization had stabilized itself in the new forms to be found along the Nile, Tigris and Euphrates, Indus, and Yangtze rivers. Then before Western civilization, there is the Aegean dark age of 1400 to 800 B.C.E., which expresses the shift from

Gebser's mythical to mental epoch. Before Western European civilization, there was the dark age of 476 to 800 C.E. And now, before the shift to the integral, we seem to be experiencing our own dark age in which our civilization is disintegrating. So if we line up Gebser's structural transformations of consciousness with dark ages, we get this:

1. Archaic	1. Mesolithic Dark Age, 9500 B.C.E.
2. Magical	2. Kurgan Invasions, 4500 B.C.E.
3. Mythical	3. Aegean Dark Age, 1400-800 B.C.E.
4. Mental	4. European Dark Age, 476-800 C.E.
5. Integral	5. Contemporary Dark Age

In the loss that is characteristic of a transition to novelty, the dark age seems to, paradoxically, open up a new possibility: the loss of the magical in the shift from sacrificial, matristic cultures to militaristic, patriarchal cultures, or the loss of the mythical in the shift to the mental in Greek philosophy, or now the loss of literate civilization in the shift to the electronic noetic polities of a decultured planetization. Naturally, this shift is opposed by traditional and reactionary forces, from Islamic jihads to Aryan nation attacks; but as enemies adopt the electronic technologies of their opponents in order to fight them, they are inevitably pulled into the culture they abhor. Televangelists like Reverend Jimmy Swaggert may hold the good book in one hand while they gesticulate against rock music with the other, but to the degree that they use television to promote themselves, they become isomorphic to rock stars and become just another sports star or celebrity.

In chaos dynamical theory in mathematics, it is the accumulation of noise that pulls a system from one attractor to another. So in our transition from industrialization to planetization, it is the accumulation of noise that is pulling civilization apart. In industrialization, the global marketplace was the phase-space of human culture that defined the value of all human transactions. The new phase-space, however, is not the marketplace but the catastrophe, for it is the catastrophe that brings us together in a condition that now defines all our human transactions. This evolutionary catastrophe bifurcation of "up or out" compels us to look on human culture with a new, deeper, and more compassionately spiritual level of understanding. Those who are oriented to the marketplace will resist this transformation of world view, so the accumulation of noise will have to be great indeed before they are pulled into the basin of a new attractor. Nevertheless, noise is the transition to the noetic polity; it destroys the solitude necessary for the philosophical reflection characteristic of the mental epoch. But before we can effect the transition to the integral to stabilize our condition in the angelic musical polities of the future we will have to learn how to make our way through the demonic states of possession of our present. My contribution to this effort is to offer—in the face of the disliterate,[8] electronic world of MTV and *Wired* magazine—this study of specific works of literature as expressing the true markers along the way of the evolution of human consciousness.

2

THE PAST
EVOLUTION OF
CONSCIOUSNESS:
FROM SPIROCHETE
TO SPINAL CHORD

When the artist Christo packages a subtropical island off the coast of Florida or the Bundestag in Berlin, he shifts our normal perception into a different cognitive domain. This displacement of natural and historical objects and their traditional scales of reference is descriptive of our new culturally displaced humanity. But since this process of displacement can become quite disorienting, one either has to trust the artist, in an act of faith that turns a Christo into Christus and makes him messianically more important than nature or traditional culture, or one seeks to avoid such megalomaniacal inflation by working in concert with others. What the culturally disorienting shift in scale of reference calls forth is friends who can help one climb above the field to see with the mind of a mountain or the eye of a Landsat camera. The friend who lifted me up to a new Gaian understanding of the planetary dynamics of microbial life was Lynn Margulis. Margulis is the Distinguished University Professor of Biology at the University of Massachusetts at Amherst; along with Jim Lovelock, she is the author of

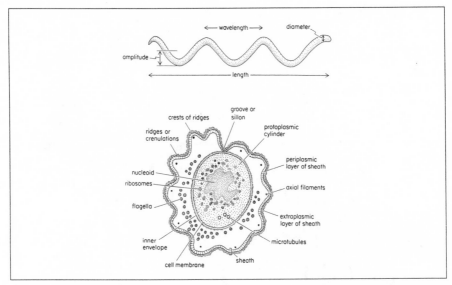

Figure 2.1 Amplitude, wavelength, and cross section of the spirochete. Drawing by Laszlo Meszoly; with permission of the laboratory of Dr. Lynn Margulis.

the Gaia theory of the evolution of life on Earth. She is renowned for her book *Symbiosis in Cell Evolution,*[1] and Freeman Dyson, in his book on the origins of life, calls her one of biology's immortals.[2]

So sensitized have I been by Margulis's work that I now can appreciate how bacteria have been treated like invisible serfs working in the fields while we humans dined in the manor house and talked about the evolution of consciousness as if it were only about the hominization of the primates and the emergence of the human brain. But brains are made up of neurons, and when Margulis looks at the long axons attached to neurons, or at mitotic spindles transporting genes in cellular division, or at spermatozoa attaching themselves to ova, she sees a variant of the biological architecture of the attachment of the spirochete to the larger cell of the protist. So let us begin our story of the evolution of consciousness with the spirochete — that simple helix-shaped bacterium that has neither tail nor head.

Margulis has a general theory of evolution in which these ancient bacteria are seen as fundamental building blocks of symbiotic evolution. Bacteria are cells without nuclei, or prokaryotes; the cells with nuclei, the eukaryotes, came later on down the line of evolution and were the product of an evolutionary symbiosis that Margulis has helped us to understand. The simple rods of the bacterial spirochete that pulse in a wavelike motion attach

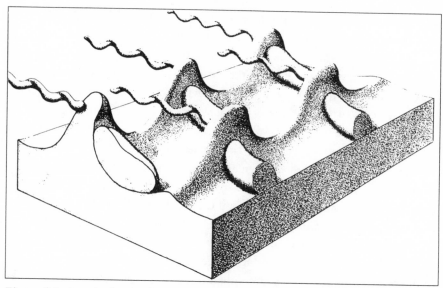

Figure 2.2: Attached spirochetes. Drawing by Christie Lyons; with permission of the laboratory of Dr. Lynn Margulis.

themselves to the surface of larger cells, as well as to the insides of larger cells with a nucleus to become flagellating engines of motion.

Margulis is a scientific visionary, and her theory is that this process of spirochete attachment and incorporation is a very general process that branched out in many directions, from the propellant for the protist to the fertilization of the ovum, and even to the development of the long axon attached to the neuron. Her theory is an imaginative vision of the architecture of life, and I was fascinated with it the very first time she described it to me. At that time, I was living in Bern, Switzerland, and she came to pay a visit to me on her way to a scientific conference in Basel. Appropriately for these studies of morphogenesis and life, she was staying in a hotel where Goethe once spent the night—down the street from where Einstein lived when he was working on his Special Theory of Relativity. Of course, I didn't understand Margulis's theory at first, and her quick moves from spirochetes to mitotic spindles to axons was confusing to me. But later when I saw her films of bacteria at the Lindisfarne Fellows meeting in Perugia, Italy, I got it.[3] I saw the rodlike bacteria go "boing!"—like a plucked guitar string—in the films that she showed, and then something went "boing!" in my own imagination as the legendary dying words of Pythagoras popped into my head: "Study the monochord." The image that flashed into my mind was the statue of

Pythagoras from the royal portal at the cathedral of Chartres, where we see Pythagoras hunched over in his study of the monochord.

Pythagoras studied the monochord to work out the system of ratios and proportions between the length of the string and change in pitch. The physical matter was a catgut string, but the dynamical properties were mathematical. Similarly, in Margulis's films of spirochetes and protists, one begins to see beautiful corkscrew spirals as all the spirochetes attached to the protist begin to synchronize their flagellations. These patterns are what now are called, in the new sciences of complexity, "emergent properties," or examples of "self-organization from noise." Each single spirochete beating against the spirochete next to it knocks about randomly until the incoherence begins to knock itself into patterns, to entrain synchronization, and then these emergent corkscrew spirals bring forth another emergent property of propelling the nutrients in the environment down along the surface of the protist toward its mouth. In the case of the protist *Mixotrycha paradoxa*—the protist that lives in the hindgut of the termite—this symbiotic arrangement is critical because the protist breaks down cellulose that is indigestible to the termite into an acetate that the termite can digest. So the spiraling corkscrew motion of the thousands of spirochetes attached to the surface of the protist is a beautiful example of patterns of self-organization from noise, and these patterns of spiraling motion are as mathematical as they are material. In the words of the title of Maria Muldaur's song: "It ain't the meat, it's the motion."

Margulis's synthetic theory shows how these spirochetes and other tiny bacterium that once swam at large were absorbed into the living architecture of larger cells. From the wild, unorganized, noisy behavior of bacteria, self-organization began to emerge, and the hitherto free-ranging bacterium became an organelle within a larger cell. Organelles are critters such as mitochondria and chloroplasts. Margulis did all this work in the late 1970s and 1980s, and although it was repeatedly ignored or rejected by her colleagues, it was prophetic of studies of self-organization that were to follow by other scientists such as Manfred Eigen, Francisco Varela, and Stuart Kauffman.

I first I saw Margulis's films of bacteria at a Lindisfarne Fellows gathering near Stimson Beach, California in 1981—one that I organized around the theme of the new biology[4]—and I was fascinated, but when I saw new footage in 1988 at the Perugia meeting, I became completely entranced. At the 1993 summer meeting of the Lindisfarne Fellows in Crestone, Colorado, our new fellow, Stuart Kauffman, from the Santa Fe Institute for the Study of Complexity, saw these same films and agreed with me that the material showed wonderful and important examples of self-organization from

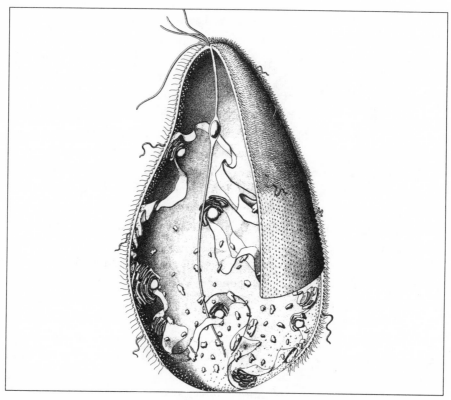

Figure 2.3: The protist with attached spirochetes. Drawing by Christie Lyons; with permission of the laboratory of Dr. Lynn Margulis.

noise. Stuart Kauffman's new book, *The Origins of Order*,[5] is a highly technical effort to study these principles at the molecular level that preceded these bacterial patterns and were, in fact, responsible for the origins of life.

Now what we see in the case of the spirochete is the most basic and fundamental form of life; it is simply a single rod without a head or a tail; it is a single rod without a nucleus or a nervous system. As the rod moves, it becomes a spring or a helical coil. The spirochete simply writhes about in its thick viscous aqueous medium in the hopes of opportunistically thrusting itself into a richer solution of nutrients. When it contracts it forms an undular form that looks like a plucked guitar string. It goes "boing!" and vibrates, moving randomly about in search of food. Thus we have the meat, the rod of the spirochete, and the motion, the wavelike pattern, and the waves it makes in its liquid medium by writhing in space.

So we begin our story of the evolution of consciousness with the earliest and most simple form of life we encounter. But notice that even at this primitive level, we begin to encounter a distinction. There are two ends to the rod of the spirochete. Let's say that food in the aqueous solution is richer in one direction, that the glucose gradient is richer, say, on its right side than on its left. So if one end encounters what it needs, it becomes still as it attends to "sucking" it in. The other end, which has not yet encountered a sufficiently strong presence of glucose, keeps writhing in repetitive spasms. So even at this most basic level, we have encountered a distinction and an emergent property of behavior, for when one end attends to the glucose gradient and the other end keeps on beating wildly, the emergent property is directional motion. The little critter becomes just like a spermatozoon in that one end becomes like a head—even though it has not yet evolved to the point that it is actually a head—and the other end becomes a flagellating tail. So we have the emergent property of directional motion along a glucose gradient.

Now please keep in mind that we got this emergent property without benefit of conscious purpose, conscious choice, a nervous system, or a mind. Just by "doing what comes naturally" in random and spasmodic movement the spirochetes begin to express self-organization from noise. This bilateral pulse that gives head and tail, eating and motion, is the very first distinction. The one becomes two, as one half of the spirochete functions in one way and the other half in another.

We know in the case of more complex nerve cells that certain chemicals act as inhibitors. So let's imagine that the presence of food—glucose, simple sugars—acts as an inhibitor. It inhibits motion or the spasmodic writhing at one tip of the spirochete. So we can say, from our point of view, but still putting the human words in quotation marks, that inhibited tip becomes still, attends to the difference in the glucose gradient, or "listens." The other end hasn't yet got the message, so it keeps beating wildly, and that, as evolution would have it, is just fine with the other end because that beating actually serves to push the other end in the direction of the food. It shoves it farther on down the glucose gradient. Now, remember, we don't even have the chemotaxis here of an amoeba sliding around in search of food. This spirochete form of activity is even more primitive than that, but, nevertheless, the spirochetes are exhibiting order out of noise, because if one ·half is still and the other half is beating like hell, then the spirochete is going to move in a direction. *So directional motion is the emergent property of this fundamental distinction between one end of the spirochete and the other.*

Contemporary science tends to be strongly biased toward chemical explanations for triggering or inhibiting behavior, so cellular biologists will talk about chemical inhibitors, but as I saw the rod go "boing!" in Margulis's film, my poetic imagination was triggered and I remembered the words of Pythagoras and began thinking in terms of wave amplitudes and ratios. Consequently, my own Irish intuition makes me suspect that the wave dynamics are as important to these patterns of self-organization from noise as chemical inhibitors or attractors are. I have a hunch that the stilling of one end of the spirochete is coming from the impact of a wave bouncing back onto the sensitive tip. When the spirochete goes "Boing!" it sends out a wave into the aqueous medium. Does this wave come back by bouncing against something else — which would be a fundamental, almost archetypal "encounter with the Other" — and does this bounce or echo cause the tip to become still and attend to "the Other"? Imagine the spirochete vibrating like a plucked guitar string, but there is nothing out there; it is alone. Then suddenly a wave comes back like a sonar wave in a submarine, and that echo means that "something is out there"; it means there might be food around. So the wave in coming back touches one end of the spirochete and inhibits that side. It becomes still and "listens." Whether this process comes from wave dynamics or molecular reaction along a chemical gradient or some interesting interaction of the two on the membrane of the bacterium is a good subject for research. However the spirochete behaves, whether it swims, tumbles, or flexes, the emergent property is the same: impelled directional motion along a chemical gradient.

Now, to understand what all this has to do with the evolution of consciousness, we need to appreciate how large and complex notions like "mind" or "consciousness" are built up out of simple reactions, such as the "attending" of the spirochete to a presence. It is helpful to come to an edge so that one can distinguish between what is mind and what is not. So in taking awareness down to this fundamental level of the form of the first distinction, this primitive reactivity between the nondifferentiated ends of the spirochete, we come to an appreciation of the nature of "form" itself. Buddha did the same thing when he tried to approach an understanding of mind and consciousness. He sat down under the tree and began to perform an archaeological excavation of consciousness in which he stripped layer after layer of mind until he came to the biological bedrock that came before human settlement. Only in Buddha's case, he did not use the word for "layer," but chose instead to use the word *skanda*, which means "heap" or "pile" or "aggregate." Buddha found that there were five of these aggregates, or *skandas*, as one moved downward from complex to fundamental, they were: forms, feelings, perceptions, dispositional attitudes, and consciousness.

At the 1993 Lindisfarne Fellows summer meeting in Crestone, Colorado—at which both Francisco Varela and Stuart Kauffman were present—
one of the biologists at the Crestone Mountain Zen Center, David
Greenway, noticed that the progression of the five *skandas* was actually an
evolutionary progression. In the individual consciousness, Buddha was
coming upon a principle of ontogeny recapitulating phylogeny. The five
skandas, thus, represent the pattern of the historical evolution of consciousness. In trying to uncover the roots of human suffering, Buddha went down
into the roots that held the organism to perceptions of its world. It was an
amazing achievement, a work of pure genius that is inspiring cognitive
scientists to this day.[6]

So, taking the suggestions of Varela and Greenway, I want to identify
this fundamental bilateral distinction of the spirochete as a *form*, as the first
skanda. The type of behavior in which one end of the spirochete is inhibited
as it "attends" to the glucose gradient or the dynamical echo of the wave
coming back to touch it, while the other end continues to flagellate, is our
archaeological bedrock. Beyond this point we are no longer dealing with
the organization of life; we have passed back across the evolutionary
threshold of life from cells to molecules. What we discover at this most
fundamental level of bacterial life is that random, noisy behavior begins to
express patterns of self-organization and emergent states appear that require no teleological direction or conscious purpose superimposed on the
material by some external, hypostatized force, some Bergsonian *elan vital*.
Here is a fundamental *form* of behavioral response that does not express
feelings, that does not express a condition of *perception*, or of an organized
central nervous system with *consciousness*. We are not up to the higher level
of the nematode when we are dealing with the case of the spirochete. And,
of course, we are nowhere near the primary consciousness of an animal or
the reflexive self-awareness of a human being. We are down at biological
bedrock, down at the level of the first *skanda*, of *form*. So we can say in the
words of G. Spencer Brown's Laws of Form: "We take as given the idea of
distinction and the idea of indication, and that we cannot make an indication
without drawing a distinction. We, take, therefore, the form of distinction
for the form."[7]

The distinction is precisely this distinguishing between 1 and 0,
between the inhibited state of one end of the spirochete and the motility of
the other.

As directional motion appears as an emergent property of this form of
behavior, the spirochete moves in its encounter of "the Other," the Other

seen as food. But if this Other is another sort of cell that has emerged in evolution, it may look upon the spirochete as Other to it, as food. Each tries to incorporate, or eat the other. But let's imagine out of millions of years and gigabillions of such encounters, that an unsuccessful encounter, one in which neither cell is able to digest or incorporate the other, results in a situation in which one end of the spirochete is stuck, while the other end keeps on wildly beating. One end of the spirochete "thinks" it is eating into the membrane of the other cell, and the other end of that cell, the membrane, "thinks" it is eating the head-end of the spirochete. You get a standoff, like the Cold War between the United States and the U.S.S.R., in which the structure of conflict became an emergent property, a relationship. In the case of the defense industries conglomerate, it was a form of planetization, a form of transnational technology that through the Cold War created Sputnik and the American space program, a new metanational cultural emergence. In the case of the attached spirochete, the emergent state is symbiotic evolution. The attached spirochetes beating wildly next to one another begin to bang up against one another, and in the entrainment of the wave dynamics of that behavior, this wildly flagellating behavior begins to knock them into order, into synchrony. And so in Margulis's gorgeous film we see this moment in which a dozen or so attached spirochetes begin to express synchronization of their motions. Personally, I think there is a Nobel Prize waiting for someone who can understand the relationship between the chemistry of this process and the physics of it—the feedback between the wave dynamical behavior and the chemistry of the inhibitors at the two membranes of the encountering cells. If we can understand this encounter at the surfaces of the two cells, spirochete and host, then we will begin to have a new understanding of the role of axons, neurons, and synapses in the growth and development of the nervous system, as well as new possibilities for the design of connectionist architectures for networks of artificial intelligence. Tim Kennedy, another Lindisfarne Fellow, is working on the morphogenesis of axon growth,[8] so perhaps he can be one of the ones to come up with something new and exciting here.

Tim Kennedy's approach is a biochemical one that studies the role proteins such as netrin play in guiding the growth of axons. Another and quite different approach is that of the physicist Roger Penrose and the anesthesiologist S. R. Hameroff, one concerned with a possible role for quantum effects in the microtubules within neurons.[9] So we need to take another look at figure 2.1 and notice the indicated presence of the microtubules and flagella. Part of the beauty and mystery of the universe comes from its nested quality in which the little becomes the large again as another vast domain is revealed to be within it. Within atoms are quarks, within proteins are amino acids, within spirochetes are microtubules. A form is, therefore — as G. Spencer Brown indicated — a form of a distinction. But the distinction is ours; it is a threshold we set out to stand on when we wish to observe nature. What we see is generated by that threshold. If we drive by the oil refineries on the New Jersey Turnpike, we will see "ugliness and pollution"; if we shift our threshold from the human to the molecular, perhaps that imaginary landscape will become one of entrancing beauty in which molecules dance in creative transformations of sound and light. Similarly, the spirochete within our blood that is giving us sphyllis is not at its threshold of activity within us to kill us off; it is not an agent of attack. So the form of a distinction or of a definition is always a kind of language performed within a linguistic domain. As the biologist Humberto Maturana has said "Everything is said by an observer."[10] If we make the microtubule rather than the spirochete our primary *form*, then the form of the distinction is isomorphic, for now the two states are not the flagellating and still halves of the spirochete, but the ring of dimers and the hollow they surround. The "tubulin dimers can exist in (at least) two different conformational states that can switch from one to the other."[11] The emergent property here is not directional motion, but the single quantum state that the quantum physicists are seeking to discover in these superconductors within our cells.

So whether our story begins with the dimers of the microtubules or the spirochete, the beginning of a narrative for the evolution of consciousness is the basic *form* of a distinction. As the dimers synchronize or entrain one another, an emergent property of coherence takes place. Similarly, when a dozen or so spirochetes begin to flagellate next to one another, they begin to entrain one another and begin to beat in synchrony. And so we get yet another example of self-organization from noise; we get another emergent behavior, for now the effect of this wave pattern of synchronization is that it stirs up the nutrients in the aqueous solution around the cells and helps to direct them toward the cells. So, the first emergent behavior is directional motion of the free-ranging and unattached spirochete, and the second emergent behavior is directional motion of the waves along the surface of the larger cell to which the spirochetes have become attached. As these cells become more successful in finding food in this manner, the Darwinian consequences are that they flourish. The wave synchronization phenomenon itself, as a successful strategy, also continues until we come to the point that we see in Margulis's films at which thousands of attached spirochetes are on the surface of a huge cell, a protist, and these thousands do not simply beat in synchrony, but in a wave pattern of formation that becomes a corkscrew spiral, and this spiral is a perfected form of directional motion that literally propels the food toward the mouth of the protist. Given a million years and a gigabillion occasions of random encounters between flagellating spirochete and larger cell, there is sufficient time and space for this pattern of corkscrew spirals to emerge on the surface of the larger protists, on which hundreds of thousands of attached spirochetes beat in synchrony. And just like slaves chained to their oars in a Roman galleon who pull in tune to the slave master's drum, the effect of synchronization is directional motion through the fluid medium.

The Roman slave ship has a slave master with a drum to enforce the rhythm of the synchrony, but in the case of the protist we don't need such an individual, for it is simply the collective effect of one spirochete entraining with the others that brings them into synchrony. But when we observe these patterns of self-organization from noise, we do need to ask ourselves, "What is the ontological status of *patterns*?" Are these "principles" Platonic ideas or mathematical laws? When I asked Stuart Kauffman this question at the 1993 Lindisfarne Fellows meeting, he looked at me with intensely concerned and honest eyes, and answered: "I don't know."

What we see in Margulis's footage is another beautiful example of Maria Muldaur's song, "It ain't the meat, it's the motion." There is the meat, the cells, and there is the motion of all these critters crammed together in the biological soup. When we imaginatively look down the logarithmic spiral of Penrose's rendering of a microtubule, or look down on the protists through Margulis's microscope, we see all these incredibly beautiful patterns that only emerge from their collectivity. We see waves and spirals and concentric rings of waves so that it looks as if we were seeing ions in an electron microscope instead of cells through an optical microscope. At the level of the meat, the protoplasmic flesh of the cells, we have Plato's "sensible realm," but at the mathematical level of the geometrical patterns of the Fibonacci series that we observe when these cells come together, we see Plato's "intelligible realm." The math, not simply the meat, brings us to the threshold of another domain, an ontological realm in which *principles* of self-organization from noise allow new modes of being to emerge. The coordinated cells begin to become overlaid by mathematical patterns, states of being whose form of "incarnation" is not meat but math. This is how I understand "angels"—beings of the intelligible realm whose incarnation is made out of music and math, out of structures of vibration that are constellated by molecules, or cells, or trees in a forest, or animals in the wild, or human minds in a collectivity one might wish to call, after the thinking of Rudolf Steiner, a *folk-soul*, if it is tribally embedded in place, or a *Zeitgeist*, if it is more distributively spread over a space but specific to a time.

At the twentieth anniversary meeting of the Lindisfarne Association at the Cathedral of St. John the Divine in New York, the chaos mathematician Ralph Abraham gave a performance of his mathematical quartet, *MIMI and the Illuminati*. At this performance, Abraham explained that his supercomputer was going to project on the two-story-high screen on the high altar fractal patterns that would enable us to see sections of time that were so small that they were unavailable to human experience. If their temporal structure were transposed from time into space, we could see them in the gorgeous patterns of light and sound that his quartet would perform for us. And that is how I understand "angels." Their temporal structure is not the same as ours, so, normally, we don't see them. We use various reorganizations of time and space to provide a threshold of emergence for them from their ontological domain into ours. A cathedral is one way to do this, because the building of a cathedral is a temporal project that requires the coordination of several generations or centuries. It is macrotime, whereas Ralph Abraham's quartet of supercomputer and three mathematicians performing musical externalizations of their temporal structures is microtime. My bringing artists, scientists, and contemplatives together in the Lindisfarne Fellowship is yet another way to express an emergent state of consciousness in which a noetic polity emerges from our collectivity; an ontological domain becomes accessible to us, or one can say, more mystically, that an angel or folk-soul begins to overlight the group. A great concert often has the quality of presence that makes the audience feel as if the space had suddenly become transformed or inhabited. In the cosmologies of Jewish Cabalism and Christian Neoplatonism, angels are organizations of mind that enter one ontological domain from another, when the conditions become sufficiently coherent to foster the emanation. The Buddhist way to describe this is to say that these conditions are emergent and not emanative. Varela is for emergence, Abraham is for emanation. So you can take your choice.

Most contemporary scientists will opt for emergent properties in place of mystical cosmologies of emanation, for emanation is simply too much for them to handle while still keeping a hold on the scientific materialism to which they are bound by acts of faith. So cognitive scientists like Patricia and Paul Churchland will assert in childlike faith that if you connect enough neurons you will get "mind" as an emergent property. For these connectionists, mind is not an expression of the mystical mumbo jumbo of an immortal soul, but rather an emergent property no different in kind from the emergence of those gorgeous corkscrew spirals of the synchronized spirochetes on the surface of the protist *Mixotrycha paradoxa*.

In the symbiotic evolution of the larger, eukaryotic cell, the larger critter discovers that the smaller one is more interesting and useful to it as architecture than as food. Presumably the larger cell first surrounded the smaller mitochondrion or chloroplast in the hopes of gobbling it up. But the little cell resisted digestion, held on to its own ancient DNA, and insisted on having its own life inside the larger cell. The larger cell began to "notice" in its frustration in breaking the smaller one down through digestion, that the little cell was producing food or oxygen, and that this process actually helped the larger cell in the process of respiration and metabolism that the hefty nucleus demanded. Therefore this new form of incorporation instead of digestion enabled the new eukaryotic cell to grow to gigantic size. The little cells continued on with their traditional life as organelles inside the new cell with a nucleus, and this process of producing oxygen, as in the case of the mitochondria, or photosynthesis, as in the case of the chloroplasts, worked out better for everybody. Israel and Palestine are trying to relearn this lesson. Since it took the eukaryotic cell almost a billion years of evolution, I guess it will take a little more time for Israel and Palestine — or Ulster and Eire — to get the picture, but it might help if politicians read Margulis's book *Symbiosis in Cell Evolution* and stopped to consider the political implications of biology for the politics of life.

By doing what comes naturally, the spirochete helped the slow and sluggish archaebacterium to get at its food; together, they became the protist. So this encounter with the Other in which both are intent on annihilating the other in a simple immediate unconscious response of "Eat it!" changes into "Hold it!" The spirochete only goes through half of the process of chewing its way into the membrane of the other, and then is forced to stop. And, of course, this is the great trick in life: knowing when to stop. So the inhibition is as important as the excitation. First, you excite something, and then right at the point of maximum excitation, you inhibit the function and it spins into its opposite in a new emergent state. That is also the process of Tantric yoga. First, you excite sexuality, and then at the point of maximum excitement, you inhibit it, and this precipitates the unconscious. It's like speeding up in a car, only to slam on the brakes so that everything behind you in the backseat is precipitated into the front: the unconscious is hurled into consciousness where it can be dealt with—not as a hidden infantile program that unconsciously controls adult behavior, but as an open compulsion that can be illuminated and eliminated. So this process of excitation followed by inhibition is an archetypal process that is constituent of multiple architectures of being.

Now, I do think that it is important to keep in mind as we consider all the beautiful waves and corkscrew spirals in Margulis's film that the wave dynamics are as important as the chemistry, that if one wants to write only a materialistic description of behavior, it is not enough to talk about GABA inhibitors and neurotransmitters, or whatever. One really has to talk about the mathematics of wave dynamics, the phase-portrait of the geometry of behavior, and the novel states of emergence in which self-organization begins to appear out of the abundance of noise. In terms of the language of the new science of chaos dynamics, one would say that it is the buildup of noise that pulls a system from one attractor to another. So out of the noisy confusion of entrapped spirochetes beating next to one another and knocking up against one another, wave synchronization begins to appear, and this new emergent property enables enhanced directional motion and food ingestion to take place.

At a later time in evolution, the attached spirochetes become a permanent possession of the larger cells, the protists. But the evolutionary lesson of archaebacterial symbiosis has been well learned, as one domain of life becomes nested within another like Russian dolls. The spirochete is nested in such a way to become the protist. The mitochondrion is nested inside the eukaryotic cell. The protist *Mixotrycha paradoxa* is nested inside the hindgut of the termite. By itself, the termite cannot digest the wood that it eats, but thanks to the protist *Mixotrycha paradoxa* that lives inside it, it can. Now this protist is not an organ of the termite; it is a completely different organism that has taken up its residence inside the termite, much in the same way that the termite is inside the log. So we have a nested universe: the spirochete is in the protist, the protist is in the termite, the termite is in the log, the log is in the forest, the rain forest is in Gaia, and Gaia is inside the solar system, and on and on it goes, and where it stops, nobody knows.

Now, if we are going to throw around terms such as "the evolution of consciousness," then we have to have some sense of what we mean by evolution. The importance of Stuart Kauffman's work, and the reason I wanted to have him join our intellectual chamber music ensemble of Lovelock, Margulis, Abraham, Varela, and Kennedy, is that he provides a good way of understanding that evolution is not simply a matter of sexual competition and dominance through time of the reproductively successful, but a play (*lila* in Sanskrit), a game of life, in which "principles of organization" provide the playing field and rules through which the competing reproducers are struggling to win time for themselves and their progeny. In order to understand why and how life evolved in the prebiotic soup, we have to have a vision of molecular complexity as a relationship between noise and patternings of order. Sociobiologists keep using the metaphoric language of late capitalism to talk about male reproducers investing in their progeny, but this new thinking of Kauffman and Margulis is really postcapitalist and postsocialist and is more appropriate for the emerging polity of the millennium. In his talk at the Lindisfarne meeting, Kauffman used the wonderful metaphor that "order is available for free in the universe." I suspect that when we understand what that truly means, our vision of economics will change dramatically.

The first step toward such a new understanding would be to begin to ask the sorts of questions that reveal our prejudices and blind spots. The first question, obviously, would then need to be: Just what do we mean when we say "principles of self-organization"? Clearly, these principles are not the meat but the motion; they are not the material stuff of the molecules and cells, but the mathematical and vibratory properties revealed in all the beautiful patterns we see in Margulis's films. Is a principle of organization like a Platonic idea, or is it like a scientific law? This is a question that Kauffman is interested in, but that he cannot yet answer. The question is fascinating because it takes us right back to Pythagoras, hunched over the monochord, studying the relationship between the math and the meat, the proportional system and the catgut string. Change the length or tension of the string or shift the position of the frets, and the vibratory music changes. So the proportional system is not explained in just a discussion of the meat. And in the same way, the behavior of the spirochete is not explained in a simple discussion of the glucose gradient. When the spirochetes go "boing!" together, banging up against one another, then the wave dynamics and the vibratory medium begin to affect the patterns of their synchronization. The geometry of the phase-portrait of their wave synchronization is an emergent property.

But just what is "emergence"? It is not simply the appearance of a new piece of stuff, but the appearance of a new level of organization. Into the prebiotic soup of molecules comes this new patterning we call life. Whether we are talking about the origins of life, or the origins of language in the hominization of the primates, we are talking about a big mystery. All of these new ideas and new questions bring us to the edge of knowledge and a horizon in which perception and imagination, like earth and sky, meet.

When one looks at Margulis's films, one sees this horizon expressed not as earth and sky, but as cells and geometrical patterns, as meat and math. This cellular imagery gives us a new biological way of coming at the old Platonic distinction between the intelligible realm and the sensible realm. The wet stuff is basically the meat, and that is the sensible realm. The geometrical patterns, the math, the dry stuff, are the intelligible realm. Another form of cellular architecture that expresses this relationship, one that is very related to music, is that of the hair cells in our inner ear that enable us to hear and listen to music. The undilupodium's[12] major protein is tubulin; the hair cell's major protein is actin. The proteins are similar, but not the same; they are homologous, not identical. The hair cells in the inner ear stick out in the air like the tails of spirochetes attached to a protist, only the hair cell is attached to a neuron. When a vibration comes in as a wave in the air, the hair cell tingles in response, but the part of it that is embedded, that is attached to the neuron, transforms that wave dynamical function into an electrical impulse that moves into the neuron, and then on down the line across synapses into our brain to be heard as music. As these hair cells stand in rows in the inner ear, they are not in straight lines, but in curved ones that create, once again, another world of organization through pattern, through curve and spiral. As the sound wave comes in, the physical wave property, the mechanical, is translated into an electrical impulse. So one part of this hair cell is sticking out and looking exactly like an attached spirochete on a protist, but in this case it is not vibrating in an aqueous or liquid solution, but in a gaseous solution of air. As it vibrates in air and moves back and forth, it becomes excited or stimulated, and this transmits to the other part that is embedded within the neuronal cell; but through that loss of motility, through embeddedness, something new is gained in the form of information. The mechanical is transformed into the electrical as an impulse of *difference*, the ions of sodium that build up on either side of the surface of neurons at a synapse. Then the synapse flashes and the pure information of difference moves through one neuron after another.

So what we have here is something very basic to the whole architecture of life, from spirochete attachment and synchrony to hair cells attached to neurons, and synaptic activity analogous to synchrony. Even before we get up to the level of consciousness, we encounter fascinating relationships between meat and motion, matter and music, that are basic to the nature of mind. This architectural structure is also the form of the spermatozoon attaching itself to the ovum in fertilization. It is the basic story of how we all got here, how we all came to be. We have this spunky, dynamic, little spirochete moving around, doing its own thing, and then we have this slow, colossal, sluggish protist, *Mixotrycha paradoxa*. Or we have the gigantic human egg, the Great Mother, and the tiny, flagellating spermatozoon, trying to get in, wildly beating, and yelling: "Hey, Mommy, look at me! Mommy, look at me!" The gigantic ovum rotates very slowly among the thousands of tiny sperm that are trying to win her favors and be allowed in to penetrate her membrane and perish into her interior life. How does the ovum decide which sperm has the genes she wants? Is there a vibration within her chromosomes that vibrates in resonance with the chromosomes within the head of one sperm more than another? In this dance of mating, is it, once again, the music, the motion, the vibration that determines which one among many the Great Mother is going to choose?

When a pattern shows up in several different instances, a popular song, a story, a myth, a statue, a protist, an ovum, a neuron, then we feel that something truly basic is going on, so we call the story typical or archetypal. This pattern of the vanishing, dynamical male, the spermatozoon, and the enormous, enduring Great Mother, the ovum, the basin of attraction, is one we are going to encounter again and again in this analysis of literature and the evolution of consciousness: from the paleolithic goddess of Laussel to the Sumerian goddess Inanna to Homer's Penelope and Joyce's Molly Bloom and Anna Livia Plurabelle. The dynamical and dying male moves through space and has his story, whether he is Gilgamesh or Odysseus. Penelope, surrounded by all the rioting suitors trying to beat their way into her bed, waits for the One, and while she waits, she weaves and unweaves. Molly stays in bed while Leopold Bloom wanders around Dublin. These narratives are not simply stories, but forms of cultural storage that tell more than they know. So by bringing all these stories together, I am not simply writing on the history of literature, I too am telling more than I know. With myth and science, I am constructing a metamyth, a metascience that is a new kind of genre—oral and written—that is a performance of the very reality it seeks to describe.

In courtship and conception, the Great Mother decides. The choice is hers. She decides "this one." And then that one breaks through and in vanishing into her immensity, he perishes—like a dying star in orgasmic supernova exploding into space, giving off its genetic inheritance in the form of the radioactive materials that fertilize the dust clouds of evolving solar systems. The heavy metals that we have here in the interior of our Earth are proof of that ancient supernova event. In diploid conception, the female must throw away half of her own genes in order to make a genetic dialogue possible. Persephone is taken from Demeter, and the maternal steady-state condition of ancient existence is lost. But out of her descent into the underworld, Persephone will generate the new periodicity of seasonal time. So each partner has to lose in order to move up to the next level of order. Once again, this is something that Israel and Palestine are trying to figure out.

So as you lose one particular level of definition, you open yourself to emergence, to *novelty,* for now, out of the basic act of the incarnation of life, a new story is possible. A new generation that is not like the old one comes into being. So here again we are getting principles of self-organization from noise. Noise, then, is not a menace to order, but a rich background of random associations that provide open potentialities for novelty. Rigid crystallization locks a system into one form in which change is not possible; it can only repeat itself ad infinitum, ad nauseam. The mother-daughter pair will clone themselves forever in an eternal steadystate, the feminist utopia of changeless Amazonia. But the appearance of the deadly and dying male disrupts all that through the introduction of loss and noise. A chaotic system in which noise draws a system from one basin of attraction to another is, however, a more complex system in which evolution and novel emergent states become possible.

In the case of the spirochete, we encounter the most basic distinction of dividing the one into two by halving it. This registration of a fundamental distinction gives us a form, the *form* of the first *skanda* in Buddhism. Now let's imagine that we have a situation of sensitivity, not simply that of one end of the spirochete that is stilled while the other end is flagellating, but that of a bacterium that in following its glucose gradient has developed a sensitivity to the pH scale of acid to base, as well as light to dark. The action of sunlight can be imagined to break down or enhance the presence of certain chemical rich solutions that the bacterium finds favorable, or unfavorable. Or it could be that the photosynthesizing bacteria, such as cyanobacteria, feed on light and excrete material that is a nutrient for other bacteria that will therefore prefer to stay in the light to find these nutrients. In one of Margulis's films, we actually do see a long, spiraling spirochete that moves back and forth in a circle of light, and when it comes to the edge of darkness, it reverses its spiral to move back in the opposite direction to remain in light.

The important point to notice at this level is that there are now *two* channels of information coming in, and not simply the one distinction of the more basic *form*. Let's further imagine that the condition of light plus a pH base means food, or the action of "Eat!" and that the opposite condition of dark plus acid means danger, the danger of being eaten or having your cellular membrane dissolve. This situation means "Be eaten!" The creature must flee into safety. This existential situation is the fundamental one of eat or be eaten, fight or flight. But notice, now, that when we have two incoming channels of information and cross them we get something new. The emergent property here is one of *meaning*, and not simply reactivity. The condition of safety in which one can eat is an interpretive domain and not simply a reaction without meaning. In their landmark work *Autopoiesis and Cognition: The Realization of the Living*,[13] the biologists Humberto Maturana and Francisco Varela put forth the radical notion that cognition had to be taken down to the level of the cell. I would propose that the great divide comes in the move from the rodlike spirochete to more differentiated bacteria such as cyanobacteria, which react to light through photosynthesis. With the short spirochete, you have a simple fundamental *form*, but with lengthier spirochetes and other bacteria that react to chemicals and respond to light, there is a move up to the second Buddhist *skanda* of *feeling*. What feeling is, is precisely this crossing of two channels of incoming information, acid and base, glucose-rich and glucose-poor, light and dark. When a line moves from one dimension to two, geometrical figures emerge as a novel condition, and when cells pass from one dimension to two here, they shift from mere chemical reactivity that requires no feelings, no interpretation, and certainly no mind, to an existential condition of interpretation: safety or danger; eat or be eaten. At this level, we have not yet encountered perceptions, and certainly not a mind. We have no differentiated organization of a nervous system, but, nevertheless, we are dealing with feeling, so I would agree with Maturana and Varela's landmark work of over twenty years ago.

Now, I want to make it clear that this is a technical definition, that feeling is to be defined as the cross-referencing of two channels of information that generate the moiré pattern of the interpretive domain of safety or danger. In moving from Buddha's first *skanda* of *form* to the second *skanda* of *feeling*, we have moved up the evolutionary ladder of life from the spirochete to the cyanobacteria, to what used to be called blue-green algae, but are now called cyanobacteria. These more differentiated single cells have platelets within them that are aligned in rows. They respond to light and excrete oxygen, and their presence on Earth served to shift our planet from a methane atmosphere to the beautiful blue sky we now have, or used to have before cars came along to eat oxygen and excrete ozone and hydrocarbons.

Let's take hold of the next rung on the ladder of life. Let's imagine that these two channels do not come in with their information at the same time. Let's imagine that the sense of reaction to light is fast, but that the sense of reaction to the pH scale of acid-base is a little slower but more lingering. It lingers, and this afterimage or echo creates a delay-space that then has to be cross-referenced with the reactivity to light to give the interpretive domain of safety or danger.

Now let's complicate the conditions slightly to have a glucose gradient, a pH scale, and reactivity to light, all with slightly different time-processing in the milliseconds. For example, reactivity to light may be instantaneous, but detection of the glucose gradient or the Ph scale may take a few milliseconds more to register. To generate an interpretive domain of feeling "now," one has to stabilize the delay-space so that the echoes or afterimages overlap to generate the moiré pattern of the interpretive domain. One has to have a metalevel in which one develops a feeling for the *forms* and the *feelings*. If one cross-references three channels in this way, the delay-space between the times of the different channels becomes an extensive field of reference. This cross-referencing of channels in a delay-space is *perception*. Perception is Buddha's third *skanda*: forms, feelings, perceptions.

When we come up the evolutionary ladder of life from feelings to perceptions, we encounter the dynamical world of time. A perception is a judgment of time, for an animal doesn't want to confuse the dangers of past and present; it wants to perceive what is going on *now*. The very nature of the extensive field of the delay-space that emerges when channels process information at different rates is about nothing if it is not about time. Neuroscientists who have measured our human sense of "now" report that it is an extensive field that ranges between one-fifth and one-quarter of a second. A longer duration belongs to the next moment, the next sense of "now," and a shorter duration is too fast to be available to consciousness. It becomes what Gregory Bateson used to call "a process rather than a product of consciousness." These rapid processes support the functions that enable us to have a field of awareness, but they are not accessible to consciousness itself.

With the emergence of this sharp phenomenology of time, we have crossed the Great Divide, or what Christians might like to call the Fall. On one side of the Great Divide, we have an undivided world in which beings are saturated with Being. Eternal Atman rests in eternal Brahman. But once we slice up the world into distinct perceptions, into distinct rates of time, we take an ontological step that separates the unique being from the universal Being. Of course, from another perspective, this process of temporal differentiation is ambiguous, for the emergence of the extensive field of the delay-space that orchestrates the afterimages and echoes of impulses is taking one giant step toward individuation and the emergence not of life — which we have had for billions of years — but of living beings: of nematodes and not simply spirochetes and cyanobacteria.

In the work of processing time, of cross-referencing channels of information that come in at different rates, of stabilizing the delay-space so that the afterimages don't dissolve before they can be accessed for perception, a pathway of activity comes about that we can call a nervous system. The more all these channels of information from forms, feelings, and perceptions are cross-referenced, the more the extensive field of the delay-space becomes stabilized. The delay-space endures not simply as a perceptual afterimage or echo, but as a virtual engine of perception that begins to evolve into an organization of perceptions, a system with a natural history of its past processing and judgments. In other words, it moves from after-image or echo to identity. With this meta-level of cross-referencing of perceptions, of perceiving perceptions, we take the step from perceptions to patterns of association, habits of connections, histories of patterned connecting determined by the neuronal synchrony that orchestrates the network that is brought forth in response to this excitation. This neuronal synchrony that has been reported on by Wolf Singer, Rodolfo Llinas, and others is within a range of oscillation of twenty to forty hertz (Hz),[14] and so its behavior is within a range of time that is a "now." But this neuronal synchrony that orchestrates neurons into a network in an experience of "now" is a learned and selected pathway with a history. It is what Gerald Edelman calls "neural Darwinism"[15] — a group selection patterning of response that becomes reinforced and develops structures through repeated performances. Kittens raised in the dark from birth do not, and can never, develop certain neural structures that normal kittens do. "Wolf children" raised by animals in the wild without human language cannot develop linguistic ability after they are discovered by humans and brought back into human society. These patternings of associated responses through a network of what the Enlightenment philosopher David Hume liked to call "customary conjunctions" take us from the third *skanda,* of Perceptions, to the fourth *skanda,* of dispositional attitudes.

As the habits of associated perceptions persist through time, as they become a customary response to activity, they are themselves perceived, and this metalevel of perceiving perceptions and associating perceptions gives us the new emergent state of the fifth *skanda,* of consciousness. Francisco Varela likes to distinguish between primary consciousness—the consciousness of the animal—and the reflexive consciousness that generates an awareness of selfhood, a state that we most probably share with chimpanzees. When this consciousness becomes thus reflective on itself, we have the emergent condition of the ego or the self. But, notice that this condition of alienation of time from eternity, of beings from Being, is even more basic than the human ego. Before there was Adam there was "war in heaven."

And so we can see now that the five *skandas* of Buddhism present a developmental model of the evolution of consciousness: from the *form* of the spirochete to the *feeling* of the cyanobacterium to the *perception* of the nematode to the *dispositional attitudes* of the slug to the primary *consciousness* of the animal and the reflective self-consciousness of the human.

If we look back at this evolutionary process of emergent states in the movement from forms, feelings, perceptions, and dispositional attitudes to consciousness, we should be able to construct a dynamical model or phase-portrait for the geometry of behavior. We could construct a five-dimensional model for consciousness with each channel of information coming in defined as a dimension or axis. We then could define consciousness as "the state-space of the perceptual system." "State-space" is a technical term that I have learned from Ralph Abraham; it is a mathematical concept used in the new sciences of complexity and chaos dynamics.

Now here I need to give a caveat to those New Age folks and mystics who like to talk about the consciousness of stones and crystals or, after the evolutionary theories of Sri Aurobindo, wish to speak about the universal consciousness of matter. That language is fine as long as you don't travel outside New Age circles, but it will get you into trouble if you try speaking to cognitive scientists. Since Lindisfarne is an "association" of artists, scientists, and contemplatives, our fellowship depends on using a lingua franca that permits communication. When you go to Paris you speak French or suffer the consequences. When you go into the domain of cognitive science in universities or scientific institutes, you cannot use the language of the yogic ashram. In this context, consciousness means awareness of awareness, and it is in this context, when I am talking to Stuart Kauffman or academic philosophers such as Dan Dennett, that I define consciousness as "the dynamical state-space of the perceptual system."

Let each sense channel be defined as a dimension, create a mathematical description for each of these five senses, and then orchestrate all of these senses together and you get the state-space of the perceptual system. The extensive field of the delay-space that orchestrates all these channels of perception is what I want to call consciousness. This extensive field is like a standing wave in a river; it is there, but from another point of view it is not really there in the same way that the water is there, or that the banks of the river are there. This extensive field is the ego; the Christians will say that it is there and that it is precisely the dynamic that is doing all the work, but the Buddhists will say that it is not really there, that it's simply an impermanent patterning in the way the water reacts to the turbulence of encountering the resistance of rocks and riverbanks. But if this standing or slowly moving wave is another example of principles of self-organization from noise, then the ontological status of "principles" can lead us to asking all sorts of Platonic questions. And this brings us "by a commodius vicus of recirculation back" to the old Hindu-Buddhist debate about the ontology of *atman*, the reality of the self.

The Buddhist emphasis is on the impermanence of this standing wave of the ego in the riverine flux of time. For the Buddhists, our suffering and our pain come about precisely because our automatic reaching out to stabilize the extensive field of the delay-space of all the "nows" of our different sense-channels has created a sense of attachment and fixation, a crystallization of identity. We have become captured by our own perceptions and our unique excellence, *areté*, has become our tragic flaw, *hamartia*. Picture a woman seated in a chair watching a soap opera, but a woman so sensitive and imaginative that she identifies with the character and projects into her situation and forgets she is in the chair and becomes that character to suffer its agony. This, you will recognize, is another version of the trope of the "two birds in the tree" of the *Rig Veda* and the *Upanishads*. For the Buddhists it is this grasping in our perceptions that creates the *duksha*, or suffering.

The Christian tradition argues that the self is not a pathological aberration emerging from grasping, reification, or misplaced concreteness, but that the ego is actually the emergent domain of the extensive field of the delay-space, and that the higher self or soul is the mathematical domain of the principles that determine self-organization from noise. "It ain't the meat, it's the motion." The ego is this temporal field of all the "nows" held in synchrony by a natural history of processing, a sense of a past that is constitutive of identity. If an ego is an emergent state that arises in the stabilization of the "nows" in the delay-space, then it is not necessarily a pathological phenomenon of "grasping," but rather a part of the architecture of life. It is the relationship between the mathematical domain, "the principles" and the meat domain of the flesh, the neurons and the network in synchrony at forty Hz.

If one has an inappropriate vision in the imagination, one generates an inappropriate "phase-portrait for the geometry of behavior" of the self. Our culture, lacking a vision of a multidimensional model of consciousness, simply oscillates back and forth between an excessively reified materialism and a compensatorily hysterical nihilism. This Nietzschean nihilism, in all its deconstructionist variants, has pretty much taken over the way literature is studied in the universities, and it also rules the cognitive science of Marvin Minsky, Dan Dennett, and Patricia and Paul Churchland, in which the self is looked upon as a superstition that arose from a naive folk psychology that existed before the age of enlightenment brought about by computers and artificial intelligence. This materialist/nihilist mind-set controls the universities. Although there is no authorial intentionality in deconstructionism, and although there is no single author or Cartesian theater of the self for "the multiple drafts" of Dennett's philosophical deconstructionism, I choose—in the words of Berkeley, who said, "We Irish think otherwise"—to think otherwise. I choose to focus on precisely what the metaphors bring forth when we use words like "principles" and "self" in this contemporary language that speaks about "principles of self-organization from noise." In this emanation versus emergence debate, the Buddhists don't want to have emanation from some other mathematical, platonic domain, for they fear that it reifies an eternal soul or *atman* outside the very relationships of *withness* that bring forth an identity in time. So the Buddhists opt for emergence and claim through their great classical philosopher Nagarjuna that if the soul or self were outside and transcendent then it could have no relations with anything. But the Hindu and the Christian traditions of the higher self or eternal soul see the self as having a different modality of time. There is a vanishing mode of perceptions, but there is the other bird in the tree, the bird that only witnesses the bird that actually tastes the fruit. Once again, it is the condition of the intelligible and sensible realms. The Buddhist tradition that Francisco Varela and my son Evan Thompson articulate in their book *The Embodied Mind* holds that when one looks for a self, it is not really there. In their language, there are selfless minds in worlds without ground.[16] But this doctrinal contentment with selflessness eliminates the opportunity to understand precisely the dynamic in which a self does emerge in "*self*-organization."

At the Lindisfarne Fellows conference in the summer of 1993, Evan Thompson said that he is no longer satisfied with this formulation, so in the books to come one can expect to see a generational divergence between Francisco Varela and Evan Thompson, just as there was, before, a generational divergence between Humberto Maturana and Francisco Varela.

There are many reasons not to be satisfied with this first extension of Buddhism into cognitive science, for now Kevin Kelly, the editor of the hip Silicon Valley psychedelic review *Wired*, is proclaiming that there is no self in the brain or anywhere; there are only "swarm mentalities." This strikes me as something of a projective self-description of the collectivity of *Wired*, *Mondo 2000*, and Howard Rheingold's *Whole Earth Review*; but the difficulty with this sort of trendy boutique Buddhism is that it serves the corporate electronic state only too well, for it eliminates the politics of the European Enlightenment in which our practice of individual civil liberties are based. The Western esoteric tradition in which I am situated would see the ego as an emergent phenomenon that is coming from precisely this interface between the music and the meat, so it has more of an angelic, emanationalist quality to its descriptions of the self that emerges in self-organization from noise.

Literature gives us a wonderful way of coming at this problem of the multidimensional nature of the self, and this is one of the reasons why I have constructed this narrative not simply with philosophical works but with the major literary texts of history. If you want to think about perception, time, and the nature of identity, then it is not enough simply to read Edelman's *Remembered Present* or Dennett's *Consciousness Explained*;[17] to be a good cognitive scientist you also have to read Proust. From my point of view, what we have been talking about with the idea of the delay-space is really what Proust's famous scene with the madeleine is all about.

Let's consider this scene for a moment. Proust sees the madeleine, and nothing happens, but then he smells and tastes the moist madeleine drenched with tisane, and the whole complex of lost memories of Combray springs into his consciousness. The tea-drenched madeleine served by his mother makes him recall another time when the same small cake was served to him by his aunt. Recall how in the book Proust is an entirely feminine-obsessed man. He waits at the top of the stairs for his mother to come to kiss him and put him to bed, or he waits in the park in the Champs-Elysées for Gilberte to appear. The primary act of birth imprints us with the sensuous numinosity of the female body through which we first become startled by light into consciousness. In that intimate facial relationship with the female body in birth, we encounter our first smell, taste, touch, and sight. The formation of consciousness becomes imprinted by this carnality, and so the act of writing is not a shift into abstraction but an archaeological excavation of conscious- ness—a *recherche du temps perdu*—to recover this primary connection to the feminine, Goethe's *ewige Weibliche*. Proust waits for his mother to kiss him good night so that he can sink into the reverie that is like the dreaming reverie in the womb from which he awoke into bright consciousness when his mother's other lips kissed him into birth. His consciousness is literally embedded in the senses—"Longtemps, je me suis couché de bonne heure"— trying to recover the past, and the perception that triggers the recovery of the past is an extensive field of the relationship between two different times, the time of the tea and madeleine with the mother and the time of the tea and madeleine with the aunt. Now notice that this experience of recovering lost time is not triggered by the mere sight of the madeleine. It is the synesthesia of taste and smell that is affective. In fact, most of the powerful epiphanies of consciousness in Proust come from the archaic, connecting power of smell and not the abstract and distancing power of sight: "La vue de la petite madeleine ne m'avait rien rappelé avant que je n'y eusse gouté."[18] The recovery of the vision of his past and Combray required the much more evolutionarily primitive sense of smell, a sense that depends on the olfactory bulb, which is located so close to the limbic ring, underneath the higher rational mind of the cerebral cortex. The recovery of past time required smell and taste. But what triggers this experience of smell and taste is this tea-saturated madeleine. The madeleine is named after the Madeleine, Mary Magdalen, the sacred prostitute and consort to the Messiah. This doubling of prostitute and priestess gives us the energy of two in one. The plump and richly greasy cake is encased in the pleats and folds of a nun: "les formes—et celle aussi du petit coquillage de patisserie, si grassement sensuel sous son plissage sévere et dévot."[19] Remember that in ancient times the bakery was situated next to the temple of the sacred prostitutes, for baking was a performance of one of the ancient mysteries of the goddess *Ceres*. To honor the goddess as the source, the place of origin, the loaf was incised with a line to make it appear like the labia majora of the sacred vulva. So this madeleine of Proust, with its fold and pleats and its shell-like shape is not just any ordinary cake; it is impressed with the magic of time and the power of the feminine that is contained in its name. The shell, whether because of its labial shape, or because of its interior pink color, has traditionally been a symbol of the female genitalia. "Elle envoya chercher un de ces gateux curts et dodus appelés Petites Madeleines qui semblent avoir été moulés dan la valve rainurées de une coquille de Sant-Jacques."[20]

So what Proust is presenting to us, in his most delicate, sophisticated, polite, courtly, and ever so French manner, is a form of symbolic substitution for the female body. What is being presented in the birth of memory is the unconscious compulsion to recover the numinosity of the birth of mind itself. What triggers the numinous experience of the recovery of lost consciousness is precisely this reconstitution of the delay space between one channel of sense perception and another. Proust sees the madeleine, but nothing happens until he smells the tisane and tastes the cake. With richly suggestive words such as *dodu, grassement sensuel,* and *plissage,* Proust is talking about the female vulva, about birth, about the birth of consciousness. So what is going on in Proust's reconstruction of lost time is not simply an effete, fin de siecle nostalgia for la belle époque, but a profound work of research into the nature of perception, memory, and consciousness. In the evolution of consciousness, smell and taste are archaic senses that take us back to the mysteries of hominization, to the shift from estrus to menses in the new pheromonal environment that surrounds the birth of the human species itself—the evolutionary reorchestration of the sensorium in the shift from olfaction in the leaf-darkened forest of the primates to sight in the open and sun-drenched savanna of the hominids.[21] Very often in Proust's narrative, the epiphanic moment is an evolutionary reversal in which the cortical dominance of sight is overpowered by a limbic explosion of smell. For yogis as well as artists, a mystical experience of the *siddhis* (special powers of grace that can appear during heightened moments of consciousness) can reorchestrate the sensorium so that one smells a person's aura and does not simply see it. Rilke too, in lines from his "First Duino Elegy," contrasts the consciousness of angels, animals, and humans, and says that the animals are aware that we humans don't feel at home in our interpreted world. In yoga and ecstatic states of mystical experiences, or in normal human experiences of intense sexual trance, we drop down out of our abstract, interpreted, perspectival world and come into a more basic, primordial, non-perspectival world, where senses resonate with one another and intimately participate in an intensely emotional consciousness.

In Proust's excavation of consciousness, experience is an extensive field between two modes of perception, sight and smell, and two times, the time of the madeleine with the mother and the time of the madeleine with the aunt. These two different times set up a horizon between them, like the linkage of the rising full moon and the setting sun, and trigger the recovery of consciousness of Combray. But what Proust is really playing on is the theme of the recovery of the emergence of mind, the origins of consciousness, the birth of the self, the embeddedness of his consciousness in the feminine. The stabilized extensive field of the delay-space between different channels of sense perception is, therefore, literally, the *matrix* of identity, of the ego. And so you can see why it is appropriate for me to begin my narrative about the course of literature and the evolution of consciousness with Proust.

3

SCIENCE AND THE CONSTRUCTION OF MYTHIC NARRATIVES ABOUT HUMAN ORIGINS

A narrative about human origins is not a historical record of sequentially identified "facts." The origins of humanity are at a horizon so remote from our present, and the fossil remains so fragmentary, that the construction of these remains into a theory and then into a narrative requires an exercise of the imagination, a form of storytelling that is isomorphic to mythmaking simply because it is a form of mythmaking. Mythic thinking, scientific or religious, is a form of macrothinking that seeks to present answers to the big questions of "Who are we?", "Where do we come from?", and "Where are we going?" Any answers to these questions, Marxist, mystic, or sociobiological, are performances of imagination and mythopoeic thought.

The domain of specialized, technical thinking is the more common realm of socially constructed facts.[1] Even sorcerers require socially constructed facts to ply their trade; they need to know the facts of the case and the symptoms of their patients to know what procedures to undertake or recommend. Factual thinking is microthinking, and it takes for granted quite a lot, and that lot is generally the common lot of the humanity of the moment, be they chemists or alchemists. But whenever we look closely at the act of perception, the perception becomes figured against a horizon, and things begin to become mythopoeic as we find that there is a constructivist dynamic that involves the imagination in the temporality of the act of perception.

An act of perception of the experience of what we would call a moment of "now" is by the neuroscientist's measurements no more than about a fifth to a quarter of a second in duration. Anything that doesn't come within that periodicity falls outside of it and becomes either an unconscious process that supports or generates the conscious product of neural activity or an event that is sequentially deferred to the next instant, the next instance of "now" in the moment just after the preceding. But a slice of temporality finer than a quarter of second is not an event of consciousness. So the whole notion by which we constitute one "now" succeeding another becomes very granular. Whenever we come to a horizon at which we really extend our perception in an all-encompassing way, we approach the limits of the perceivable in time and space, and the imagination is triggered to coordinate the sensorium, with taste helping out smell — as we saw in the case of Proust's madeleine — or sight helping out sound. Unregistered submoments too fine to make it into a normal "now" whisper "unheard melodies" that make us intuit or have hunches about what we cannot perceive directly. All the sensory signals that are coming in at different times are not always related in the extensive field of the delay-space — in the state-space of the perceptual system that I have suggested can serve as one definition of consciousness — but linger or haunt the edges as marginal events. This kind of edge activity of the temporal delay-space is its own kind of interior horizon of consciousness. Projection can serve to make some of these ghostly haunters of edges accessible to consciousness, or we can become conscious of them through the subtle process we call intuition. In our perceptual world, we live in a four-dimensional world of time and space, but our complete being is configured in topologies that are multidimensional and not so easily collapsed into height, length, breadth, and duration. When we become sensitive to these multidimensional domains, as poets and mystics do, then the horizonal space gets reconfigured in a non-Euclidean topology as the simplicity of the ego attends to the complexity of the spirit. The ego experiences the daimon — as Socrates describes it in *The Apology*.[2] Or Rilke passes beyond the conventionality of his sight-interpreted world to the All of the archaic acoustical space in which the Angel of the "Duino Elegies" emerges.

There is also a more common, extroverted, and American way to shift from ego to daimon that can occur when we are driving a car in the vast landscape of the Arizona desert. As we are driving the car and the monotony of the hours and vast distances takes us over, there is a reversal of figure and ground, much in the manner of a Zen *seshin*, and we realize that for stretches of time we are no longer situated consciously in our ego, our personality, but as we drive the car, we shift out into the hyperspace of the daimon in which it is driving the vehicle of the ego itself. Our situatedness in time and space in a body with a name and an identity becomes complex as we suddenly are taken up by a consciousness whose experience of time and space is much vaster than the ego with its linear limits of the birth and death of a thing conventionally called by a name.

Part of what we take for granted in the perception of the world is really learned and culturally shaped. If children see auras, but their parents do not, they learn not to attend to that part of the ultraviolet spectrum and shift to the range that is defined as normal by those around them. Marshall McLuhan was fond of the story about the first time movies were shown in a village in Africa. The people did not know how to read the imagery, and when somebody walked off screen to the left, they would get up to look behind the screen to see where that person went. They hadn't been trained to see movies as an imaginatively created continuity. "Cut to the chase" is something we have come to expect in the movies, but it is not necessarily the grammar of happenings. Perception is an imaginatively learned act, so when my twenty-month-old son looked down at his spoon, lying face down on the dinner table, and said "Night, spoon!", I was delighted to have my first confirmation of my earlier reading of Jean Piaget on the language and thought of the child.

We can get a sense of what movies must have looked like for the African villagers when we walk down the street and see someone's television flickering through the living-room window. The discontinuity of the light and images becomes apparent; for the passerby outside on the street, the images on the screen no longer represent a narrative sequence of events. From this vantage point, one can see the incredible sequence of disturbing interruptions that is television and see, perhaps, for the first time that McLuhan was right when he said that "the medium is the message." Television destroys solitude, reflection, peace, and tranquility; it is a system of subconsciously irritating interruptions, and the content of the program is irrelevant to what is occurring in the perceptual activity of consciousness. Actually, content is destroyed by the medium, and noise itself becomes the new environment. So children raised on television grow up to prefer noisy discos to pubs where one can hear and have a conversation; they grow up to prefer excitement, interruptions, and violence rather than reading, reflection, solitude, and meditation. It isn't just the crime on television that generates violence; it is the complete environment of instantly shifting imagery, disrupted sequences, and heightened levels of noise that amount to a violent assault on the nervous system that also contributes to our new social medium of noise and violence.

So if one were to stand outside the culture of the American living room, looking through the window at life in the suburbs, or if one were to hang out in another space looking down on oneself listening to the Navaho language on the car radio as one drove through Monument Valley toward Tuba City, then the conventional reality that others take for granted because they are so deeply situated within it would become apparent. Once one is involved in those conventional living-room spaces, one loses one's edge, one's horizon. One is totally into conventional reality and imaginatively connects the dots to supply the continuity that obscures just how disconnected, fragmentary, and granular the "world" really is. Mystics are people who attend to the graininess, who look at the gaps between the sequences of "nows," who intuit around the three-dimensional constructs of their fellows the angels of multidimensionality who are everywhere about them.

So imagination is always present in the act of perception, but there are moments when we begin to be much more sensitive to the role it plays. In my first book, which was on the Easter Rising in Dublin in 1916, I was concerned with the kind of imaginative horizon in which a cultural vision of the distant past was created by Irish historians and scholars and popularizers of history who brought forth a new understanding of the ancient mythic landscape of Ireland. The project of the historians who recovered the archaic was to construct a mythic horizon, an event horizon, in which imagination transformed perception in a new definition of identity. In looking at Standish O'Grady's influence on Padraic Pearse, I was looking at how the horizon of myth affected the temporality of history through the imaginative seizures of revolution. As a child, Padraic Pearse read Standish O'Grady's mythic vision of Irish history, got down on his knees, and vowed to free Ireland from the English. Padraic Pearse was no longer half-English, he became completely Irish.

At this edge, history ends and myth begins. Another event horizon is the mythic edge of human history in the hominization of the primates, in the myth of origins of human identity itself. Science is the storytelling of our time. By telling stories about our origins, from the big bang to the African savanna, science is really telling stories about what and where we are and where we want to go from here. If we construct any narrative about who we are, where we came from, and where we are going, we will have basically constructed a myth, a myth about human identity. But to appreciate the mythic quality of the construction of narratives—to see just how a fact requires a theory much in the same way that a flame requires an atmosphere—it is useful to look at differing narratives of human identity.

Every society has a cognitive structure of permissible knowledge that is managed by an elite and forbidden knowledge that is distributed in black or shadow markets by cognitive outlaws, heretics, revolutionaries, or just plain crazies. Since no market system is ever hermetically sealed off from the society in which it operates, there is always some traffic between the two systems, a gray market, that is tacitly allowed or overlooked. In our society, artists are the cognitive wanderers who are allowed to go back and forth between the elitists centers and the lunatic fringe. As long as they don't take themselves too seriously by setting up a new economy or a new religion, they are tolerated as a commercial property or ignored as an idealistic irrelevancy. Obviously, my role as a *Wissenskünstler* in an informational, electronic society is to be a wanderer and never truly belong to the societies in which I move. In 1971, when I first described some weird things that were hanging out "at the edge of history," I was accepted and praised by the normal world of *Time, Harpers,* and the *New York Times,* but as soon as I moved a toe over the edge from journalism about the evolutionary news to intellectual commitment to spiritual communities such as Findhorn, Auroville, and Lindisfarne, I was ostracized from the world of official notice and literary reviews. For the critics, I had fallen off the edge of history to dwell henceforth in outer darkness.

This oppositional culture of the critics is not entirely unjust, for those who make a commitment to a movement, religious or revolutionary, often do lose their good sense. Propaganda replaces philosophy, and a belief in a particular guru or in "art and the sacred" becomes a way of camouflaging mediocrity. "Sacred" art or architecture is often just simply bad art and architecture—not that you don't get bad art in exhibitions at the Whitney Museum, but on the whole, the kind of art one sees at places like Findhorn and Auroville is just spiritual kitsch. A dominant world-city such as New York is committed to excellence. Every time I go out to San Francisco, I always suffer culture shock as I encounter the psychedelic theme park of the Haight-Ashbury or feminist nativistic movements concerned with "the goddess and women's spirituality." The experience makes me understand and appreciate why the *New York Times,* the *New York Review of Books,* or the *Nation* wrote me off as just another crazy New Age mystic who had lost his sense of discrimination. As an academic critic once said of me in the *Partisan Review,* "The most recent book by William Irwin Thompson is evidence that neither a trained intellect, an expensive education, nor the study of history can protect you from a will to believe."[3]

Edges and centers are, of course, an expression of only a two-dimensional model, and as soon as one shifts to a multidimensional topology or universe, one encounters Jorge Luis Borges's recursive sphere in which the edge is nowhere and the center everywhere. Imagine the universe as a torus in which the center is not a big hole—the cosmic bagel—but a dimensionless point. This point is the beginning of time and space—the big bang—as it expands to infinity, it folds back on itself, so the outside surface recirculates and infolds to become the inside surface of the torus, until it reaches the dimensionless point again and circulates back to the outside of the torus. I see this cosmic topology as a curious paradox: the "inside" is matter—stars and elementary particles looking outward at the spatially extended universe; but the "outside" is mind, the surface of the torus is mind reflecting back on itself in the cosmic solitude of the daimon or windowless monad of Leibniz. If one imagines this torus as a cross-section of a 3-sphere in topology,[4] and then thinks of it in such a way that every point on its outer surface is the center, is *the* Point, then one ends up with a holographic universe in which each point reflects the whole. Something like this is what is going on in the vision of the candle reflected in the hall of mirrors in the *Hua Yen Sutra* of Chinese Buddhism, or the Primum Mobile of Canto 28 of Dante's *Paradiso* .

What has all this got to do with the hominization of the primates? It means that scientific narratives of human origins are myths and, in their deep structure, are recursively involved with other religious or weird and crazy narratives of human origins that exist in the hypertext spaces of our culture. When we line them all up and read them as mythic narratives of human identity, then more complex cognitive structures begin to emerge than when we simply read one narrative—Richard Leakey's or Donald Johanson's—and take it as the gospel truth. Certain motifs or themes begin to show up in more than one narrative; it is as if one were watching a play in which the character exits stage right but returns stage left in a new costume, with a different accent and a different tone of voice. Let's imagine an interesting play in which crazy ideas are put in the mouths of properly attired and responsible professors, and truth is put in the mouths of absolutely unac-

ceptable characters: bums, lunatics, god-crazed prophets. In such a play of
the sociology of knowledge, the whole notion of "forbidden knowledge"
would begin to become artistically interesting.

And, in fact, I think that just such a drama is being played out in our
contemporary culture. In the university of today, there is definitely such a
thing as forbidden knowledge. Make a mistake and you are denied tenure
or fired. Outside the dominant centers of accepted knowledge is a "twilight
zone" in which science, art, and forbidden knowledge, and imagination and
paranoia converge and separate.

But precisely because this horizon is murky, it is dangerous, and you
can fall off into insanity, so I don't wish, after the fashion of R. D. Laing, to
celebrate the schizophrenic as some sort of Promethean culture hero bringing fire to the suburbs. There is such a thing as insanity and it hurts; it hurts
the crazy as well as the people around him or her. So I am not going to try
to celebrate paranoid narratives as the ultimate secret code for what human
identity is all about. I am interested in paranoia as a structural performance
of narrative that is generated out of an ontological anxiety, but it is the
dramatic condition of epistemological terror that fascinates me as a writer.
As a *Wissenskünstler,* I am fascinated by the epistemological ambiguity of
marginal ways of knowing. Paranoia is a response to the condition of
epistemological terror, but not an answer to that terror. It is a scream of pain,
but not the answer to the pain of human existence.

I want to begin my analysis of literature and the evolution of consciousness with academic books about the origins of humanity, books that
have the necessary *nihil obstat, imprimatur,* which is Catholic talk for kosher
knowledge, but I intend to make these works part of a larger collage, and
their truths will be kept in quotation marks along with those of all the other
works, mystical or crazy. The structure of the narrative will, therefore, not
be revealed in the linear narrative of this book, but in the hypertext in which
all the texts are stacked in the imagination of the reader. In this more
complex space, permissible and forbidden knowledge cross in ways that
excite the artists but disturb the academic clergy. So when I shift from one
zone of knowledge to another to say, "Now, let's consider forbidden knowledge, crazy knowledge, artistic knowledge, responsible knowledge, dominant knowledge, the narratives of the powerful and the narratives of the
powerless," the reader can take them all in, in the way that Lévi-Strauss
recommends that we take all variants of a myth as performances of the myth.

Our starting point is Misia Landau's *Narratives and Human Evolution,*
in which she attempts to use the concepts of folklore to assess the archetypal

structures that appear in the scientific narratives about human evolution, from Darwin to the present: "I suggest that all these paleoanthropological narratives approximate the structure of a hero tale, along the lines proposed by Vladimir Propp in his classic *Morphology of the Folktale* (1928). They feature a humble hero who departs on a journey, receives essential equipment from a helper or donor figure, goes through tests and transformations, and finally arrives at a higher state."[5]

Folklore is one way in which a popular culture persists in an elitist and literary culture. You have high literature and you have fairy tales told by nannies to the children at bedtime. In the original edition of Grimm's fairy tales, the Brothers Grimm call their collection *Hausmärchen*. *Hausmärchen* is a form of marginal knowledge; it is what the maid tells the children under the stairs, or in the kitchen, or in the nursery at bedtime. Now the maid is a person of the lower class, and therefore she is more likely to be in touch with peasant lore and superstitions than the professional classes she serves. So we end up with a series of oppositions: oral versus written, peasant versus bourgeois, fairy tale versus science, female versus male, or matriarchal lore versus patriarchal science and technology. In the case of each of these dyadic sets, the valuation is on the left side, on the powerless, the voiceless who are whispering the truth to the children before dreamtime, while the powerful men gather in the study to speak loudly about stocks and bonds, invasions and inventions.

Two things happen to the male imagination from this kind of *Hausmärchen*. One is that the distaff side of the social weaving—the feminine, the intuitive and mystical—is carried by the lower, serving class. The other is that the body and the dreaming mind at bedtime carry the charisma of this forbidden knowledge. The knowledge is encoded into the body physically, as the maid or nanny scrubs the naked body of the child and prepares it for its immersion into the immensity of the dreamtime. If you are an aristocrat, your mother comes in to give you a dry peck on the cheek before you go to sleep, but it is the nanny with her peasant dialect or her lower-class accent who has cleaned your bottom, rubbed your body all over with a towel, and set you into the dreaming womb of the bed. In some folk cultures, the way to get the male child to stop crying and drift off to sleep is to sing it a lullaby and fondle its penis. In other peasant cultures, the mother or wet nurse fondles the infant's penis while the child is sucking at the breast. The upper-class male who grows up in such cultures often finds the women of his own class desexualized, but the women of the lower class—the attractive Other—appear charged with eros. Accordingly, whites in the South are attracted to blacks, the English are attracted to their Irish or Cockney nannies, and when they go slumming in the red-light districts of London, they seek out the women who have the accent and carnality of the women who first fondled them, loved them, and set them down into the dreamtime. Sexual fantasies become an adult way of recovering the dreamtime. The embeddedness of Proust's mind in its reverie in bed is a recovery of the lost time of the very birth of his consciousness; the madeleine is a symbolic displacement of the vulva, and the primacy of the archaic senses of taste and olfaction are the charismatic senses that deliver him from the conventional sight-interpreted world of abstractions and take him back into the primacy of the dreamtime. When the upper-class Victorian Englishman married, he found or was assigned a woman of his own class so that he could propagate the family line. The woman of his class would close her eyes, do her duty as she endured the horror of sexual penetration for the good of England, but neither she nor he were supposed to be deeply touched by the act. True companionship was to be found by men in the male-bonding of the club, the army, or the academy. Sexual intercourse was part of a family routine and not a mystery of ecstatic transformation in a charismatic mystery school. Think of Ruskin on his wedding night, shocked into impotence by the sight of his wife's pubic hair; he had thought women were like statues, pure, white, chaste, cold marble. The horror of the female sends many of these British public school boys scurrying back for cover into homosexuality. But if the gentleman feels the pull of his infantile mate, he sneaks out into night town on a quest for the secret life of the body. If he is really to have a mistress who speaks to his heart, it is not going to be a woman of his own class; he is going to go slumming and look for a Cockney woman of the night, or he is going to have an exotic Creole or Jamaican mistress or something of the sort. You find this pattern over and over and over again, from President Jefferson with his octoroon mistress to the television evangelist, who when the Klieg lights of the television set were turned off, would sneak out into night town to look not for feminine beauty, but for the most sordid and tacky forms of cheap sex he could buy with the donations from his flock of sheep.

So the *Hausmärchen,* the fairy tale whispered to the children at bedtime, is one kind of performance of forbidden knowledge, and this analysis of literature and the evolution of consciousness is another. I take what students learn in university and give it a peculiar twist or spin, in this new genre of mind jazz for an age in which nature is not the forest but a vast horizon of information. The nanny takes the specialized narrative of what children learn in Sunday school from the middle-class minister and brings it back to the archaic culture that predates Christianity. The parables of Sunday school frighten but don't enchant; however, the Nanny's fairy tales and old folk songs do. They speak to the imagination, and if one should chance to grow up to become, not a soldier or a businessman, but a poet, a painter, or a composer, then one will feel the pull back into the folksoul of the dreamtime. Perhaps one artist will write symphonies that are based on folk melodies, as Dvorak and Bartok did; or another will be like Yeats and leave London to celebrate the peasantry of the west of Ireland. So *Hausmärchen* is no trivial chatter.

Now what Misia Landau has done is to subsume scientific narratives under folklore, and that is an enchantingly subversive act. If we go back to the nineteenth-century narratives of Thomas Huxley and Charles Darwin, we find that even scientific narratives, morphologically, have the structure of folktales. Very cleverly, Landau takes the monkeys down out of the trees, sets them into a little table of hieroglyphs that captures the basic structural features of all the different evolutionary narratives, and suddenly big science becomes folklore.[6] Here is this hominid swinging in the trees in the old stable forest environment, but then comes the weather change that brings desiccation and a shrinkage of the forest. What is the poor creature to do, but miniaturize the old environment in the clump of trees in which the females gather food, chatter, and hold their young in their newly freed arms. Will it cling to the last branch, or dare to move out, naked and exposed, into the terrors of the new environment? One animal either dares or is forced out into the new environment. It goes through various changes and as it departs from the old world, there comes the test; but somehow or other there is someone who comes in as a kind of guardian angel and makes a donation that helps the hominid along the new path of evolution. In one narrative, the donation is encephalization, the big brain; in another narrative, the donation is the bipedal gait. Darwin says that we were bipedal before we had a big brain, but others insist that it is the other way around. Johanson's narrative is close to Darwin's because Lucy had a small brain but a bipedal gait, so Johanson sees the big brain as coming later on down the line. There is the transformation, the shift from the primate forest to the hominid savanna, and with it another test and a new donation. Now we see the hominid in Landau's hieroglyph holding aloft a tool, a rock or a bone. Technology has appeared. We are on our way, and human begins to replace hominid.

Landau's application of the folkloristic scholarship of Vladimir Propp to evolutionary narratives is like Vladamir Bogoras's application of Einsteinian relativity to shamanistic lore. Bogoras noticed that the stories Siberian shamans in Russia told about time and space were very much like the parables the Russian mathematician Minkowski told to explain the Einsteinian relativistic time shift. The shaman climbs a pole, enters another timespace, and when he returns, centuries have gone by on Earth. This relativistic time shift occurs all around the world, from India to Ireland. In the ancient Irish poem, "The Voyage of Bran," the hero sails out beyond the known world, he leaves the world of men and warriors, comes to the ahistorical world of the Island of Women, and then returns to Ireland. As he is docking his ship, one sailor jumps on land and decays into ashes as if he were centuries old. The people on the dock ask Bran in his ship who he is, and when he identifies himself, they respond by saying: "Ah yes, we have heard of you, for 'The Voyage of Bran' is one of our most ancient sagas." So the poem we are reading, like an Escher drawing in which a hand draws the drawing we hold in our hand, is contextualized in the most amazing way. One can see here that our modern science fiction as a new form of folklore has roots in these ancient Irish voyage poems, the voyages of Bran, Brendan, and Muldoon.

What Landau is doing is showing us how folklore and scientific narratives are all performances of myth; they are macrostructures that are setting up explanations of who we are, where we come from, and where we are going. So around the time of Kuno Meyer and Vladimir Propp in Germany, and Vladimir Bogoras in Russia, we begin to get a study of folklore and folk myth as way of understanding the full range of expression of our human identity. The narratives of hominid and human evolution are a way of understanding how science is brought forth as a consensual domain. The normal way for an undergraduate to read a textbook on human evolution is to think, "This is the truth! This is what the big boys in graduate school know." But once we begin to understand how a seemingly coherent narrative is constructed out of a few teeth and half a skull, and that knowledge is a really a political domain, then the whole construction of a consensual domain begins to take on a much more human character. There are many different ways to construct a narrative about human origins because any description is as much a performance of human identity as it is a description of it.

If one wants to appreciate this quality of ambiguity, just try writing an autobiography. As one gets into it, one begins to see that the narrative is an adult construction of memories, and therefore a narrative structure of time that one did not experience as an infant or a child. As one begins to organize the material into a narrative, thematic structuring—the grammar of grammars rather than simply of words—begins to exercise its influence. The underlying ideas often do not even need to be consciously expressed, for they can simply determine what one thinks is important, or what one takes for granted as the nature of reality. One sort of person will construct a narrative organized around individuals, from parents to teachers to charismatic and influential leaders. Another person will choose a narrative organized around places, neighborhoods, cities, landscapes. In one narrative, the idea of class may be determinant; in another, sexuality and the drama of the body. One soon realizes that in one narrative, one could talk only about money and power and come up with a coherent story, and in another, only about sexuality, or religion. Each story would be, naively, about the "same" person, yet each autobiography would generate a completely different narrative character. When one writes an autobiography, one may start out as a good Christian or Hindu, determined to tell the secrets of "the higher self," but ends up a good Buddhist as one realizes that one doesn't have a fixed self: there are unending processes of relationships in all directions, and there are at least a dozen different ways to construct the description of personal identity. What is true for the autobiography of the person is even truer for the autobiography of the human race. So when one reads a narrative that tells the story of human evolution from Australopithecus afarensis to Homo sapiens, one becomes aware that one is reading a kind of novel, a work of imaginative fiction. For example, in considering the appearance of metaphors, ask yourself about the imaginative act that has joined the fragments of bone into a coherent narrative. The good doctors Roger Lewin and Richard Leakey confidently proclaim that "the evolutionary momentum that propelled *Homo erectus* toward *Homo sapiens* must have left behind some pockets of *erectus* and have caused some *sapiens* populations to move down biological blind alleys to their own extinction."[7] Notice both the mixing of metaphors and how the whole narrative depends on a suspension of disbelief in an act of scientific faith. What is "evolutionary momentum"? What is a "biological blind alley"? And what is "extinction"? Are the thirteen colonies extinct? Is the Neanderthal extinct in the way that the Edsel or Tucker is extinct, or in the way that the Polynesian is extinct on Oahu, or in the way that the baroque is extinct in modern architecture? Leakey and Lewin go on to say "Joining Neanderthal man on his ill-fated journey was Solo Man and Rhodesia Man both of whom likewise paid the penalty of over-specialization."[8] Because limited funds did not allow the anthropologists to find some bones in the areas they chose to dig in, does that mean that Rhodesia man ended up in a blind alley of evolution, or does it mean that their research team ended up in a blind alley?

The paleoanthropolgists tell us that the Neanderthals had brains bigger than ours, but somehow the big louts got overspecialized to the cold and died out when the climate became warm again. So fantastically intelligent were the Neanderthals, with their Pleistocene culture of fine tools, their innovations of clothing and shelter, their spiritual culture of burial and imagined afterlife, that they just couldn't handle it when the weather improved.

I don't really "know" what Leakey and Lewin are talking about, but I do know that they are telling a story. No matter how many equations scientists use to camouflage their narrative, the lattice of mathematics is just so much barbed wire around a concentration camp to keep the poets away from the scientific class that is in charge of the management of human identity.

A scientific narrative is a cultural construction and the whole thing is built out of metaphors and mythopoeic ideas. Sometimes the metaphors are incredibly mixed together and piled onto one another. For example, consider this one from Leakey and Lewin, and let me number a word every time a new metaphor is introduced:

> One of those crucial [1] refinements [2] in brain circuitry [3] was the evolution [4] of the ability to speak a complex language. . . . The explosion [5] of new cultural patterns [6] and the acceleration [7] of material [8] advance [9] during the past fifty thousand years, which are sometimes cited [10] as evidence [11] of a very recent invention [12] of language, are much more likely to stem [13] from a more effective exploitation [14] of what was already wired [15] into the brain from an improvement of the wiring itself. The biological machinery [16] for the advance [17] was well established fifty thousand years ago, and its speed [18] was fired [19] by the steady accumulation [20] of knowledge which finally hit [21] a critical mass.[22]"[9]

Brain surgery, wiring, hitting, explosions, speed, critical mass. This narrative is not simply metaphoric, it is a tossed salad of mixed metaphors. When one looks for metaphors in a narrative one notices, in much the way that George Lakoff and Mark Johnson have pointed out, that words like "ability" and "language" are old physical metaphors that have become worn smooth in their usage through the centuries. Language is inherently metaphoric, so any narrative, scientific or folkloric, is a road paved with conscious metaphors on a path of unconscious metaphors worn down by our ancestors.

Leakey and Lewin's book is basically a work of fiction. It is, of course, based on an external reality of artifacts, but, then, so is Homer's *Iliad* or Tolstoy's *War and Peace*. In fact, some novels are actually more scientific than Leakey and Lewin's narrative. But because this book is coming to us empowered by the magical name of Leakey and embossed with the insignium of the editor of the *New Science Journal,* it cons us into thinking that it contains the scientific truth. This is partly what science is all about: power and the fund-raising confidence game of fame. The arbitrariness and the imaginative quality of scientific narratives are hidden from the laity. Only those allowed into the professional meetings are allowed to see the doctrinal battles, to watch Leakey and Johanson fight it out over a bone. But when they come out to face us they have to pretend it is all more solidly scientific than it really is, because if we sensed just how arbitrary and how imaginative their narratives were, then we might feel a little insecure about giving them the big bucks they need to do their thing. Keep in mind that Johanson's institute in Berkeley is funded by the Getty family.

In the great story of how we came to be human, the opposable thumb and the mouth are central characters. Because the forest canopy thinned out in the glacial cold snap, the early hominids had to stand to peer out over the tall grass before they scurried to safety in the next clump of trees. To hold her infant securely as she dashed for cover, the hominid mother could not knuckle walk on all fours but had to stand and make a run for it on her lower limbs. The dominant males could scurry away on all fours, but the poor mother, burdened with her infant, had to stumble into something new. And because of the primal bond between infant and mother, the terrified infant would not forget the image of its mother, upright and running on two feet. It also would not forget the babbling song of its mother while nursing. So to the female of the species, we should credit our bipedal gait and language. The "hominization" of the primates should really be called the feminization of the primates, because it is never the dominant male hierarchies that introduce innovations that upset the system; if knuckle walking was good enough for the old boys, it will be good enough for them. It is also unlikely that hunters were noisy on the prowl, so the chatter that serves to bond the group together is probably a female innovation. Language is about community and not simply communication; once again, McLuhan was right: "The medium is the message."

So one can see how seductively easy it is to make up these *Just So Stories* about how we came to be human. It really doesn't matter whether we settle on the aquatic ape story of Elaine Morgan and Alastair Hardy,[10] in which upright posture, loss of body hair, salt tears, full breasts, and instinctive infant swimming are brought forth in selective response to the shift from the dried out savanna to the seashore; or settle on Leakey and Lewin's *Field and Stream* stories about man the hunter whose big brain was brought about by clever killing and the high energy diet of meat. These are good stories that tell us as much about the storyteller as about any extinct hominid.

Here, for example, is what Leakey and Lewin write on the origins of language: "A mouth that is adapted to help procure food, to carry objects and threaten or exert aggression is not likely to be able to make complex sounds."[11]

The dominant notion is that one has to have the great opposable thumb and a mouth that is free to articulate sounds. But what about dolphins? They have a big brain. They, like us, have abandoned estrus and are open to sexuality at all times. They don't have an opposable thumb, but they have communication. It just doesn't make the easy sense that the paleoanthropologists claim, and sometimes even they realize that when they honestly confront the inherent darkness of the subject they have to admit that they do not know what caused the chimps to stay chimps and the hominids to change. As Donald Johanson and Maitland Edey admit: "The only thing we have not discussed up to this point was the biggest enigma of all: How did it all get started? What pushed those ancestral legs up on their hind legs and gave them, some of them, an opportunity to evolve into humans. That question is basically the entire story of hominization."[12]

For Johanson and Edey the story is, not surprisingly, one of a great technological leap:

> How do we account for Homo erectus' sudden jump from Homo habilis? Was it actually all that sudden? Why was it made? Was it a matter of a quick evolutionary spurt taken in tandem with the development of a new and better tool culture? If so, where and why did the new culture start?
>
> Then, an even more interesting question: why did that culture — and the man who made it — stagnate for another million years? Homo erectus, it is fairly clear, evolved practically not at all during that immense time. Then, suddenly, humanity took another spurt. About two hundred thousand years ago there occurred a second technological leap, and out of it rose Homo sapiens.[13]

When one reads the narratives of Leakey and Lewin, Johanson and Edey, one is conned into belief by magical invocations of "technological leaps." Scientific narratives are composed of technological metaphors that seek to convince us that they are "real" and up-to-date.[14] Johanson and Edey speak of technological leaps, and Leakey and Lewin talk about brain circuitry, just as Freud, in his day, spoke of repression, as if the mind were a steam engine. Freud used steam engines, and Lewin uses computers; for one, the mind is a locomotive engine of heat and compressed steam, and for the other, an electronic information-processing computer. These dominant metaphors are literally dominating and force us into the submission of belief in the doctrinal narratives of big science. We submit to the technology of explanation because the explanation is technological.

Technologies have stabilized a consensual domain for us moderns more effectively than faith, doctrine, or poetic visions. We all look at buildings that don't fall down and rockets that go to the moon and we think that something is going on in science and technology; so we worship science and technology in an idolatrous fashion. Scientists can actually stabilize a consensual domain more effectively through superstition than through force. If one stabilizes a domain through compulsion, then one has to use the scimitar or the torch, to be put to the sword or burnt at the stake. Medieval and contemporary religious societies require violence, immediate violence, to stabilize a consensual domain. In Islamic societies, writers, satirists, and feminists are denounced and placed under a sentence of death. But once the magical apparition of technology has taken hold of society, then the masses fall into line and believe in science because they can see the rockets' red glare and the bombs bursting in air. So people vote to give money to big science with its scientific laboratories, universities, and researchers who keep the faith. Ours is a technological culture, so our myths of origin are constructed out of technological metaphors in the media, incantatory rituals that enchant us.

Here one can see that the description of the Other often really is a projective self-description. The Other is appropriated by the empire of big science; so the animal, the wild, the primitive, the female, the alien all become resource colonies to the empire of science, to the factories that produce explanations for one generation and pollution for the next.

Scholarship and science are often forms of disguised autobiography; therefore, we need to be careful and not simply take the narrative for granted, as naive freshmen might take the material handed to them in textbooks by their teachers. Textbooks describe the sociology of the class in power. For example, for the last thirty years in the universities, we have had deconstructionism in literary criticism. Basically this subculture, which was created by Barthes, De Man, and Derrida, describes the postwar sociology of the shift from the writer to the university salaried critic. Around the 1960s, the romantic notion of the artist— a Thomas Mann or a Yeats, artists from the generation of the 1930s, before World War II—began to die off with the men whose works had sustained it. The independent author, supported by his large reading public, could be alone in his study—a Yeats in his tower or a Thomas Mann in his home above a Swiss lake. There in his cosmic solitude, he could get in touch with the mysteries of the universe, write great books, and be empowered by the charisma of literary fame. But after World War II, the power of the universities to build atom bombs and win wars against ideologies made collective technologies more important than individual beliefs, be they those of Marx or Hitler. Money began to pour into state universities, and places such as Berkeley became as powerful as Oxford or Harvard. With these new universities came not the old elitist humanities, but the new social sciences. In hundreds of departments of literature, a new bureaucracy of critics took over and the solitary artist became an ecosystem supporting an industry. There was no longer Yeats, Mann, and Joyce; there were Yeats, Mann, and Joyce industries. The critics proclaimed that their criticism was more important than art, that meaning was an illusion, and that the only thing that really mattered was the information processing of critical reading that transformed the ore of the author into the gold of the critic. The routine of the literature department was more important than the charisma of the artist; so Barthes proclaimed the death of the author. Yeats was dead; De Man lived. And what was true of literature was also true of philosophy. The age of the solitary pipe-smoking philosopher strolling the greens of Oxbridge or the *Holzwege* of the Black Forest—be he Russell, Whitehead, Wittgenstein, or Heidegger—was over; the age of cognitive science in computerized laboratories had arrived. When Dan Dennet says that there is no self, no Cartesian theater of the cogitating ego, but only "multiple drafts,"[15] he is really giving us a self-description of a modern philosophy department in which there are no real philosophers but only clerks passing memos back and forth in the collective information processing of modern cognitive science.

So Landau is right in applying folklore studies to paleoanthropology, because these best-selling scholarly narratives are a popular form of storytelling. They are a good read and a new genre of pop science that tells us something about the nature of contemporary humanity. In the nineteenth century, clergymen would play to the general religious culture by writing popular sermons, and these printed sermons could sometimes even become bestsellers. In the nineteenth century one also had the dime novel as a pop genre. The dime novels created the myth of the Western as a new folktale. They were then followed by science fiction in which Jules Verne gave us a more technological vision of the new frontier.

The current popular trade books about human origins, such as *Origins* by Lewin and Leakey and *Lucy* by Johanson and Edey, provide us with another example of the cultural shift from religious visions of human identity to scientific performances of human identity. Rather than saying God created man on October 14, 4004 B.C., or that woman was taken out of Adam's rib—all those old kinds of literalist things—science tells us a new story. Except for provincial backwaters in the South or places where the fundamentalists of the religious Right are trying to take over school texts and curricula to put their own creationist doctrine into the public schools, science has for the most part become the new story that we tell to keep ourselves together in a multicultural society. This story is believed to be a collection of facts and not superstitions, but the closer one gets to a fact—like the closer one gets to the one-fifth to one quarter of a second unit of "now"—the more granular the fact seems to be. In Ludwick Fleck's *Genesis and Development of a Scientific Fact,*[16] a fact is shown to be a social institution. A fact requires a theory. One cannot even conceive of a fact without a theory to support it. So if one is looking at a skull, if one doesn't have the right theory or vision or myth or story in one's mind, one might just toss it back into the ground and say that it was the skull of a cretin. A nineteenth-century Frenchman might look at a Neanderthal skull and say it that it was just a German soldier killed in the Napoleonic wars. In the sixteenth century, when meteors were observed striking the Earth, the perception was denied, because stones just did not fall out of the sky. So to look at a skull and see it as a fossil requires a theory, in just the way that a flame requires an atmosphere.

Science as storytelling is perhaps much more apparent in physical anthropology than in physics. To take a few teeth and bones and construct a fossil,[17] and then make that fossil a character in a narrative of development, is an imaginative act like writing a novel. Johanson talks about the division between "splitters" and "lumpers"; some scientists keep splitting the lines of development, and others keep lumping them together in a single line. Mary Leakey was a good Christian, and so she wanted to keep apes on one side, and humans on the other to maintain the great divide between animal and human. But Johanson is a lumper, and his radical move was to construct a single line of development. We have little Lucy, Australopithecus afarensis, and then the evolution to Australopithecus africanus. But then we come upon this grey area and out of this mist comes Homo habilis who keeps on marching toward Homo erectus, and on to archaic Homo sapiens. According to Johanson and Edey, "We do believe that the emergence of human beings began some time about 3 million years ago. By 2 million, it had been accomplished. By then creatures recognizable as Homo walked on earth. So did their cousins, the robust australopithecines." So for Johanson and Edey, we have this great divide between Homo habilis starting out on a new adventure and robustus getting caught in a dead end. "By one million, there were no australopitheces left. They had all become extinct."[18]

What we end up with in this narrative is a performance of an archetypal couple, one that is going to stay with us in literature for a long time. We have Gilgamesh, the god, and his hairy companion Enkidu; we have the brothers in the Old Testament, smooth-skinned Jacob and hairy Esau. "And the Lord said unto her, Two nations are in they womb, and two manner of people shall be separated from thy bowels" (Genesis 25:23). We have Robinson Crusoe and Friday, Natty Bumpo and Chingachagook, Ishmael and Queequeg, or in our own time, the pair in the movie Star Wars, Han Solo and his hairy copilot, Chewbaca. This narrative structure is so fascinating that we never seem to escape it. It appeals to the imagination as if there were something archetypal about it—a memory of lost time, an unconscious reading of the akashic record by the artist turned clairvoyant.

Art is emotionally compelling, but science is emotionally confusing. It cons us into thinking it has answered the question when it hasn't. Just what keeps a chimp a chimp but shoves Australopithecus into Homo habilis? This grey murky area is exactly what I am referring to when I talk about a horizon in which perception and imagination are ambiguously related. This ancient horizon at the edge of our identity is not just a historical horizon, it is a mythic horizon. When Johanson lumps all the fossils together, he is imaginatively creating the mything link. Myth will always be the event horizon between fact and theory. After reading hundreds of pages of material, we find that we still don't know why brains get bigger, why a culture that is adequate for survival is abandoned in favor of some new culture that hasn't been tried out yet. Various explanations are given, but the explanations are all basically self-descriptions from the cultural assumptions of the writers.

The projections from unconscious processes of the human personality account in large measure for the nature of scientific narratives, but we should not dismiss the part played by the up-front, in-your-face nature of the competitive, conscious personality. Male dominance accounts for the fact that although Mary Leakey found the fossil, the B.B.C. film about the discovery gives the credit to her husband and is entitled "Dr Leakey and the Dawn of Man." As paleoanthropology develops, it plays out a drama straight from the pages of Freud's *Totem and Taboo,* for we pass from the patriarch of the primate herd to the sibling rivalry of the *Bruderbund* as we watch young Richard Leakey fight it out with Donald Johanson. And in his book, Johanson makes the reader quite aware that Timothy White is a brusque and nasty primate who has not much use for opinions that are not grasped in his own fist-hatchet. White is described as afflicted with an arrogant personality and unable or unwilling to communicate his ideas in a tolerant and cooperative manner. As would be the case in a novel by Tolstoy, we can see that character is destiny and creates its fate uncon- sciously. The unconscious character experiences his or her fate as external to its consciousness and laments the seemingly external infliction of the events of its life. The character cannot see that, like Anna Karenina, destiny is an emanation of character. The social process of doing science depends enormously on human interactions and arbitrary things, such as funding in America and revolutions in Ethiopia, but the closer one gets to science as it is played out by scientists, the more it looks like a wild west saloon of males in display and conflict.

The closer one comes to the storytelling of paleoanthropology, the more one sees that it really is another version of science fiction, that science faction and science fiction are not on opposite sides of the world, that they both are performances of mythopoeic storytelling. When one reads Owen Lovejoy's descriptions of "The Origin of Man,"[19] one remembers Donna Harraway's sociology of knowledge in *Primate Visions,*[20] and recognizes that Lovejoy is projecting the American suburbs back onto the African savanna. For Lovejoy, the entire story of hominization is about the emergence of the nuclear family at the dawn of time. Weak females with dependant infants needed big strong men to protect them. The narratives of primatology emphasize the systems of male-dominance of baboons and chimpanzees, and conveniently overlook the system of female-dominance in the case of the Bonobo chimpanzees.

Even though female lions and cheetahs do most of the hunting on the African savanna, and the big powerful males tend to do nothing more than loaf in the sun, steal other animals' catches, and fight with other males, the male anthropologist's vision of hominid females is of helpless southern belles. Lovejoy's is a Kipling *Just So* story of how the nuclear family of mom and pop came to be. But the U. C. Santa Cruz anthropologist Adrienne Zihlman doesn't see a family back there in three million B.C.E., but something much more like the female-centered cluster of the pygmy chimpanzees.[21] So the alpha males at Berkeley see a kind of macho protoculture at the dawn of man, but the feminists at Santa Cruz see a more cooperative and female-centered culture at the dawn of humanity.

> Contrary to many reconstructions of early human social
> life that picture women burdened with young, sitting back
> at camp waiting for the hunters return, hominid mothers
> must have been moving actively around the environment,
> getting food and carrying infants while doing so. . .
> I argue here, as I have elsewhere, that gathering and not
> hunting was the initial food-getting behavior that
> distinguished ape from human.[22]

What we are determines what we see. It is not so much what we think, but what we are not really thinking about that is shaping what we see. Technologically oriented men will tell us that culture comes from males and tools, but then the female scholars enter the discussion to say, with Adrienne Zihlman, that these hominid males were not selected for aggression and brutality; that, *au contraire*, it was the females who really did the selecting and chose males that were cooperative, helpful with infants, and nurturing. So back in two million B.C.E., we had sensitive, vulnerable, New Age males who stayed home to help out with the kids. Lovejoy portrays the suburban faculty wife back at the dawn of time, and Zihlman the kind of male that a female faculty member would have for a spouse. Both narratives are examples of self-description. If one is a religious zealot, then one is going to come up with a biblical narrative and say God did it. But God ends up being another self-image: he is a white patriarchal male who is in charge of everything and is able to keep women in their place.

The whole structure of the men's club of anthropology is full of these tacit assumptions that generate stories, and the stories have a lot to do with the way the researchers live. Before Jane Goodall and Diane Fossey went off to live in the wild with the chimpanzees and gorillas, the normal way of life for researchers was to drive to work, torture the animals for a while, then drive home to the wives and kids in the suburbs. The animals were forced out of their own context and made to do things that would confirm what the researchers had in mind. It was very much the way in which priests of the Inquisition would torture women to get them to reveal what the Inquisitors had in mind. Living in the wild was too sloppy and out of control, so it was easier for the men — and we are talking about men here — to keep the chimps on file in places like the Yerkes Primate Lab and work them over from nine to five. Donna Harraway's study of the good behaviorist Dr. Harlow in *Primate Visions,*[23] is a powerful indictment of this unthinking mentality.

What Harraway's work enables us to see is just how important gender is in the engendering of knowledge. On one side, you have the Nobel laureate biologist Barbara McClintock with her "feeling for the organism,"[24] and on the other, the manipulations of genes as discrete objects by Francis Crick and James Watson, or Jacques Monod and Francois Jacob. In the female context, we have living plants, whole organisms growing in slow and seasonal time within the soil; in the male context, we have discrete objects taken out of their context and subjected to manipulation, control, and sometimes even torture. We have narratives of "symbiosis in cell evolution" with Lynn Margulis, or we have dramas of power and deception with the selfish gene of Richard Dawkins. We have Harlow and the Yerkes Primate Lab versus Goodall and Fossey in the wild.

Male science tends to focus on discrete corpuscular objects — be they elementary particles or genes — and seeks to reduce ecologies of being to single causes that it can identify and control. Female science seems to be pattern based, interactive, and more cooperative than competitive. This gender-based culture even carries over into sports, for male coaches have commented on television that when they shift to coaching women in sports they find that women are much more group spirited and cooperative than the individualistic and competitive males they have been used to. It's the difference between the obstetrician and the midwife. The obstetrician gives the woman a drug to induce labor so that he can keep his appointment at a professional meeting or on the golf course; the midwife waits and works more sympathetically with the mother. I speak from direct personal experience of these two approaches to childbirth, one at the Boston Lying-in Hospital, the other at the Maternity Association in Manhattan. This opposition, like the opposition between the concept of light as a particle or a wave, seems almost archetypal: the women gather and the men hunt. The male has a linear target for his spear or bow and arrow, the female has a child on one hip and a collection sack on the other. The anthropologist Mary Catherine Bateson has explored this gender difference in her book, *Composing a Life.*[25]

The violence and technology that was used in hunting was carried over into cattle raids, then organized warfare, then the organization of the military-athletic-industrial-scientific complex. And in all of these cases, the superiority of a male culture of competition and dominance is taken for granted. As Harraway describes Harlow, his cruelty is invisible to him. It takes Harraway as a sociologist of knowledge to come in and expose the invisible sadism that is part of his project. He would never think of it or see it. He simply thinks his research is just routine science. Sadly, he is right; it is routine science.

Because *Primate Visions* sensitizes us to the political dimensions of the practice of science, it is, I think, a very important book. Unfortunately, it is written in a very inconsistent style. Sometimes Harraway is very literary and strongly metaphoric, and in those cases, I, of course, like her writing, but at other times she has been captured by the diction of postmodernist lit. crit. In the last twenty years, literary studies have tried to distance themselves from the disgrace of being in the humanities by crossing the quad and moving away from the ivy-clad stone buildings of the past into the aluminum and glass office buildings that house the behavioral sciences. The old Mathew Arnold liberal arts college approach of studying literature as the storehouse of the best that has been thought is too embarrassingly elitist for today's teachers and is felt to be merely an apology for the canons of taste of a white male upper-middle class. The critic is now not a judge of what is fine, but a political representative for an imagined oppressed minority. Any minority will do: women, blacks, Native Americans, Hispanics, gays, or lesbians. Since for feminists, "the beauty myth" represents a Madison Avenue oppression of women as a commodity, politically correct women have hair longer on their armpits and legs than their heads, tattoo their arms, and try to cultivate the "ugly" look. The beauty myth in writing, too, has to be uglified and purged of those old-fashioned bourgeois notions about prose style, those antique elitist notions from Flaubert, Joyce, and Lawrence — all white European males — that have so "disempowered" us. So literary critics now write about engenderment, "foregrounding the vehicle," and constructed discourse.[26] Professors of literature are now social scientists and not purveyors of the good, the true, and the beautiful. This bureaucratic subculture has infected Harraway, and she has marked herself as an outsider beyond the pale of the establishment.

Harraway is interesting for several reasons. One is the sociology of knowledge by which feminism has rearticulated the intellectual landscape. When I was teaching at MIT in the 1960s, the Lévi-Strauss 1950s notion that women existed in culture only as instruments of exchange by men was pretty much thought to be the way things were. Then later in the 1960s, Robert Ardrey, Lionel Tiger, and Robin Fox all wrote popular bestsellers about man the killer-ape and men in groups. Men ate steaks and women ate salads because men were hunters and women were gatherers. Technology was the driving force of culture, and women were the prizes and the spoils of the evolutionary battle, but they themselves were not part of the creative dynamic that formed culture. So even into the 1960s there was this received wisdom that nature and primitives were feminine and that technology was masculine. Modernization, therefore, was always masculinization.

Harraway comes at her feminism from a totally different philosophy from that of the reconstruction of the Great Goddess by Marija Gimbutas, Merlin Stone, Riane Eisler, Elinor Gadan, Charlene Spretnak, and Starhawk. Harraway says if God is dead, then the Goddess is too. She is not going to have any truck with this new nativistic religion in which women create their own rituals of women's mysteries to dance on the Venerean hill and chase the men away. Harraway's tough sociology of knowledge serves as a cleansing of the whole sentimental mush of the New Age movement. *Primate Visions* is a solid, forceful book that is very thorough in its analysis of the whole imperial construction of physical anthropology. Her analysis of the American Museum of Natural History in New York is amazing. In a wonderful essay entitled "Teddy Bear Patriarchy," she discusses the statue at the entrance — the statue of Teddy Roosevelt on a horse with the "redman" walking on one side and the "blackman" with "savage" spear on the other. She analyzes the representation of the gorillas in the Museum's diorama as well as the whole image of Africa as it is was constructed in the rise of anthropology. Then she goes through the whole history of the rise of man the hunter and the blindness by which whole fields of scientific knowledge were totally unable to perceive nature. Men went out into the field and what they saw was a description of what they were. When a primatologist was describing baboons, he was also describing the behavior of alpha males in the control of knowledge in the university. When a scientist was marking out an area as a research subject, he was declaring it to be a wild natural resource for his own scientific culture, as raw data to the empire of pure science. This is as absurd as Christopher Columbus planting a flag and claiming to "discover" America.

What starts with animals or savages is easily extended to nonscientists in a scientific culture. Citizens can become raw data to science, can become a resource colony to the empire of someone else's description. This first came home to me when I was an undergraduate and was forced to take the

Minnesota Multiphase Personality Test. The entire freshman class at Pomona College was ordered to take the test and there was never a question of whether this might be a violation of our civil liberties. We were all used as subjects; we were marched into the auditorium and given machine-scored tests that consisted of questions like "Do you look at your feces before you flush the toilet?" "Do you wipe the doorknob before you open the door?" "Have you ever had a mystical vision?" And I thought, now that is a very interesting juxtaposition. A mean-spirited little master of white rats was in charge of us all, and when I asked him about the context and the manner in which the questions were clustered, he didn't get the point but tried to turn the discussion into an inquisition to find out if I ever had a mystical experience—no doubt, so that he could alert the counselors in the dean's office for possible future behavioral problems. C. S. Lewis has written about this academic take-over of religion and the humanities by the empire of behavioral science in his science fiction novel *That Hideous Strength*, but people have dismissed him as just an old High Church Anglican Tory caricaturing the postwar Labour government. Harraway, however, cannot so easily be dismissed by the Left, for her leftist analysis of the empire of behavioral science is useful in showing us that something is really going on in science that is not simply scientific. So I think *Primate Visions* is an extremely important book. It is not mystical; it is not New Age; it is not Jungian and mythopoeic, but it has a critical power to it that—except for the critiques of Ivan Illich—has been missing in the whole alternative or New Age movement of the last twenty years.

All of which is simply to say that science is human, all too human, and that the science of human origins has perhaps the most savage and prehuman culture of them all. To pretend that physical anthropology is a more scientific discipline than English or folklore is naive in the extreme. These popular bestsellers, such as *Origins* and *Lucy*, are a form of fiction, and it would be better for us all if we read them with the sense of humor and irony that Italo Calvino has taught us in *Cosmic Comics*. When the physical anthropologists start taking themselves too seriously, they begin to attract the fundamentalist creationists into their orbit, and as these two gangs of males go into display with invocations of the sacredness of science and religion, these sanctimonious members of the clergy begin to deserve one another.

Literature, and here I mean the literature of the artist, the writer, and not the critic in the university, has an artistic delight that allows us to dwell—without ever settling down—on and in the mystery of human origins.

WEIRD MYTHS ABOUT HUMAN ORIGINS AS EXPRESSIVE OF THE EVOLUTION OF CONSCIOUSNESS FROM THE TERRITORIAL NATION-STATE TO GLOBAL NOETIC POLITIES: THE STRANGE CASES OF ZECHARIA SITCHIN AND RUDOLF STEINER

M any different sorts of imaginative people are now living perilously close to the edge of reality, and from this perspective the world certainly looks different than it does when seen from within the normal centers of learning. Reality is not all it's been cracked up to be, and some people have to have a crack-up to find that out. One can live at the center of things and do business in the common consensual, nailed-down reality of the conventional culture defined by Harvard, Wall Street, or Washington. As long as one stays in the center of things with people who agree on one single epistemology or worldview, then one is all right and conventionally sane. But as soon as one begins to move out of the dominant worldview of the institutions that are defining the civilization, then one runs into trouble.

For materialists who have no awareness of psyche, no experience of the astral plane and nonmaterial states of consciousness, the move becomes particularly disorienting, for there is no place to go but *out*. So they go out of their minds instead of into them. They project their discoveries in the most literal and materialistic forms of explanation. Complexity becomes simplicity in the single paranoid code that explains everything. Here, there can be no question about the ambiguous relationship between perception and imagination at the horizon of consciousness. In fact, there can be no ambiguity whatsoever, for great explainers don't like ambiguity, complexity, or humor. "They are out there," and "They are out to get us."

As luck would have it, Zecharia Sitchin was lecturing at the Harvard Club in New York the very week I was scheduled to discuss his book *The 12th Planet* in a Lindisfarne Symposium at the Cathedral of St. John the Divine. I went to hear him speak and found him fascinating because I never before had heard anyone who was so totally like his book.[1] He spoke in a soft voice and read his text in so slow and methodical a manner that my mind became restless and began to wander during the pauses between sentences. The library of the Harvard Club, in which he gave his lecture, provided many visual opportunities for distraction. Certainly, one could not pick a more dramatic contrast for his presentation about the gods in their rockets coming to Earth from the twelfth planet than that library, which called to mind a nineteenth-century men's club. Everything was sane, sober, gentlemanly, and as far away from a *National Enquirer* UFO contactee story as one could get. It was only when Sitchin began to discuss the Gulf War that his mania appeared, as if in reaching from one edge of history to the other, he strained himself and his psychic hernia popped out. When it came time to relate the mythic landscape of the dawn of Sumerian civilization to the contemporary edge of history with the Gulf War, the recent battle became part of a grand conspiracy theory about ancient titanic forces that clash by night. And Sitchin's passionate Zionism also popped out along with his idée fixe about extraterrestrial intervention in human history. This great battle between the forces of good and evil had been fought before in the Near East, only before, according to Sitchin, in ancient times, the war of the gods was fought with nuclear weapons. For Sitchin, the past is an event horizon in which imagination and perception collaborate in a classic maniacal narrative of cosmic synthesis. He is the code-breaker who has cracked the enigma of human life on earth; he can read the secret conspiratorial code that holds it all together, and for those who have eyes to see, it was revealed once again in the Gulf War.

When one comes to the edge of consciousness in dream or meditation, one can watch the mind shift from ideas to imagery; things that were drifting through the mind as thoughts become films or dramas. What was at one moment merely an abstract thought becomes an existential drama in which one is more vividly and experientially situated. One is no longer simply thinking, one is projecting a world. Some projections are part of an unconscious agenda that was laid down in the formation of consciousness at birth, before we had language. Our consciousness was dynamically formed in the process of birth, with its sensate bonding of mother and infant,[2] but because we didn't have language, we couldn't file those experiences in little linguistically neat packages that our memory could access. It takes some unusual form of excavation to get at them: tantric yoga, trance writing, hypnosis, rebirthing, holotropic breathing, or psychedelic drugs. The process is a bit like the experience of writing with a computer when the window comes on screen to say: "An application cannot be found to open this document." When the normal ego tries to access preverbal states of consciousness, to recall birth or infantile experiences before language had evolved to shape and store them, an application cannot be found to open the document, for the experience is before documents were set up and arranged by a verbalizing memory. One can keep looking in memory, but what one finds are the linguistically formed memories of the *narrative* of the personality that one has constructed over time. This narrative is basically the egoistic sense of who one is, but what one is trying to get at is more like the ground that is under the filing cabinets, the preverbal foundation of consciousness.

History is the written form of our collective memory. When one tries to create a memory for what occurred before written history, a civilized application cannot be found to open the document. We come to the edge of history, and it is a world of other spaces and dimensions, a world of myth and madness. To open oneself to these spaces requires not civilized programs, but some unusual form of excavation.

It is naive to think that there is such a thing as an objective, neutral science that can give us access to these spaces. Since the scientist is always culturally situated, the description of one culture is always a performance of another. Why does a historian or a scientist choose this topic of research over another? Why is one particular explanation compelling? If we were to do a content analysis on the terms and metaphors that crop up in a scholarly narrative, we would begin to see the outcroppings of the hidden strata of the scholar's interior landscape. The reason the scientist has been drawn to a particular field has to do with very deep-rooted unconscious compulsions and fascinations. For example, in their book *The Way Men Think:: Intellect, Intimacy, and the Erotic Imagination,* Liam Hudson and Bernadine Jacot perform a sociology of knowledge analysis of all the different fields that tend to be gender specific and gender reinforced.[3] Why are more men interested in molecular biology, atomic physics, and engineering, whereas more women are attracted to organismic biology, ecology, and sociology? Male science tends to isolate discrete particles — genes or subatomic particles — and then seek to manipulate them in an effort to control or replace nature with culture. Female science tends toward a more participatory mode in which culture is embedded in nature, but both culture and nature are enhanced through the intimacy of understanding. Once again, this archetypal difference is the difference between the genetics of Francis Crick and Barbara McClintock. Hudson and Jacot are Jungian psychoanalysts; their explanation for this archetypal pattern is that the male suffers from a wound of difference, a developmental crisis that separates boys from their mothers. The mother-daughter pair, Demeter and Persephone, share a similar body and do not feel this anxiety of difference; consequently, they require no hero's journey or myth of individuation — no technological replacement of nature to substitute for the sensuous maternal intimacy that stimulated and then abandoned them. I have explored some of this turf in an essay on the robotic scientist Hans Moravec in my last book, *The American Replacement of Nature.*[4] The male compulsion to get away from "the mere jelly" of biology to create a perfect "postbiological world" in downloading the soul into a computer can be traced all the way back to the Gilgamesh epic, in which the male-bonded pair of Gilgamesh and Enkidu attempt to slay the spirit of the forest and deliver themselves from the goddess Ishtar's power over life and death. Moravec and his robot are just another example of that old archetypal pair, the male-bonded couple.

So the career choice one makes says much about one's unconscious agenda. The autodidact, the lonely person in the library compulsively constructing a revisioning of human history, figures himself against the stars as a solitary and misunderstood genius. He alone has discovered the secret that connects everything together. He can show how the DNA code, the hexagrams of the *I Ching,* the molecular structure of mushrooms, and the geomantic lattice of the power-points in the Earth's crust are all part of a grand puzzle that proves that the gods are out there. The grand paranoid cosmic synthesis is always a fascinating narrative of occult connections, and this mad compulsion to find the single code that explains everything does not necessarily invalidate the entire narrative of the work, but it does render a darkness visible.

In his books, Sitchin doesn't allow himself to slip into paranoid narratives, but, of course, a book is easier to control than a lecture because by the time a book has gone through a copy editor and an editor, the manuscript has been cleaned up and made to look more socially responsible. But when the person is right there in front of you, as Sitchin was, you can see what is really going on in his compulsion to explain the universe. I found the lecture to be more of a revelation of the man than the book.

What I also found fascinating, and the reason why, ultimately, I find Sitchin's theory unconvincing—even though I am interested in myths of origin of all kinds—was his literalization of the imagination. Sitchin is nothing if not a literalist. One clear giveaway that Sitchin has been taken over by Whiteheadian "misplaced concreteness" is expressed in his book by his fondness for casting the gods from the twelfth planet in cheap 1950s B movie rockets and space suits. The ancient Sumerian goddess Inanna's headdress is a space suit helmet; the straps on her back are for a space backpack. Precisely in murky areas in which there is a lot of room to doubt, and more than enough space to wonder, Sitchin is constantly invoking absolutist language like: "The complete package of instruments—for this is what they undoubtedly were—is held in place with the aid of two sets of straps that crisscross the goddess's back and chest."[5] One can make a good case that the statue of Inanna pictured on page 125 of Sitchin's book is a Sumerian version of the neolithic icon of the "phallic-necked goddess" that Marija Gimbutas has discussed in her books.[6] The Sumerian statue of Inanna appears to be just such an epiphany of the goddess, with the head visually punning as the glans penis. And what Inanna wears are those objects that she must take off, one by one, as she passes through the seven gates of hell, as described in the Sumerian poem, "Inanna's Descent into the Nether World."

What Sitchin sees is what he needs for his theory. So figure 15 on page 42 is radiation therapy, and figure 71 on page 136 is a god inside a rocket-shaped chamber. If these are gods, why are they stuck with our cheap B movie technology of rockets, microphones, space-suits, and radiation therapy? If they are gods, then why can't they have some really divine technology such as intradimensional worm-hole travel, antigravity, starlight propulsion, or black hole bounce rematerializations? Sitchin has constructed what appears to be a convincing argument, but when he gets close to single images on ancient tablets, he falls back into the literalism of "Here is an image of the gods in rockets." Suddenly, ancient Sumer is made to look like the movie set for *Destination Moon*. Erich Von Däniken's potboiler *Chariots of the Gods* has the same problem. The plain of Nazca in Peru is turned into a World War II landing strip. The gods can cross galactic distances, but by the time they get to Peru, their spaceships are imagined as World War II prop jobs that need an enormous landing strip. This literalization of the imagination doesn't make any sense, but every time it doesn't, you hear Sitchin say "There can be no doubt, but . . ." One can be certain that when Sitchin says that, there will be a lot of "buts" and plenty of cosmic space in which to doubt.

Sitchin wants to make the *yad* and the *shem* rockets that take us up, but *yad* and *shem* may simply be another version of lignam and yoni, one pointed, the other oval. "That which is highward" need not be a rocket; it could be the erection of Osiris, a symbol of the regeneration of time. In Samuel Noah Kramer's translation of "Enki and the World Order," Enki lifts the penis and out flows the seminal waters of the inundation of the Tigris and Euphrates; in Sitchin's translation, Enki lifts the microphone.[7] For Kramer the crown of Inanna, the "Shugarra" is "the crown of the steppe," or the wild grasses from which agriculture comes; for Sitchin it is "that which makes go far into the universe," or a space helmet.[8] There is plenty of room for doubt here, for each cultural historian sees what he wants for his theory. My reading will fit in nicely with the approach I have taken in *The Time Falling Bodies Take to Light,* and Sitchin's will fit in with 1950s movies such as "They Came From Outer Space!"

There is a hermaneutics to the imagination, and its images can never be taken literally. The imagination is the intermediate realm between matter and spirit; it is the realm of psyche. The economy is also an intermediate realm between matter and spirit; on one hand, there is nature, say the veins of gold in the earth, and, on the other, compassion. A paper dollar is not a literal hunk of value; it is a consensual instrument that allows a cultural domain to come into play. So it is with an image from the realm of the psyche. The image one creates of an angel or an extraterrestrial is not a literal hunk of life; it is a negotiable instrument that allows domains that are multi-dimensionally transcendent to the human evolutionary body with its sensorium to enter into relationship, to allow a new culture to come into play. What we cannot see we can imagine. What one imagines is what is in one's storehouse of imagery, so some sensitives see angels as insipid girlish boys with giant pigeon wings. Others cannot conceive of angels, and so they imagine extraterrestrials appearing at the foot of the bed as they go to sleep and abducting them into flying saucers. Since human males have erections when they are in the dream state, their minds cross these two conditions and lead them to imagine that the extraterrestrials are performing genetic experiments on them and drawing out samples of semen. This is a modern version of the medieval legend of the succubus.

In his book *Cosmic Memory*, Rudolf Steiner claims to be able to take us to the edges of history in an archaeological excavation that he calls "reading" the akashic record—the etheric image in the structure of space-time that holds the record of the past. But one needs to remember that the template for registering this crystalline structure is Steiner's own imagination. The akashic record is not like a CD-ROM; even for an amazing clairvoyant like Steiner, there is a hermeneutics to the imagination, and what Steiner "sees" is a negotiable instrument that brings forth a relationship between himself and the akashic record of the collective unconscious. Steiner's imagination is a product of his time; it is influenced by Ernst Haeckel's nineteenth-century Darwinian narratives and by the physics of the turn of the century. I don't think that one should take a clairvoyant's reading of the akashic record as gospel truth. Steiner himself admits that "reading" the akashic record is a very difficult and complex act—that it is not like the Mormon leader Joseph Smith finding a piece of angelic script engraved on metal and buried in the hill of Comora. The literalism of the Mormons, or of Zecharia Sitchin, comes about precisely because they do not understand the nature of psyche and the imagination and always seek to literalize, to concretize in a simple and idolatrous fundamentalism.

The imagination is an intermediate realm between the ego in its perceptual body of senses and the intuition of higher, multidimensional states of consciousness. Information moves in both directions. Some kinds of intuitions come down to the ego, and some kinds of peripheral perceptions are transformed by the imagination as they surface into awareness and become rendered into an imagistic narrative. Take, for example, a man who has been exposed to a flu virus; while the virus is still incubating and he is unconscious of its presence, he has a dream that shows that his body is, at some level, aware of the infection. The narrative of the dream, however, is a symbolic, imagistic construction. It is not an objective reading of a meter.

To come up with a myth of origins, a story, a work of art, a scientific theory, is definitely a creation of the imagination. When we say that Eve was made from Adam's rib, or that Isis and Osiris made love in their mother's womb, we are using language — which, as George Lakoff and Mark Johnson have shown, is an inherently metaphoric system to begin with[9] — as a symbolic expression. We can translate metaphors in multiple ways, and in the case of a myth, the narrative is always a fugue containing several lines of meaning at once. So we can think of Isis and Osiris in the womb as the Earth and the moon in the stellar nebula before they evolve into distinct planetary entities. Or we can think of Eve as the moon being pulled out of Earth, a rib taken from Adam. To take mythic narratives literally, to think that some old man named Jehovah pulled a rib out of a man to make a woman, is pure superstition. It is an insult to the nature of the creative imagination; it is a mistake that no real artist would ever make.

For example, when Steiner talks about the ancient body of man swimming in the sea, we should picture not some comic book Aquaman swimming around in a submarine Atlantis, but the evolution of the cell. In *Cosmic Memory*, Steiner also talks about a Lemeurian epoch in which the human was half fish and half man. Well, Sitchin, on page 259 of *The 12th Planet*, shows us a picture of the fishman Oannes and says it represents a submarine that the gods used in the Persian Gulf. In Steiner's act of seership, the image is brought forth through a meditative dreaming with and through the akashic record and then is intellectually reconstructed into a narrative. Steiner's narrative is sensitive to the entire evolution of life, and one has to go back to the time when life was still in the ocean and not yet on land. Steiner is seeing Haeckelian visions of planetary evolution. Take this description from *Cosmic Memory*:

> Thereby this likeness of man is in a position to attract certain substances from the environment and to combine them with itself, secreting them again later by means of the repelling forces. These substances, of course, can only be taken from the animal realm described above, and from the realm of man. This constitutes a beginning of nutrition. Thus these first likenesses of man were eaters of animals and of men.[10]

When Steiner uses the word "man" here, one should think of the German word *Mensch* or, even more generally, of "creature." Steiner is describing the cell, the chemotaxis of the amoeba. We were the cell. The origin of life is the origin of us. Steiner's vision is one in which humans are deeply embedded in the whole natural history of the planet and the solar system. And he's right. The biosphere is an extended body politic; properly speaking, it is part of our incarnation. Like a flame that requires an atmosphere, we require Gaia. Steiner is an amazing visionary, but if one becomes a fundamentalist follower of his, an Anthroposophist constantly intoning "Der Doktor hat gesagt," then one destroys the spirit with the letter of literalism.

Literalism is very often the affliction that followers inflict on their more imaginative leaders. The followers degrade the movement, and everything the leader has tried to do becomes a rigid and ridiculous caricature of itself. Steiner fell into the sacrificial role of leader and played out the tragedy of followership for all of us to see. One disgruntled follower burned down his Goetheanum, and another probably poisoned him. A remnant of his followers have embalmed his remains in a humorless cult of nineteenth-century folk romanticism, in terrified flight from the demon Ahriman and his servants in the modern electronic world.

There is a shadow side to all leaders that gets unconsciously picked up and acted out by their followers. When a great initiate such as Steiner drops into incarnation in too heavy a fashion, he creates a big splash, and that cultural splash creates the opposite reactions of followership with the Anthroposophists and decayed German romanticism in Hitler's fascination with the occult. It is better to slip into the waters of human incarnation silently, like a frogman, and swim out to attach magnetic bombs to the battleships of industrial materialism. Steiner certainly was no Fascist; in fact, the Fascists were out to get him, so he had to make his base in Switzerland. Steiner lived with a Jewish family, was a teacher of a hydrocephalic Jewish child, and actually took this eight-year old who was considered a vegetable and worked with him so that the child grew up to become a doctor—which is certainly an impressive achievement. But the cultural reaction of the intense leader-led romantic movements of spiritual renewal created the shock waves that gave us Wagner and Hitler. The cult of the great Germanic artist went from Goethe to Wagner to Hitler, the artist manqué. There is a lesson to be learned in the phenomenology of revitalization movements and in the religious effort to institutionalize the ineffable. When one allows oneself to become dogmatized into an institution or a movement, then one ends up with a leader, a cadre of elites, and a mass of followers, all of whom degrade the movement and turn it into its opposite. One goes from complex multidimensional Steiner to humorless cult, or, worse, from Jesus to the

Inquisition. As Jesus once said "in transmission" to the contemporary seer David Spangler: "It isn't what they did *to* me but what they did *with* me that really killed me."

But no matter what strategy one takes, that strategy will have its shadow. I like to envision Steiner deciding to drop down into a body and a culture, and thinking, "Oh my God, look what they are going to do with all of this!" But out of compassion he drops in anyway. What he was able to do is amazing. His creation of the Waldorf schools would be enough for the life of one man, but add to that his contributions to medicine, and we have two lives, then add to that his reforms of the treatment of the mentally retarded, and we have a third life; and on it goes throughout all his work in biodynamic gardening, philosophy, and literature.

In spite of the simplistic and escapist culture of his followers, Steiner himself was a very complex and multidimensional personality. He hung out in the coffee houses of Vienna, where he would meet and have intense discussions with the likes of Leo Froebenius and Stefan Zweig;[11] he went to visit the dying Nietzsche and recognized the Fascist mania of Nietzsche's sister long before anyone else. He edited the scientific writings of Goethe, wrote numerous works of philosophy, and pioneered new and very practical work in agriculture, medicine, and the treatment of the mentally retarded. But such is the antispiritual culture of our universities that a nihilist like Nietzsche is turned into a literary avatar and Steiner is not even given a passing footnote in the cultural history of the turn of the century. He deserves better. He certainly deserves better than followers, but now in the work of Arthur Zajonc he is beginning to get the understanding he deserves.[12] But in some ways, Steiner brought his general cultural rejection on himself, for his second wife, Marie von Sievers, who belonged to a well-to-do and upper-middle class family, was determined to make the good Doctor Steiner thoroughly respectable in the terms of German nineteenth-century academic culture. She took a bookish rabbinical-like scholar who didn't know how to dress or present himself to the world, and constructed the German Herr Professor Doktor. Steiner never discusses his marriages and sexual experiences, and he seems not to have thought very highly of the temptations of the flesh. Some historians, such as Richard Tarnas, feel that Steiner might not have been so much asexual as a repressed homosexual who had mothers instead of lovers for wives. Living in a time when homosexuality would have invalidated his whole religious movement and mission as nothing but ideological camouflage for perversion and heresy, he simply clamped down hard on sexuality. The jealousy and competition for the ownership of Steiner by the women around him, however, was evidently pretty intense. Frau Doktor Steiner, Marie von Sievers, was the leader of the movement's traveling eurythmy dance company, but Frau Steiner did not like Steiner's collaboration with Ita Wegman, the leader of the anthroposophical medical movement. All of which is to say that Steiner was human, all too human, and very much the product of his time.

But what we can take from Steiner for our time is his visionary cosmology, in which human evolution is expanded into cosmic evolution. We can extend the narratives of our human identity far beyond the hominids of the African savanna to the origins of the cell, and beyond to the origins of our solar system. We can reverse the literalization of the creative imagination of Steiner by his followers to appreciate that Steiner, inspired by Goethe's science of morphology and growth, was trying to articulate, along with Henri Bergson and Alfred North Whitehead, a new philosophy and art based not on physics but on biology.

To read Steiner sympathetically, we need to expand our own imaginations so that a reading of the akashic record becomes a psychological participation and not an objective meter reading. For example, when Steiner talks about a time when man was bisexual and could reproduce offspring out of himself, he is not talking about Lemeurian hominids but about the cell. Here we need to compare Steiner with Darwin to get a truer historical feeling for these evolutionary narratives that became the cosmogonies of their day. Here is Steiner:

> In the course of time, the material substances become denser; the human body begins to resemble the subsequent shape of man, the other that of woman. When this difference had not yet appeared, every human being could produce another human being out of himself. Impregnation was not an external process, but was something which took place inside the human body itself.[13]

And here is Darwin:

> It has long been known that in the vertebrate kingdom one sex bears rudiments of various accessory parts, appertaining to the reproductive system, which properly belong to the opposite sex; and it has now been ascertained that at a very embryonic period both sexes possess true male and female glands. Hence some extremely remote progenitor of

the whole vertebrate kingdom appears to have been hermaphrodite or androgynous.[14]

Darwin's narrative is a scientific variant of the myth of Plato's androgynous dawn man from the *Timaeus*. In the hermeneutics of the imagination by which facts are gathered up into a narrative, myth, science, art, and visionary experiences of "reading" the akashic record are not universes apart. The myth of the prehistoric androgyne is a mythic transform, a dream image. When Steiner is talking about the human body, he is really talking about the eukaryotic cell.

But since the evolution of the cell requires an ocean, and the ocean requires an atmosphere, and the atmosphere requires a sun and a solar wind, one cannot discuss the evolution of life without discussing the evolution of the planets and the solar system. And that is exactly what Steiner does in *An Outline of Occult Science*[15]—which is as weird a narrative of human origins as you could possibly ask for—but it is also a deeply ecologically embedded narrative that doesn't have the Cartesian split between the *res cogitans* and the *res extensa*. When Steiner was in a meditational state and "reading" the akashic record, what he received he transformed into imagery, precisely because reading the akashic record is an act of the imagination, and this process is always an act of translation and never one of literalist transcription.

Steiner's efforts are interesting because as a mystic he tried to heal the breach between science and mysticism, and his whole life work was a rejection of the nineteenth-century materialism that said that thoughts are to the brain what urine is to the kidneys, that consciousness can be reduced to a chemical process. This world view is still with us; it is basically the cognitive science of Patricia and Paul Churchland and others. In response to the materialism of his day, Steiner went back to the poets and the tradition of the nineteenth-century German idealism. He tried to root his philosophy in a hermeneutics of the imagination inspired by the great German idealist poets such as Goethe and Schiller.

Steiner's is an intellectual approach to heal the rift between elitist scholarly knowledge and folk knowledge. It is an attempt to create a sensitivity to the astral plane in reaction to the materialism of his time. Unfortunately, much of anthroposophy has remained stuck in the fin de siècle art nouveau of its founding era. If one goes, as I did in Bern, to a eurythmy performance, one notices that eurythmy is all astral and psychic. The women move about in pastel nighties with their arms flailing about in the air—supposedly to manifest angels in the ether—while to the side a woman in Birkenstocks, homespun smock, and a Dutch boy haircut intones Novalis with a deadly serious expression and takes five minutes to extend each vowel so that the angels can get out of the vowels to join in with the movements of the dance. Every gesture of the dancers reaches up in a gnostic effort to get out of the body and catch the vibrating vowels the woman is blowing to them like so many soap bubbles. There are no loins, there are certainly no genitals; and there is no ground; it is all in the air. Eurythmy is just about the mirror-opposite of flamenco. Flamenco is rooted, grounded; the dancers strike the earth with strong feet and full, muscular thighs. Recall Carlos Sauras's movie of the flamenco version of *Carmen*, in which the older teacher tells the younger woman to stick her tits out like the horns of a bull. This is the mirror-opposite of Steiner and Marie von Sievers, and of Balanchine, too. Young ballerinas in New York would, like Amazons, have their breasts cut down because Balanchine didn't like big breasts sticking out in violation of the purity of line. Russian mystic that he was, he wanted his dancers to be androgynous angels. So this fin de siècle spiritual rejection of sexuality is an expression of the culture of the first half of the twentieth century. You find it in Steiner, in Balanchine, as well as in Sri Aurobindo and his yogic consort Mira Richard.

Because the imagination is the realm of psyche, the realm of what the theosophists call the astral plane, it is an ocean of shifting and shifty imagery. When one is in the ocean, there is a level underneath, the crust of the Earth, and a level above, the sunlit air. In the water, one sees only the shimmering of the light; one dwells in an intermediate realm of light and shadow. The psychedelic sailor who becomes entranced with this intermediate world falls overboard and falls in love with the mermaids. This enchanting world of erotic seduction is, however, infantile: the mermaids have beautiful breasts to fondle, but they are scaled down from the waist, so sexual intercourse with them is not possible. Which is another way of saying that enlightenment is not a psychedelic experience. The experience of light is going to be very different if one is looking at the reflections of sunlight from within the turbid waters and swimming with the monsters of the deep.

Just as the ocean is an intermediate realm, a template between the crust of the Earth and the atmosphere, so is the imagination an intermediate realm, a template between matter and spirit. And just as the ocean is the participatory realm that produces clouds and rain for the islands and continents, so is the imagination the participatory realm that produces the imagery of art and science that nourishes the civilizations on land. What is brought forth through the imagination is a structural coupling between the self and the Other, between the individual and the *Umwelt*. Like clouds, imagery is not fixed and solid. If one looks at the clouds and tries to read a secret code in their movement—to say, for instance, that because this cloud is in the shape of the Korean peninsula joined to a mushroom cloud we are going to have nuclear war in Korea—is to slip into a paranoid consciousness. This is one of the traps along the way for the imaginative or mystical person. If instead, one looks at the clouds and sees the geophysiological process of circulation from sea to clouds to rain to rivers that flow back into the sea, then one can begin to appreciate the process of relationship without trying to lock the process into a literal code or a literalist object.

So there is a hermeneutics to the imagination, a way of reading the clouds or the akashic record, and fundamentalists of all and any stripe always get it wrong. They reify the imagination and they deify their chosen leader; they turn their leader's act of creative imagination into a cultic code and demote art into religion. It is as if one took a dollar bill and turned it into an icon, took it out of circulation and set it on top of an altar in a temple. What was meant to be a negotiable instrument that could bring forth a consensual domain or a cultural experience of multiplying processes of activity becomes useless. Steiner admits that the hermeneutics of the imagination is a creative act and not a case of meter reading. But in the case of Sitchin, we encounter a literalization of the imagination in which the intuition, unable to deal with complexity, simplifies the past into a fixed narrative in which ambiguity is replaced by technology.

When complexity, ambiguity, and humor have been eliminated from culture, one ends up with a cult, and when humor leaves a group, it is a good time to go out with it. In the transformation of culture into cult, anything will serve. You can start out with Jesus and end up with the Inquisition, or start out with Marx and end up with Stalin. The process of transformation of culture into cult seems to happen universally, whether it is with Freud, Jung, Steiner, and Balanchine; or Sri Aurobindo, the Mother, and her follower Satprem.

Paranoids and cosmic code crackers cannot laugh at themselves or at their obsessions. Since paranoia is a response to terror, the condition of anxiety is not conducive to laughter. The dynamic of the imagination is polysemic, complex, and multidimensional; it is never simple, linear, fundamentalist, and literal. Every single time there is a mystery in Sitchin's narrative, that mystery is eliminated with a simple cause. And the simple cause is always technology. Everything can be explained by technology.

Jacob's ladder and dream are about rockets and space ships. Actually, Jacob's dream is a good place to stop to consider the nature of perception and imagination. According to Sitchin, "The 'Lord's Abode,' the 'ladder,' and the 'angels of the Lord' using it were not there when Jacob lay down to sleep in the field. Suddenly, there was the awesome 'vision.' And by morning the 'Abode,' the 'ladder,' and their occupants were gone."[16]

Dreams, religious experiences, and angels are not acceptable forms of human experience for Sitchin. Only technology is real, so rather than having Jacob falling asleep and having a dream, Sitchin has to say that the quiet place that Jacob chose for a snooze was next door to some ancient Cape Canaveral.

One good way to get a feeling for the hermeneutics of the imagination is to watch one's mind cross over from the waking state into the hypnagogic. J. Alan Hobson's *The Dreaming Brain* is a very good book on sleep and dreaming.[17] Hobson is a professor of medicine at Harvard. In his sleep research lab at Harvard, Hobson has studied the neurochemistry of dreaming, of how just before we begin to dream, muscle inhibitors are secreted that stop us from running in bed when, for example, we dream that we are running. In this transitional state, sensory perceptions are transformed into imagery. If our hands are on our chest, we dream that some succubus is sitting on our chest. If we hear our heart beat, we transform it into footsteps and have a nightmare that someone is walking down the hall to the door of our bedroom. Sometimes, when we are not yet deeply asleep, but the muscle inhibitors have been triggered, we dream that we are paralyzed, and we struggle to awaken. We feel the weight of our hands on our chest, dream that something is sitting on our chest, and we struggle to knock it off, but we cannot move and become frightened that we are paralyzed and struggle to wake up, to reverse the inhibitors and to move our body once again.

This transformation from percept to imagistic drama is really quite fascinating. Once after I had cleaned up the kitchen from lunch, I lay down on a Le Corbusier chaise longue; as I became completely relaxed, I began to hear the Cuisinart running in the kitchen. As I stared up at the ceiling, I began to reason: no, that can't be, I'm alone in the apartment; no one is in the kitchen. What had happened was that for a second I had drifted into sleep with my eyes still open and the sound of my own snoring had been imagistically transformed into the little drama of the Cuisinart grinding away in the kitchen. If I had been a hominid in the African savanna, I would have probably turned the sound into the image of a lion roaring. Steiner writes about this as well. He writes about a watch ticking on his bedside table. The ticking is experienced in a dream as the clickety clack of a train, and suddenly he finds himself in the middle of a drama in which he is on a train.

The etheric body, and its hypnagogic state, is linked to the old reptilian brain, a brain with a past that is a storehouse of images. The images we create depend upon our own storehouse of memory. Mediums and psychic channels are people who shift out of the waking state into trance and then begin to think in dreams, but, unfortunately, they have no understanding of symbolism, so they take their psychic experiences literally. Jacob dreams of a ladder because that is the common instrument in his daily life for moving from one level to another. To think that angels need ladders to get down to Earth is as ridiculous as thinking that they need 1950s rockets.

If I were to generate a paranoid narrative, I would say there was a demon in the kitchen who had turned on the Cuisinart; suddenly the whole aspect of the imaginative participation by which a sound can go through a template and be transformed into a narrative drama would be obliterated in a kind of fundamentalist, literalist, paranoid narrative. But what one learns when one watches the hypnogogic state is that at that edge between external sensitivity to the room and internal imagination in the dream, there is a real outside world, as in the case of Steiner's dream in which the watch by the bedside table is transformed into a train. But the transformation of watch into train is a metaphoric process, and metaphors should not be taken literally, whether they occur in dreams, visions, myths, sacred texts, or works of literature.

Events that are not perceivable within the time frame of the human consciousness —this little one-fifth to one-quarter of a second that we call "now"—can be intuited in marginal states of consciousness and then transformed by the imagination into dreams, visions, and mythic narratives. If the rate of happening is not in the human time of movies of twenty-eight frames per second but at one frame per second, or is occurring at a billion frames per second, or at a cosmic periodicity of once every million years, then both the infinitely little and the infinitely large are beyond our perception, but they are not beyond our imagination. So the unknown can be imagined even if it cannot be known, quantified, or measured. The imagination is a kind of extensive space of unconscious memory that can feel these cosmic things going on at the margins of our consciousness—in our multidimensional subtle bodies rather than our physical body and brain—and then transform them into imagery. But we shouldn't take the imagery literally.

For example, let's take Francis Crick's theory of "panspermism." This is Crick of Crick and Watson DNA fame. The theory of panspermism maintains that life on earth was seeded by organic molecules coming to our planet from the impact of meteorites from outer space. Consequently, the notion that life came to earth from outer space as expressed in B movies such as "They Came from Outer Space!" is an artistic intuition of planetary evolution. Crick's theory of panspermism holds that much of the material for the evolution of life came from outerspace in the form of meteors and comets and that as these objects struck the Earth they added some spice to the primal soup of the prebiotic ocean. All this stuff was cooked and simmered for over a billion years until finally there was operational closure with micelles, membranes, and, finally, living cells. Such was the evolution of life on Earth.

Now, notice that we have this transformation going on outside the time frame of human perception. How can one make this kind of story accessible? One way, of course, is through a mythopoeic construction, so we end up with a story that the Earth is like the ovum and these meteors are little spermatozoa coming in from outside and impregnating Gaia, Mother Earth. We can tell a story, and the story begins to fall into archetypal patterns, of female impregnation and masculine insemination. The archetypal pattern of sexual intercourse begins to move the narrative closer to the imaginal realm of myth and fairy tale, and we can begin to tell a story about the origins of life. Our ego in our physical body was not there at the origins of life, but each of our subtle bodies—the etheric, astral, mental, and causal bodies of esoteric lore—has more dimensions than three, so by the time we move up through the five subtle bodies from ego to Atman, from the yogic *annamayakosa* to the *anandamayakosa*—or from meat body to light body—we add multiple dimensions and cosmic time. Atman whispers through the intuition into the ego's ear the myths, fairy tales, and cosmogonies that tell the story of how we and the planet came to be. We know because "we" were there, not at the level of ego, but at the macro level of myth, of the universal consciousness that is holographically infolded in each of us. At one level, we were the organic molecules from outer space, the archaebacteria, the dinosaurs. Now we are human, but soon we are about to become something else. For Crick the gods from outer space are organic molecules riding to Earth in meteors and comets, and for Sitchin, the gods are extraterrestrials riding to Earth in 1950s rockets from the twelfth planet.

These sorts of big picture stories can't be told except through myth, mysticism, and art. The trick is to know how to read myths or works of art.

The scientist tends to dismiss mythopoeic expressions as superstitious rub-
bish; the fundamentalist tends to literalize the imagination, thus collapsing
multiple dimensions into a mere two or three. The imagination is a particular
kind of membrane; it is a transformer that takes in higher dimensional
experiences and steps them down to household current to run the appliances
of our daily life. Like the membrane around a cell or the membrane around
a flame that is the dialogue between the atmosphere and the flame, the
imagination performs the relationship between the unique and the universal,
between beings and Being. Imagination can be liberating as long as one
realizes that it is a membrane and not a wall. The logical category-mistake
of the fundamentalists of any stripe is to turn that particular membrane into
a wall, a locked cell containing identity, containing truth, and eventually
containing you, not in a culture, but a cult.

    People who are at the unconscious level mystical and sensitive and at
the conscious level of socialization constrained to be materialistic are often
unable to deal with their marginal sensitivities and try to explain everything
in a technological manner. What for Steiner would be angels are for Sitchin
extraterrestrials in rockets. Consider Sitchin's explication of the caduceus.
The caduceus, the staff of Mercury with the two snakes turning into
wings—the contemporary logo of the medical profession—is an ancient
hermetic symbol of the two nerve channels of the spinal column and the two
hemispheres of the brain. For Sitchin, the caduceus is not a yogic symbol of
the *ida* and *pingala* nerve channels, but of a space satellite. Now, the caduceus
is an emblem that has been used for thousands of years by yogic initiates. In
kriya yoga, there is a particular mantra, a cool lunar tonality that is used to
bring up the energy in the moon channel from the base of the spine to the
third eye, and there is a particular mantra one intones as one visualizes the
warm solar energy returning back down in the sun channel to the base of
the spine. If one takes the time to learn this yogic technique from a serious
yogic ashram, then as one performs the visualization one feels an energy
pouring over the brain and fanning out and energizing the particular center
between the eyebrows. As it fans out over the brain, it feels like the hood of
the cobra, and then suddenly one understands the old movies one saw as a
child—of the snake in the basket rising from the sound of the flute, of it
rising and becoming straight, of its having a jewel on its forehead above its
two eyes. The imagery is an initiatic hieroglyph for yogic practitioners, not
just for Indian yogis, but also for European hermetic initiates. The spinal
column is Mozart's Masonic *Magic Flute.* The seven holes in the flute are the
chakras along the spinal column; the passing through the magic fire unburnt

is going through the initiation of raising the interior fire of kundalini at the base of the spine. What we see in the movies, or what I actually saw outside my hotel in Agra, India, is the snake charmer who, rather than performing his yoga alone in his room at midnight, is performing his art for tourists in the streets. Some snake charmers are, of course, frauds, and the snakes are devenomed, but some, perhaps, have mastered their fear, charmed the snake, and gained a certain kind of wisdom. They have literalized an esoteric practice, but in an exoteric manner they have come to a mastery of fear and a centering of consciousness. So snake charming can be a kind of yoga after all. But Sitchin has the simple and idolatrous mind of a peasant—not that peasants are bad—but the peasant's imagination, as opposed to the poet's, is a literalist one. For Sitchin, technology is the idol, and so the caduceus is a space satellite, and that's all there is to it.

When one shifts from Sitchin to Steiner, one moves into more of an awareness of multidimensionality; in Steiner's works, the gods are not rocket pilots but forces of evolution and planetary development mythologically expressed as archangels. Steiner developed his own forms of meditational practice, a form of yoga for the West,[18] and therefore his cosmology is not merely a technology. As one goes through yogic practice, whether from the East or the West, one experiences the opening of the chakras—the cerebro-spinal centers of consciousness—and encounters the richness of multidimensional space. No longer is everything expressed and structured in three-dimensional space. As one stops the beating of the heart and the pulse of the breath, one moves into fine microstructures of time in which "angels" become part of one's newly expanded symbiotic consciousness. It is a new kind of evolution. Even the current craze of angels, for all its addiction to kitsch, is a sign of this cultural transformation. In the former cultural shift, from Europe to the American frontier, the dynamic was of cowboys and Indians, from Natty Bumpo and Chingachagook to the Lone Ranger and Tonto. Now in our shift from the continental to the galactic frontier, the pairing is of humans and angels, or humans and extraterrestrials. Just as in the evolution of the cell, the mitochondria and the plastids found themselves inside the gigantic eukaryotic cell, so now the ego finds itself inside a multidimensional field of life in which beings participate in its newly extended field of consciousness. Unlike us, these multidimensional beings have bodies that seem to be made out of music and mathematical lattices of light. This elevation of consciousness is expressed in Dante's *Paradiso*, in which a cognitive bliss presents "the Angel sphere that knows most and loves most."[19] If one prefers a more contemporary version of this experience, then there is Arthur C. Clarke's and Stanley Kubrick's film, *2001: A Space Odyssey.* This work of science fiction is a more Sitchinesque vision in which initiation is technologically mediated, but when the astronaut goes through the stargate, he passes into multidimensionality and encounters rotating lattices of light and music that conduct him through an initiation, serve as midwives to his rebirth, and carry him back to his planet so that he can become the messianic starchild for an Earth in crisis.

Now even in the mystical experiences of stopping the heart in yogic meditation there is still a heremeneutics of the imagination. How does one interpret this experience? Say one has been in meditation for two hours and one has slowed down one's metabolism to the point that the heart stops and the breath ceases, and then one feels a movement out of the body through the chakra-vortex of the third eye, the stargate of 2001. Is it the case that the heart has literally stopped? Or is it the case that now our sensitivity to time is so fine and subtle that the interval between each heart beat has become vastly extended. Like Alice going through the looking glass, or a shaman climbing a pole into another world, one has moved into a relativistic time-space. One is no longer situated in a discrete corpuscular self in which the ego holds reality together. Heartbeat—gap—heartbeat. Normally, we ignore the gaps to connect heartbeat to heartbeat with a sense of continuity that we know as the ego or personality. But through meditation one reverses figure and ground and focuses on the gaps rather than the beats. The gaps are given equal time and space, and when that happens, "there goes the neighborhood." Angels move in across the stream, and it is never going to be the boring suburbs of the ego again.

Angels, like great jazz musicians, have their own kind of music. As one begins to get a feel for these multidimensional topologies, the only good metaphors for them are music and mathematics—which is why art, music, and mathematics are so critical to understanding these angelic states of emergent evolution. In our American mass culture, angels are presented as insipid celestial humans, but in the Neoplatonic and Iranian traditions, angels are called "celestial intelligences." In our age, one possible way to rescue angels from Disneyfication is through music and higher mathematics. When we shift into the musical-mathematical domains of consciousness in the gaps between each heartbeat—in the fine microstructures of human time—then angels begin to have a topological reality. And so one of the most intelligent, sophisticated, and interesting questions we can ask about angels is: How many can dance on the head of a pin? The head of a pin is a point, a dimensionless point that is the intersection of void and multidimensionality. This dimensionless point is the basin of attraction of multidimensional complexity; it is a singularity like the big bang or a black hole that opens up all sort of possibilities. The universe *is* exactly all sorts of possibilities.

What is being brought forth in the relationship between, let's say, a celestial intelligence and our own human intelligence is a constructed reality, a negotiable instrument for spiritual commerce. The image or symbol is not an absolute description of reality, but a medium of exchange, a form of currency, like the dollar bill. Now the paranoid, the literalist, will say money is valuable because gold or diamonds have powerful occult properties of vibration. If one tries to set up a Hamiltonian central bank in which the government takes the gold and gives the citizen a slip of paper, the paranoid and the literalist will get very nervous and start mumbling about cabals and conspiracies in which the evil ones are trying to gain power to lock all the occult vibrations of gold and diamonds in their magical chambers to rule the world. The evil ones can be the Jews, the Rothschilds, the Rockefellers, or the Council on Foreign Relations. Fill in the blank with the enemy you love to hate. For the paranoid and the literalist, reality is not something brought forth in relationship; it is a collection of things. So if they accept the dollar, they want to be sure that there is actually an equivalent amount of gold in Fort Knox to back it up. Nevermind that there is not enough gold on the planet to back up all the transactions one might wish to have in a vast global economy. And that is why some conservative literalists won't trust metal as a basis of value but will insist on land. Whether the literalists are medieval feudalists or mercantilists, they place their faith in objects and not relationships.

Value was once based on land, then on metal, then on paper currencies backed up by a national bank. Then in the late capitalism when Nixon took the world off fixed rates of currency exchange, value was based on nation-state futures in which a national scientific and industrial technological complex backed up the value of the nation. Foreigners weren't simply buying dollars, they were trading in American nation-state futures. This was why the moon shot was so important. It was backing up the global belief system in the American scientific and technological complex. It was a television commercial for selling American nation-state futures.

The emergence of late capitalism is coeval with the emergence of electronic systems of communication, artificial intelligence, and chaos dynamics. It is a new form of mathematical topology in which "the center is everywhere and the circumference nowhere." It is an unconscious consensual domain that allows a planetary culture to come into being, but those whose identities are fixed in the medieval religious group or the industrial nation-state start freaking out and become involved in tribal violence, ethnic cleansing, or more American forms of conservative hysteria, such as the bombing of the Federal building in Oklahoma City. The global economy is threatening because it is not mappable in three dimensions and its multidimensionality seems to be evil to both Islamic and Christian fundamentalists. They class it as demonic although it would be just as valid to identify it as angelic because it is a phase-change from one global economy to another.

Since the fall of the Berlin wall and the meltdown of the Soviet Union, we all recognize that Communism is dead. We think, rather naively, that capitalism won and is alive and doing well. Not so. We are now in the midst of the catastrophe bifurcation from capitalism to environmentalism. Global pollution and global catastrophes are having an implosive effect as disasters such the greenhouse effect and the ozone hole are bringing all of humanity together in the new planetary cultural phase-space. One result of the greenhouse effect is that there are hundred-year floods and hurricanes every year. The president recognizes a photo-op, dons a windbreaker, and takes a helicopter ride over the stricken area, declares it a disaster area, and promises millions in national emergency relief. That's just fine and dandy when there is only one disaster every decade, but when there are ten every year, and when they are coming alongside plagues and medical crises, as well as a graying population in which more people are on pensions than in the workforce, one can forget about paying off the deficit. So the feedback of the currents of the global biosphere on the currencies of the global economy is an implosion in which we are all brought together in the new body politic of catastrophe. This cultural transformation embodies the shift from an economy to an ecumene—a world space not expressed as a world church or religion, as it was in the middle ages, but as a global ecology of consciousness. At the moment, this evolutionary catastrophe bifurcation is an extremely polarized one of tribal and genocidal self-extinction on the one hand—as in the cases of Bosnia and Rwanda—and universal compassion and global involvement on the other.

World War II effected the shift from capitalism to late capitalism and established the new Pacific rim economy. If we had been enlightened we might have created our destiny with Japan instead of having our fate inflicted upon us in the unconscious form of war. Now we continue in our unenlightened state as we burn out the rain forests to have grazing land for cattle so that we can have McDonalds hamburgers, but what we get is global weather change and new airborne viruses heading to plague the megacities. The demand for a national health plan is just the first recognition of our entry into this new global ecumene of human relationships. National health is to us what the land grant acts and railroad charters were to the nineteenth century: the articulation of a new space and the entry into a new cultural domain. The natural response to this shift from one culture to another is to deny it and seek to regress: to buy an attack rifle, return to the land, and store food and ammunition; or to return to European white colonialism and declare African independence a failure; or to bash Japan and buy American; or turn off CNN and let Bosnia, Rwanda, and Somalia go to hell.

Now just as World War II was the unenlightened transition, a violent release of heat in a phase-change, from a national to a transnational culture for the Pacific Rim, so now are we going through the unenlightened transition from an industrial to an informational society. The release of heat in this phase-change is the remedievalization of society in the meltdown of middle-class, democratic society. Public health, public transportation, and public education are all breaking apart as the postwar space of the expanding middle class is subjected to "downsizing" by transnational corporations. Government is no longer about political philosophies, but becomes another variant of electronic sports, a game of opposition in which both sides are the same: Republican and Democrat, Pepsi and Coke, Avis and Herz. The content of the electronic media is based on the traditional culture they have destroyed: television destroys family conversation and so gives us the relationship conversations of Oprah; electronics destroys reading and so gives us films such as *Pagemaster*; televised news destroys government and so gives us the eternal presidential campaign as a variant of NFL and the Superbowl. In this condition of electropop Fascism, the minds of the citizens are collectivized into informational feedlots and fed the technoswill produced by such conglomerates as Time-Warner-CNN, or Disney-ABC. The informed citizen of a middle-class democracy becomes a loyal subject of the new mediocracy. To accelerate this process of collectivization in informational feedlots, masses of immigrants are allowed in to destructure trade unions and pauperize the lower middle class. This GATT and NAFTA restructuring of the nation-state is basically a hockey face-off over who is going to rule the twenty-first century: China or North America in a new formation that has corporatized Mexico and destructured Canada and pauperized the formerly middle-class United States in order to create its own internal "Third World" labor force that can compete with Asia and

Indonesia. The transnational corporation uses cheap Mexican labor to break down the middle-class civility of the Canadian economy—with its national health plan—then energizes reactionary, Social Credit British Columbia—which hates elitist old boy Ontario—and pits it against francophone Quebec, and then sits back and hopes to pick up the pieces. It is basically the "hostile takeover" strategy of the 1980s now applied to nation-states instead of corporations. Buy it out, break it up, and sell off the pieces, which are worth more than the whole: Canadian water is worth more than that old fictional Canadian nineteenth-century McDonald-Laurier railroad nation-state. So as Canada disintegrates, a new North America is able to consolidate a transcontinental economy that can compete with Japan-Korea-China and the whole Pacific Rim, or with a rising super-Europe, and have all the water and energy it needs. The great need for the future now is not oil, it's water, and Canada has the biggest reservoir of water anywhere around.

As public safety collapses in this process of the pauperization of the industrial middle class, the rich take to their neomedieval castle subdivisions protected by private armies, and the poor are held in reservations in which the police are basically armies of occupation. The end of late capitalism thus has become a caricatured death-rattle in which Dickensian poverty, the nakedly honest entrepreneurialism of crime, and the shadow economy of drugs present the world with a vision of complete cultural entropy in which no traditional human economy is viable. In essence, the situation is an evolutionary catastrophe bifurcation of up or out, a global economy or a planetary ecumene.

If value in the late capitalism of the 1960s was based on nation-state futures—the cumulative knowledge embodied in the scientific and techno-logical complex of the country—what is value based on in this new global ecumene of angelic compassionism? It isn't based on Buddhism, but Buddhism does surface as a global fascination, and the Dalai Lama becomes not a medieval theocrat, but a global teacher precisely because Buddhism captures some of the dynamics of a worldview based on relationship, dependent co-origination, and compassion. The new economy is based on states of consciousness and multidimensional upward mobility, not the power of positive thinking in the boomerism of old style capitalism, but investment of time, energy, study, and capital in noetic polities rather than nation-states. Some of these noetic polities are demonically constellated by the media, popular music, Olympic sports, and the celebrity as the apotheosis of the dying individual. And some of these noetic polities are constellated by planetary lattices of information — Microsoft, the Internet, Greenpeace. Just as the discovery of the New World extended the phase-space of Europe to create a new world economy, so the mystical entry into these angelic, multidimensional hyperspaces is extending the phase-space of America to create a new planetary biospheric mentality, a Gaia Politique. When Sitchin comes out with a weird narrative that gods in rockets messed with the primates and genetically transformed them into hominids, consider that misplaced concreteness for the intercession of one ontological domain into another. I think Kubrick and Clarke are closer to the truth than Sitchin. As Charles Peguy once said of another cultural revolution: "Tout commence en mystique et finit en politique."[20]

5

PREHISTORIC
SCULPTURES:
THE BODY AS THE
STORY OF TIME

Proust's madeleine is one expression of the recovery of past time through the symbolic form of the feminine. Now I would like to look at prehistoric sculptures of the female body as another expression of the primal source, another *grassement sensuel* form that is, like the madeleine and the seashell, impressed with the evolutionary architecture of time. Although my general focus in this book is on literature and texts as cultural artifacts of the evolution of consciousness—from our imagination of the hominids in natural history to our imagination of the posthuman future of consciousness—I want to approach the origins of folktales and literature through a consideration of the image of the female body as a reflection of myth preserved in sculpture. I want to look at the goddess Inanna by going back to the statues of the great goddess from the prehistoric settlements of paleolithic Dolni Vestonice to neolithic Çatal Hüyük. Here, I am spiraling back to some of the themes that I wrote about almost a generation ago in *The Time Falling Bodies Take to Light*.

Now, the old, high cultural, European way of describing the course of literature and the evolution of culture is to proceed from great man to

great man. You start with the murmurings of the pre-Socratics, break out
into the operatic roar of Plato, and then make your way through history,
going from Aristotle to Augustine to Aquinas to Descartes to Kant to
Einstein. No women. No Egypt. No Africa. No India. No China. This
scholarly curriculum is really the intellectual construction of identity, and
of imaginary identifications, for gentlemen of the patriarchal era in which
Oxford and Harvard dons described, indeed, *performed* Western civilization
for the benefit of all. It would never occur to a Benjamin Jowett or an F. M.
Cornford to think otherwise, but I, too, am probably guilty of some similar
unconscious limitation of worldview. The younger generation of literary
critics and cultural historians, say of my daughter's generation—she is now
working on her PhD in English at Ann Arbor—will undoubtedly find blind
spots that express the limitations of me and my time. Some future politically
correct critic may come along and say that there were not enough gay and
lesbian texts in my Lindisfarne symposium because I was blinded by my
own heterosexuality; or that there are not enough African texts, because I
was really a Eurocentric at heart, for all my gestures toward India, China,
and Mexico. Actually, I worried about this last month and consciously tried
to anticipate some of these objections. So I took down my copy of Marcel
Griaule's *Conversations with Ogotommeli*[1] from the bookshelf, thinking that
there might be some way I could work in Dogon cosmology with the other
cosmologies, such as the Babylonian *Enuma Elish* or Heisod's *Theogony*. I had
not looked at Dogon cosmology since I was an anthropology student in
college, but when I reread this cosmology, more than thirty years later, I
became furious and tossed the book in the corner in disgust. The creation
of the world is turned into a rationalization for the genital mutilation of
women. Dogon cosmogony certainly does form a parallel line of comparison
with the Babylonian *Enuma Elish,* in which Marduk, the heroic male god,
creates the world by dismembering the body of the Great Mother. But what
I had been naively willing to accept as exotic ethnographic data as an
undergraduate, I could no longer accept as a grandfather. I was disgusted
and said to myself: "To hell with p.c.; these guys are just plain savages!" The
creation of the world is made into a justification for cutting out the female
clitoris. Now in France, this whole issue of civilization versus savagery has
become much more than the p.c. battle of multiculturalism and academic
curricula that it is in the United States. Hundreds of infant girls, whose
genitalia have been clumsily razored out by their fathers, have been showing
up in French hospitals. The infants are brought in screaming, bleeding,
infected, mutilated for life, and probably also convinced psychologically for

life that they were justly punished for the sin of being female. The French minister of health, a woman, became enraged at this practice brought into enlightened France by African immigrants, so she has declared open cultural war against it, and there are signs in all the clinics warning parents that in France genital mutilation is a crime. Now if one wishes to be an orthodox p.c. advocate, one certainly does not want to be accused of being a racist, so one has to fall into line and say no culture has the right to enforce its culture on another. Therefore some might wish to claim that the French Socialist minister of health is really a racist and no better than reactionary Le Pen, the leader of the National Front. After all, no one would dream of passing a law in New York that Jews no longer had the right, in our Jeffersonian republic founded on the principles of the Enlightenment, to circumcise their infant sons — one of the practices that they have smuggled in to our bright and shining shores from the "violent and barbaric" Middle East. So one can appreciate the kind of cognitive dissonance that this practice of genital mutilation must create for liberal feminists. Which side do they come down on: the right of black Africans in white France, or the rights of women everywhere?

Let me confess my bias here and now: in this case, yes, I am for European civilization against African savagery, *pour La France* as a cultural expression of the civilization of the Enlightenment and against the powers of ignorance and darkness; I am for the celebration of the sacredness of the female body, whether it be Proust's madeleine, or the statue from Lespugue that I am about to discuss.

I accept the fact that this book expresses my biases and conventional attitudes, as well as those of my generation's vanishing literary culture. No matter how hard I might try, I could never achieve an abstract balance and a *political* representation for all the cultures and four quarters of the globe that would satisfy every advocate of any emergent ism.

When I was an anthropology student in the 1950s, I was taught that pottery was the signal of the beginning of the Neolithic era, around 9000 B.C.E. In recent excavations, however, archaeologists have discovered that ceramic figurines go all the way back to Dolni Vestonice in Moravia, from around 24,000 B.C.E. So the old, neat, linear progression simply won't work any more. Dolni Vestonice is also a very interesting place to begin our discussion because there we encounter a rather amazing arti- fact, not the usual faceless image of the Great Goddess but the head of a real, quite distinctly individualized woman. It is a small head, carved out of mammoth ivory. The woman's hair is coiffed in a bun on top of her

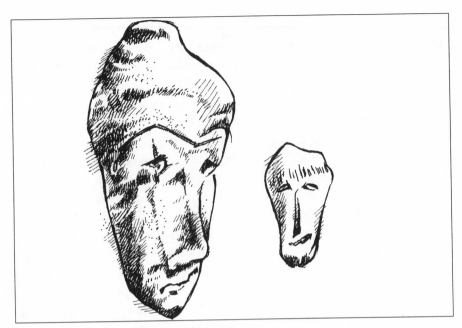

Figure 5.1: Drawing of Head of Woman.

head, and her jaw is distinctly misshapen, as if she suffered either from some deformity or traumatic accident. A skull with a similar disfigurement was found at Dolni Vestonice within the settlement of mammoth tusks that served as the fence around the encampment. The skeleton was buried within the community, but outside was found a single hut that also shows the remains of ceramic-making activities—the making, firing, and deliberate cracking of these ceramic figurines of the Great Goddess herself. Evidently the clay was mixed with water in a deliberate way so that when it was placed in the magical fire of the hearth, it would explode and lines and cracks would appear. It is thought that these lines and cracks were magical signs for divination, hieroglyphs of profound meaning, not unlike the signs that were painted on the walls of the caves at places such as Lascaux. I want to begin my story with this woman, with prehistory's first real person. She is *la sage femme,* shaman, sorceress, artist, and alchemical adept in the secrets of fire and transformation.

Women need to be credited for creating not only agriculture but also ceramics and its protochemistry. These prehistoric technologies are deeply embedded in art and the sacred, in ritual and probably in a lunar astrology. But as history develops and society becomes reorganized into the specialized castes of male priests and warriors supported by an economic surplus, the generalized female shamanic figure, who is healer, artist, and scientist at once—is shunted to the side. The male professionals take over and we get the configuration of the patriarchal society of priests and warriors. That is history, but prehistory, herstory, is something quite different. This woman, with her disfigured jaw, whether from traumatic wound or disease, is what Joan Halifax in her book on shamanism calls "the wounded healer."[2] Perhaps her disfigurement is the numinous sign of her encounter with terror and her survival of that encounter. She is a formidable figure, one who dwells apart, outside the conventional center of human society; but what she is able to read in the magical script written by fire on the earthen body of the Great Goddess is the knowledge on which her people depend. Figure 5.1 is a line drawing of her head.

In prehistory, technology, art, and the sacred are one—as I hope they will be once again in posthistory. The prehistoric ceramic technology in which figurines of the Great Goddess were mixed with water so that they would explode in the fires of the hearth is neither simply technology nor art, but a form of divination. In our culture, only technology is considered important, so archaeology is really the story of changing technologies. This is illustrated in a cover article on these ceramic figurines in the January/February 1993 issue of *Archeology*.[3] It's a professionally revealing essay because it shows the denigration of art history as a valid form of knowledge. The "new archaeologists" prefer computerized data processing to self-indulgent and romantic fantasies about ancient religions, so they prefer to stick to the more substantial reality of tools. Consequently, our history is a history of tools—from stone to copper to iron to steel and to plutonium—and what is "real" is how and with what humans killed one another in their time. Here is the voice of the professional archaeologist:

> What is reasonably clear is that the Moravian ceramics never led to the production of utilitarian objects. It is for their short-term performance value not for durability and practical use. We can only speculate on how the course of prehistory would have changed if the Pavlov had appreciated the full potential of ceramics. But this is not the only case of ancient people missing the technological boat. Upper Paleolithic people including those at Dolni Vestonice used ground stone technology to produce jewelry rather than tools such as axes and adzes so common in the Neolithic. Copper was used to make jewelry and trinkets in North America and the Near East long before it was used

in the manufacture of knives and weapons. Wheel toys are widespread
in prehistoric Mesoamerica yet neither the Mayan nor the Aztecs ever
used the wheel for transport.[4]

These poor benighted savages are limited to art and religion because they
don't understand the technological possibilities of fire for forging weapons.
Most every archaeological department in the world is dominated by this
technological worldview, and anyone who does not share it, such as scholars
like Marija Gimbutas, is ridiculed as a mystic, an amateur, a deluded
enthusiast given to utopian fantasies and idle speculation. When I was at
MIT, I worked with archaeologists from the metallurgy lab in designing a
course on the history of the city; at York University in Toronto, I worked
with one of the computerized "new archaeologists" in teaching a course on
"The Transformations of Human Culture," so I know the tone of voice that
you hear in this article. I vividly remember hearing it come forth from Glynn
Daniel when I asked him a question at the end of one of his lectures at the
Peabody Museum at Harvard. This patronizing tone for the primitives at
Dolni Vestonice who missed the technological boat by deflecting their
technology into merely artistic and religious purposes does not surprise me.
For archaeologists, only military technology is culturally real, so if one's
insights come from the field of art history, one will not be accepted by one's
colleagues. In this same journal, *Archeology,* in 1992, Brian Fagan wrote an
attack on Marija Gimbutas in which he dismissed her work as "a sexist view
of prehistory," one that indulged in feminist speculations about some fanciful
utopian culture of the Goddess. Fagan's dismissal of Gimbutas is a typical
example of the denigration of other cognitive styles — art and the history of
art are not to be taken seriously as a foundation for sound professional
judgments about the nature of human culture.

Let us consider these figures of the Great Goddess. Figure 5.2 is a
drawing of one of the ceramic statues found at Dolni Vestonice, and figure
5.3 is of the Goddess of Lespugue, found in France. Male prehistorians
christened these figures as Venuses, thus giving us the Venus of Lespugue,
the Venus of Willendorf, but, following Gimbutas's suggestions, I shall use
the more general term, goddess.

Notice that in both figures, the head and feet are narrow, and that the
overall general form is of two cones joined, where the equator of the joined
cones is the stomach, the omphalos of the Great Mother pregnant with the
All.[5] The pointed feet of the figurine from Dolni Vestonice enabled the statue
to be inserted into the soil of the hearth, where, presumably, after a critical

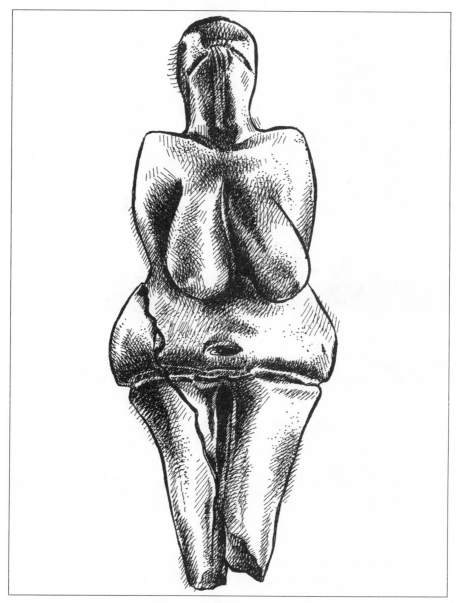

Figure 5.2: Great Goddess of Dolni Vestonice.

time, it would explode from the heat of the fire. Perhaps the shards provided some system of divination, something like the yarrow stalks used with the ancient Chinese *I Ching*, or the pattern of tea leaves in a cup used in Gypsy fortune-telling.

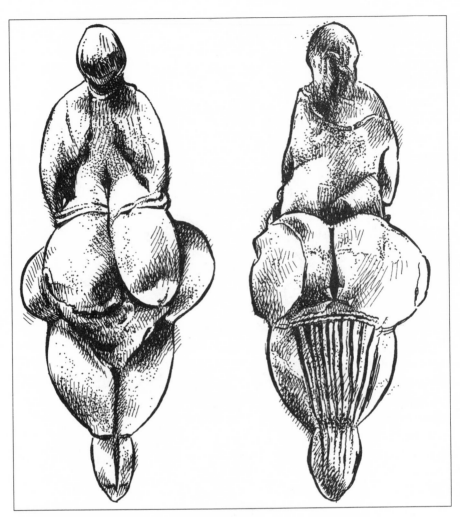

Figure 5.3: Goddess of Lespugue, Front and Back.

The statue from Lespugue seems to be more pronouncedly divided into sections: head, breast, abdomen, pubic triangle, thighs, and feet. If one were to measure each of these sections, one would probably discover a canon of proportion for the ratio of the head section to the abdominal section or thighs. The classical Greeks had a canon of proportion for the length of the head to the entire torso; it was called "the canon of Praxiteles." The proportion of the length of the head to the torso changes in life, as a person develops from fetus, to infant, to child, to adult. The musicologist Hans Keyser, in his *Akroasis*, has tried to recover this ancient Pythagorean knowledge by suggesting that these canons of proportion also correspond to a musical system of proportion and tones. If one took a guitar string and placed frets under it to correspond to the division of the body parts of the Great Goddess, one would hear the tonal analogues for the visual proportions expressed here. This would be another version of the Pythagorean monochord. I asked the mathematician Ralph Abraham at the University of California at Santa Cruz to try to do a mathematical analysis on his computer of this tonal and visual system of proportion—for Abraham is familiar with the work of the musicologists Hans Keyser and Ernest McClain. He informed me that the linear measurements do match the heptatonic scale of the Vedic Aryans and the Dorian mode of the ancient Greeks. Abraham suggested further that the lines on the back of the Goddess of Lespugue may refer to some prehistoric lute or sitar, one made from gourds or clay that has not survived the millennia. The large abdomen and buttocks of the Great Goddess would then be a resonating chamber. Since the Earth is said to give out a tone from the gigantic iron crystal that is reputed to be within the core of our planet,[6] the idea of vibration may be part of some prehistoric cosmology. Recently, New Agers, who are partial to crystals and talk of vibrations, have marketed a whistle that is said to produce the same tone that the earth does in space. Our ancient paleolithic ancestors may have had some similar religious feelings for sounds, for chanting within caves, and used these statues to construct monochords. Since there is an implicit canon of proportion here, and this canon does seem to be repeated in other statuary, it does suggest that, at the very least, more is going on here than a stone age taste for fat Venuses. What is an implicit order in the Paleolithic era becomes an explicit order in the tonal/numerical cosmology performed in the chants of the *Rig Veda*—as we will see when we come to discuss the musicological approach of Antonio de Nicolas and Ernest McClain to the *Rig Veda*.

When one turns the statue over and takes a good look at the back, one notices that it is not a realistic rendering of the female anatomy, and that something else does seem to be going on here. The key is to move beyond simple realism or linear, conceptual thinking, in which one form is merely a sign for one concept. We have to move to a polymorphic mode in which one form contains many forms—the kind of perception you can learn from the statues of Henry Moore or Jacques Lipschitz. On the back of the statue is the male genitalia as well as the female buttocks; there is a visual system of punning between buttocks and testicles, and eggs. According to both McClain and de Nicholas,[7] one ancient system of ratios and tones was considered to be female and another male, so this statue is probably a

Figure 5.4: Goddess of Willendorf.

complex hieroglyph that is expressing a cosmology, and that is precisely why it departs from a literal and realistic rendering of the human body. Gimbutas maintains that the breasts, buttocks, and thighs are in ovine form to express the containment of the orphic cosmic egg within the Great Mother.[8] From her reading, the statue is indeed a hieroglyph, an emblematic, compressed form of a cosmology. Within this cosmic form, the male is implicit within the larger female form, which only seems natural, since the male son comes out of the body of the mother. The penis here is not seen as some magical sign of warrior, priest, or patriarchal ancestor, for all those functions come later. We are back in time before there was any such thing as a priest, a warrior class, or, perhaps, even a "father." We are back in prehistory when the penis is the property of the Great Mother and is an implicit form within her body.

The presence of the penis within the body of the Great Goddess is also seen in the statue from Willendorf. (See figure 5.4). The unnaturally thin

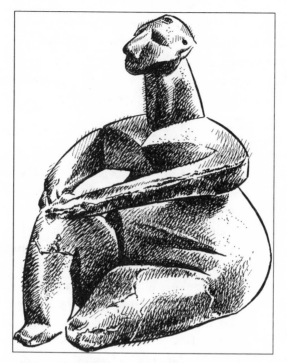

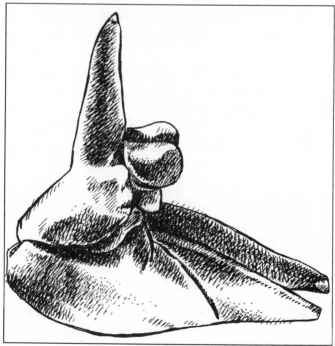

Figure 5.5: illustration of figurines from Cernavoda and Tepe Sarab.

lines of the arms across the top of the breast make the breasts appear in the form of the glans penis. In this visual system of punning, there is a logic of association. The breasts give milk, the penis gives the cream of semen. All the vital fluids, milk, menstrual blood, semen, have a numinous quality, and the magical powers associated with them survive into history and are fossilized in Tantric yoga.[9]

In the Neolithic era, this hieroglyphic system of visual punning is rendered more explicitly than in the Paleolithic, for here we do encounter the phallic-necked goddess, say of Cernavoda, or the goddess figurine of Tepe Sarab in which, as you see in figure 5.5, the breasts are made to appear like the glans penis.

When looking at all these different statues, one needs to keep in mind that one is not just looking at the fertility fetishes of a single village. The iconography of the Great Goddess is a symbolic complex that stretches from Iberia to Siberia. One is looking at the iconography of humanity's first universal religion, a profound, complex, and well thought out symbolic system about the nature of time and the meaning of human existence.

What is expressed in these prehistoric statues is a form of thinking, a visual system of homologies: the breast gives milk, the penis gives cream. The body is food, and as we will see in chapter 6, in the erotic poetry of the love cycle of Inanna and Dumuzi, when the lovers come together, they become food to each other and drink each other's sexual fluids. The goddess delights in consuming the cream and butter of Dumuzi, for he is only returning what is rightfully hers in the first place. The body of the Great Goddess is literally "the first place."

In Jack Kunz's geometrical analysis of the goddess statues for the cover of the February 1968 *Scientific American,* the body of the goddess is seen as contained within two cones joined at their common base. The form is generated from a point at the top of the head and disappears at a point where the two feet come together. In the center of the figure is the pubic triangle, the vulva as source of emergence. The resolution of the forms of the triangle and the circle is the cone. So this statue with its implicit penis, with its point and circle, is an ideogram, a performance of the central mystery, an answer to the primary ontological question: "How does the One become two?" How do the many emerge from the One? It is a rendering of the fundamental question of the philosophers, from Leibniz to Nietzsche to Heidegger: why is there something rather than nothing?

With a cone, one begins with a dimensionless point but ends up in the enormous belly of the Great Mother. The statue performs this knowledge

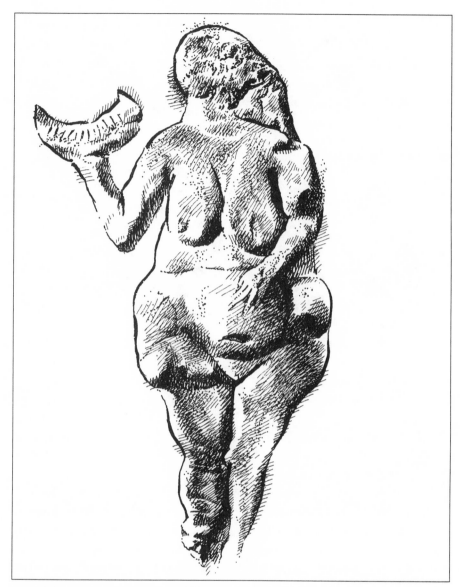

Figure 5.6: The Goddess of Laussel.

before our very eyes. Now when the male is inside the body of the female, the story of time becomes the unpacking of the many from the one; the story of time becomes the increasing separation of the male from the female.

Consider the famous Goddess of Laussel, shown in figure 5.6, an icon that brings all these elements together.

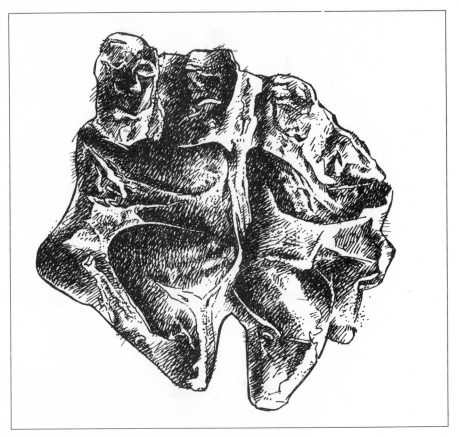

Figure 5.7: "Sons and Lovers" from Çatal Hüyük.

Notice that she holds aloft the horn as her emblem; it is the horn of plenty, the cornucopia of the vagina and womb. The cornucopia also represents the crescent moon. This iconography in which the goddess is associated with the moon survives in the icon of the Virgin of Guadaloupe, where the Holy Mother of God is seen standing on the crescent moon. There is also an ancient Sumerian poem in which the goddess Inanna composes a poem to her vulva. She calls the vulva the horn, the crescent, the boat, for the reed boats on the Tigris—similar to the boats still in use on Lake Titicaca—were made of reeds and were crescent shaped.

The Paleolithic story or mythos is one in which the phallus is implicit within the body of the Great Mother, but the Neolithic story is of the male who has moved out of her body to become the infant, then the son-lover, then the dying god.

Here is a statue from roughly the seventh millennium B.C.E. from Çatal Hüyük in Anatolia; it looks like a prehistoric Henry Moore statue of the family. On one side is the male at the breast, and on the other, the lover in erotic embrace; but both modalities of the male are of one piece with the body of the Great Mother. "Sons and Lovers" is not a recent idea given to us by D. H. Lawrence; it is an archaic notion recovered through the imagination of the writer. In a Neolithic statue of a mother nursing an infant from Hacilar in Anatolia, one can see an ambiguous embrace, one both infantile and erotic, for the mother, or goddess, holds the male at the breast and over the pubic triangle.[10]

The site of Çatal Hüyük in Anatolia was a great find because it produced a treasure trove of figurines, not just of the Great Mother, but of the male consort. The figurine of the full-grown male, however, was not found in a shrine devoted to the glories of the male, of some imaginary solar king; it was found in the vulture shrine, in a room filled with images of corpses and death. If birth is the central mystery for the female, death seems to be the central mystery for the male. The penis is a wonder, as what is small becomes great. It becomes tall and erect in dream, trance, and lovemaking; it grows like the shoots of plants, and like them it has its season, and then it falls.[11] So the penis becomes the phallus, a symbolic complex for time, for the vanishing modality of time. Since the menstruating vulva is the wound that heals itself in rhythm with the cycles of the moon in the heavens, the vulva becomes the symbol of eternal recurrence, of the enduring and not the vanishing mode of time. The male dies, and though the female may mourn, it is she who endures. So it is that the phallus belongs to the Great Mother, the vanishing mode of time belongs to the larger and more enduring mode of time.

The male goes through an intensely sharp experience of temporality—of heroic life and tragic death—and then he returns to the Great Mother. The limited phallus must pay back to the unlimited vulva according to necessity and the arrangement of time—as the Greek pre-Socratic philosopher Anaximander would later rephrase it in his secularization of this ancient mode of sacral thought. The explicit phallus returns to become again the implicit phallus within the body of the Great Goddess. So behind and within the Goddess of Lespugue is the male in the final embrace. Now one can appreciate the archetypal dimensions of Michelangelo's *Pietà*, the image of the dead Christ in the arms of Mary, and one can also appreciate how sculpture is a *form* of thinking.

This story of the dying male is expressed in the imagery of the Neolithic statuary of Çatal Hüyük, but it quite literally becomes *a* story when the appearance of writing on clay tablets in ancient Sumer allows us to read about the relationship between the goddess Inanna and her humble consort, the shepherd Dumuzi, whom she turns into a king. She endures; he dies. The clay of the figurines of Dolni Vestonice and Çatal Hüyük and the clay of the tablets of ancient Sumer participate in an enduring symbolic complex. The form of the letter is wedge shaped, and the very word *cuneiform* means wedge shaped. The wedge is the ancient pubic triangle. Our English word, "cunt" means ditch or furrow; in Spanish the word is "cuñeta." In both of these languages, the image takes us back to an ancient cosmology in which plow and furrow, sprouting plant and receiving earth, are modalities of the Great Goddess and the dying male. In the cuneiform writing on clay tablets, the phallic stylus impresses the word, the *logos spermaticos,* but even that phallic stylus is the property of the Great Goddess for what it imprints on the soft clay of the feminine earth is the wedge-shaped pubic triangle of the Great Mother. The male comes from the Great Mother and to the Great Mother he must return. "Dust thou art, and to dust thou must return." Even the Christian liturgy of burial is a performance of this ancient cosmology. One need not be surprised that these symbolic complexes can endure over the millennia from Dolni Vestonice to Çatal Hüyük to Sumer. What is implicit in Lespuge becomes explicit in Çatal Hüyük. What is sculpture at Çatal Hüyük becomes literature in Sumer.

Consider the crone of death from the vulture shrine at Çatal Hüyük in figure 5.8. Notice her hairdo; the bun is similar to the hairdo of the shamanic woman from Dolni Vestonice. This knot at the top of the head expresses a concentration of energy at the point at which the subtle body interacts with the physical body. Think of the horns on Michelangelo's Moses or the knot on the head of Buddha. The power of the hair as a kind of spiritual conductor is recognized almost universally from religion to religion, and this esoteric matter can sometimes become the source for great conflicts between diverging sects. There was a battle between the Celtic and Roman churches over the matter of tonsure for monks. The Roman church insisted on shaving the forehead, but the Celtic church, being the church of John and not Peter, and therefore, older, wiser, more esoteric, and just plain better, insisted that they shave the top of the head. The purpose of this practice is to allow light to stimulate the internal and evolutionarily ancient light-sensing organ, the pineal gland. This excitation helps the third eye to open in the experience of illumination. This experience of illumination is what Jesus is talking about when he says: "For the eye is the light of the body, and if thine eye be single, thy whole body shall be filled with light."

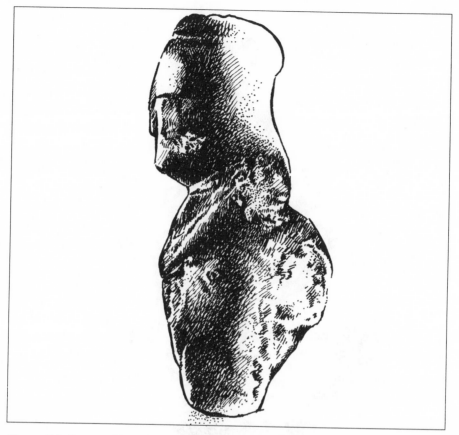

Figure 5.8: Crone of Death from Çatal Hüyük.

This point at the top of the head is also recognized in yoga, and the crowning chakra, the thousand-petaled lotus, is the most important of the seven chakras in the spine and is said to be the passage through which the enlightened soul leaves the body at death. The Roman church of Peter, not having a clue about yogic experiences of initiation and the opening of the third eye, has since retranslated this text to eliminate its esoteric meaning: "The eyes are the lamp of the body, and if your eyes are healthy, your body is healthy." The Roman church ridiculed the Irish practice of monks' shaving the tops of their heads and branded the Celts as heretics; they called their practice, after the anathematized heretic Simon Magus, "the tonsure of Simon Magus." But whether the hair is shaved, or protected from the knife—as in the cases of Shikhs or Samson—or wound into a spiral or bun—as in the case of Buddha or the crone of Çatal Hüyük or the shaman

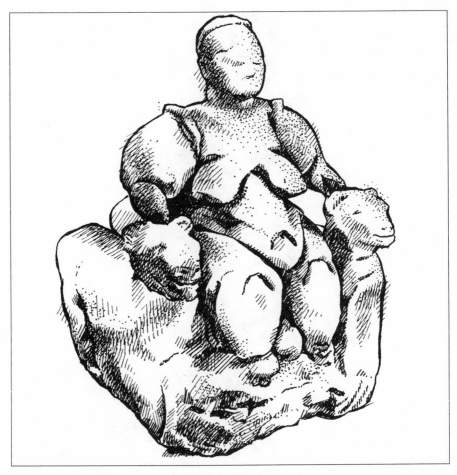

Figure 5.9: Great Mother on throne from Çatal Hüyük.

of Dolni Vestonice—the symbolism is based on sacred knowledge of the esoteric physiology of the human body.

The astonishing thing about the nature of imagery is just how long it can last. In figure 5.9, the Great Goddess sits on her leopard throne with her son emerging from between her legs in childbirth. This statue comes Çatal Hüyük and dates from 6500 B.C.E. The male is no longer pictured as implicit within her body, but coming forth as an individual.

This statue of Maitreya, the future Buddha, comes from China and is now housed in the Rietberg Museum in Zurich; there is also one very similar in the University Museum of the University of Pennsylvania in Philadelphia and two in the Metropolitan Museum in New York.

Figure 5.10: Maitreya from Rietberg Museum.

These statues of Maitreya come from China. Notice that Maitreya is also seated on the leopard throne, and that the mudra that is formed by his crossing feet is of an oval-shaped vulva. The physical world is his footstool. Similar language and imagery is attributed to Christ in medieval iconography. In Christian imagery, the oval that is formed by two overlapping circles is called the *vesica piscis*. The center of one circle is on the circumference of the other; thus, the circumference of the outer physical world is the center of the spiritual world for the Enlightened, and the center of the physical world is the outer rim of the spiritual world.

Figure 5.11: Christ in Vesica from Royal Portal of Chartres.

At the Royal Portal at the Cathedral of Chartres, Christ is shown within the *vesica*. (See figure 5.11.)

James Joyce borrowed this medieval figure and inscribed it on page 293 of *Finnegans Wake*. Understanding full well the ancient cosmology in which the vulva is the place of emergence, Joyce returns the abstract figure to its concrete origins and portrays the figure as the buttocks and vulva of Anna Livia Plurabelle.

This vulva-shaped form of the medieval *vesica piscis* represents the place of emergence of the Christ into our world. It is the matrix through

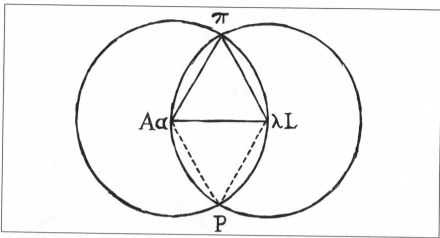

Figure 5.12: from p. 293 of *Finnegans Wake*.

which the male figure emerges into the lower world of manifestation, of time as opposed to eternity. Maitreya, the future Buddha, is not yet in our world of manifest time; he dwells in heaven and yet his emanational influence inspires those within our world who have a particular calling to his epoch. Therefore, his lowest members, his feet, are lengthened so that they can form this oval, this place of passage from one world to another. According to art historians, the peculiar hat on Maitreya's head is Iranian, so we have an indication of cultural exchange from the Middle East to the Far East. And this is precisely what we see in the continuity of this archetypal imagery going from Anatolia in 6500 B.C.E. to China and Europe.

The image of the male figure was found inside the vulture shrine of death at Çatal Hüyük, beneath the murals of headless corpses and vultures taking the flesh up in their flight. The male figurine was placed in the shrine of death because the male is the character in the prehistoric cosmology who embodies the mystery of death. The male body is a story about time, about the vanishing mode of time in which the phallus rises and falls. We see the son emerge from the Great Mother; we see him ride the animals, grow strong and flourish, and then die. He is nameless in prehistoric Anatolia, but he becomes Dumuzi, Osiris, Attis, Orpheus, and Jesus when we pass over into written mythologies.

Imagery has to be interpreted, and this is why the interpretative way of knowing is so unsettling and annoying to archaeologists and prehistorians. Imagery takes us into the realm of imagination. When one finds a tool in a dig, one can label it and say that the obsidian knife was found in level

7a; but if one unearths a statue, one has an image that has meaning, and there is simply no scientific way to limit a mythic complex to a single concept. So the scientists would prefer to avoid the whole matter and note simply that a ritual object was found at level such and such. Since the interpretation of meaning and imagery can never be scientific, it is left to the fanciful speculation of art historians, poets, and romantics who like to envision lost cultures.

Scientists claim that the interpretations of these romantics tell us more about the romantics than they do about the people of the past. But these scientists forget that science itself is a form of hermeneutics, situated in history, that natural history is always a subset of cultural history. Science is a self-description of the historical condition of the writer, whether he is Darwin or Heisenberg. In the hermeneutic circle, a narrative, scientific or artistic, is a performance of a person situated within a culture. This is one reason why I am very up-front about what I am doing in this book. I am using material from all of history to try to construct a metahistorical narrative. As we move forward in time, our image of the past changes, just as when we are driving in a car, the image in the rearview mirror changes. The way we would look upon history today is not the way a Victorian would, or the way a Marxist such as V. Gordon Childe, of just a generation ago, would.

So what should we make of all these statues? They tell us a story, that long before we have written documents and the birth of literature, we do have stories. A story is itself in its structure a performance of time, a story about time. And, of course, the most immediate symbol of time is expressed by the human body: birth, maturity, and death. The stages of growth of the human body express the fundamental architecture of time. The erection rises and falls; in one condition it points to Earth, but in the other it points to heaven. The male vanishes, but the female endures. From the "Sorrowful Ancient" of Gimbutas's Old Europe of 6000 B.C.E. to Jesus as the "Man of Sorrows" of the Middle Ages, the archetypal story remains much the same.

Now, for Jungian scholars of prehistory, for whom archetypes are their very meat and drink, the story of this dying male is one of increasing individuation. For Carl Jung, Erich Neumann, Marie-Louise von Franz, and Joseph Campbell, the prehistoric Great Mother is faceless and impersonal, and the historic hero must battle with the dragon-mother to rescue his own female soul, his anima, from nature's instinctive grip of eternal return in birth and death. Jungianism, much like Steiner's anthroposophy, is a patriarchal religion. It is founded by the great man himself, guarded jealously by his faithful female temple consorts, Emma Jung, Toni Wolf, Anielia

Jaffe, and Marie-Louise von Franz, and served by eunuch priests such as Edward Whitmont who carry aloft in procession the embalmed phallus of the great Jung before the genuflecting multitude of analysands. (But to be fair to Jung, this cultural pattern in the sociology of knowledge is much the same with Freud or Lacan; and even feminist scholarship seems to be changing the masculine face but keeping the same structures of domination through fear and power in the control of graduate students in universities.) In this truly Eurocentric Jungian myth of progress, female is past and primitive, and male is modern and developed. Even when this religion is articulated by female scholars, individuation is seen as a process of increasing masculinization. Consider the following from the recent work of Anne Baring and Jules Cashford:

> The appearance of the myth of the hero shifts the focus of attention from the great round of nature, expressed as the myth of the goddess, to "the world as the centre of the universe, the spot where man stands." It is possible to see that what we referred to as the myth of the hunter in the Paleolithic age has now become the myth of the hero. . . . The gradual separation of human consciousness from the original matrix (a term derived from the Latin word for mother, *mater*) is characteristically expressed in the appearance of a young god, who comes to symbolize this emerging consciousness.[12]

Increasing masculinization, in this Jungian narrative, means an increase in consciousness. The prehistoric is collective, faceless, and impersonal; the historic is personal and highly individuated. Now one can see why I take such delight in the face of the woman with the bun from Dolni Vestonice in 24,000 B.C.E. This little figurine is a delightful anomaly that blows the hell out of all our neat narratives of historical progression. I have sprinkled a few of these "delightful anomalies" all throughout this book. I have done this not only because I wish to indulge in a Borgesian laughter at the mad compulsions of scholarship, but also because I want to keep a healthy respect for paradox and complexity, a feeling that the universe is so vast and complex that there are multiple narratives, even contradictory ones, that can make good sense of all these voiceless artifacts of prehistory.

In Jungian prehistory, one has a female culture that is dumb and unconscious, instinctive and sensate, but as one moves forward in time one encounters highly developed individual consciousness, warrior heroes, technology, Greek rationality, and finally European science. There is much in the Jungian narrative that is compellingly attractive, and that is why it has captured scholars such as Joseph Campbell—a colossal male chauvinist if there ever was one—but because I want to avoid getting trapped, I shall point out these Jungian narratives as a way one can go, but I shall make my way around them.

There is another way to look at the Great Goddess with the implicit phallus and that is as a more complex icon of the relationship of the ego to the soul. What W. B. Yeats calls the daimon and Sri Aurobindo calls the psychic being is the higher self that does not die but projects itself into one particular incarnation after another. The ego comes and goes, but the daimon or the psychic being endures. Consequently, the ego takes on the modality of the phallic metaphor, the vanishing mode of time. But the psyche, the soul that survives incarnation and lets one recover, in the words of the Zen koan, "the face you had before you were born," that psyche is female and vast. She is Dante's Beatrice in heaven, the Gnostic's Sophia, or the Buddhist's Tara. Sri Aurobindo says that behind the heart chakra there is the psychic being, a greater self that is the sum of all our personal incarnations. The ego dies, but this being endures. So the Goddess of Lespugue is not simply a fertility fetish, an icon of reproductive time, it is an emblem of the architecture of incarnation.

Think of Plato's *Timaeus*, in which space is the feminine Receptacle and the Demiurge is the masculine creative artisan of the universe. Think of Dante in the *Inferno* and Beatrice in the *Paradiso*. Male and female are cosmological metaphors, so it is ridiculous to get too politically hot and bothered about sexism and label this as patriarchal and that as feminist. This prehistoric cosmology is at a more basic, ontological level than this little argument that men and women are now having in our culture. The body is the fundamental metaphor because the penis becomes erect in dream, trance state, tantric vision, and lovemaking, and so it serves as a symbol of the instantaneous modality of time. Because the vulva is a wound that heals itself in rhythm with the moon in the heavens, it is a symbol of cyclicity, of eternal return, of the enduring modality of time. Mystics know that there is a part of our being that is projected into time in the form of an ego that is going to die, but there is another part of our being that never incarnates. We will see this relationship between ego and psyche return in the form of the two birds in the tree—one tasting the fruit, and the other witnessing—in the *Rig Veda* and the *Upanishads*. The male dies, and the female endures. Osiris dies, and Isis gathers his remains. Sri Aurobindo dies in 1950, and the Mother Mira Richard gathers his visionary remains and founds the planetary city of

Auroville in 1968. So our story is an archetypal one that spans one end of history to the other, from Dolni Vestonice to Auroville, from one ice age to another.

What I am saying in all of this is that this mystical knowledge, with its immanental eggs of possibilities and its implicit phallus, is expressed in the Paleolithic statue of the Goddess of Lespugue from more than 20,000 years ago. I think, or perhaps I had better more honestly say, "I believe" that there have always been a few initiates, esoteric sages, who knew more than their surrounding historical culture did. This woman with twisted face from Dolni Vestonice, I believe, is one.

6

FROM
PREHISTORIC
SCULPTURE TO
FOLKTALE TO
CIVILIZED
LITERATURE

The commonplace notion of cultural development of a generation ago was that writing on clay tablets was the hallmark of civilization and that this achievement was a result of the complex culture of living in cities. Recently, however, in her essay on "The Sacred Script," Marija Gimbutas has shown that writing goes all the way back to the Old European culture of 5300 to 4300 B.C.E..[1] Andre Leroi Gourhan has shown that in Lascaux and Magdalenian cave art in general there are two parallel systems of expression, images and signs. If one keeps this in mind, one can begin to suspect that the origins of this sacred script of the Old Europeans probably can be taken all the way back into the Ice Age. So the contention of the French philosopher Jacques Derrida—that the old division of culture that sees oral as primary and writing as secondary is invalid—would appear to be true; speech and the scratching on tools, the grammatology, coevolve and influence one another.[2]

Sumerian writing should not be seen as a sudden invention, but rather as a form of activity with deep roots in the past. The clay of the tablets takes us back to the ceramics of Ice Age Dolni Vestonice, and the wedge-shaped marks take us back to the sign of the vulva in Paleolithic caves. The phallic stylus that imprints the vulva on the soft and receptive earth of the clay tablet is another version of the statuary of the Great Goddess, the phallic-necked Great Goddess in which male and female are one in the act of generation. The production of script is therefore a generative act in which phallus and vulva participate. Language is also a sexual mystery; in the words of the ancient Hermetic axiom: "As above, so below." The tongue is a phallus; the lips are labia. So it is highly appropriate that the first stories of literature that we can read off these clay tablets are erotic poems about the love affair of the goddess Inanna and the shepherd Dumuzi. The origins of literature are embedded in the origins of writing, and both are erotically embedded. Erotic literature is not some decadent invention of Henry Miller and D. H. Lawrence; these modern writers are simply romantics trying to recover the archaic roots of Western literature that had been covered up by the Christian church.

The course of literature and the evolution of consciousness begins with the love cycle of Inanna and Dumuzi. I don't wish to repeat the more detailed *explication du texte* that I put forth in *The Time Falling Bodies Take to Light*,[3] so here I would prefer to discuss how a text configures the development of a cultural ecology. Our first step, then, is to understand just what I mean by a cultural ecology.

Culture has often been described as a system of adaptations, but since adaptations are adapting to an environment, one cannot discuss them without reference to the ecology in which they are brought forth. The work of James Lovelock and Lynn Margulis has helped us to see that the organism is not clamped down into an environment in an "adapt or die!" situation, but that the organism is helping to shape and transform its environment, and that this, in turn, affects the way the organism lives within that environment. There is a bootstrapping of organism and environment in which they coevolve, codetermine one another. This concept of dependent co-origination is not simply a new idea taken from cybernetics but an ancient Buddhist notion, and it can be traced all the way back to the concept of *pratityasamutpada* in the ancient Indian Buddhist text the *Avitamsakasutra*. The coevolving complex of a society embedded in that society's sustaining ecosystem is what I mean by a cultural ecology.

If we were to take an imaginary Landsat satellite view of human development, we would see a historical sequence of human movement through several different cultural ecologies.

1. Silvan
2. Savannaan
3. Glacial
4. Riverine
5. Transcontinental (or Mediterranean for the West)
6. Oceanic
7. Biospheric

The first is the Silvan. This is the cultural ecology of our prehuman, mammalian, primate ancestry—the forest environment of the primate Ramapithecus. This cultural ecology is the primordial environment for the archaic structure of consciousness, one in which olfaction and hearing constellate the surround or *Umwelt* of the organism. The second cultural ecology is the Savannaan; this is the ecology associated with the hominization of the primates, the landscape associated with the emergence of the hominids. It is the African landscape of Donald Johanson's hominid fossil "Lucy." Global weather changes have caused a shrinking of the forest, a desiccation in which the hominids are no longer hidden within the forest, but exposed in the savanna. The changes associated with this shift from the Silvan to the Savannaan cultural ecology are the shift from estrus to menses, the shift to an upright posture, and the shift from olfaction to sight as the dominant sense. The last stage of development of this cultural ecology would seem to be the use of simple pebble tools and, perhaps, the development of some form of communication system of calls. There is evidence that food was brought to camps—clusters of trees—where it was shared. This pattern of food sharing in a miniaturization of the primary Silvan cultural ecology expresses the foundation of hominid and human culture. Food sharing is a so foundational an act of human identity that it survives into our time and we see it ritualistically preserved in the Jewish seder and the Christian eucharist. Such a form of group association would naturally encourage some form of communication. It is in the Savannaan cultural ecology that we see the evolution from Australopithecus to Homo habilis.

The third cultural ecology is the Glacial. In the movement from one cultural ecology to another there is a dynamical oscillation between expansion and compression: the expansion into a new space and the consolidation into form. The poet W. B. Yeats used archetypal imagery to express this dynamic and said that all human history seemed to oscillate between the Crucifixion and the Transfiguration on the Mount. In one there is a compression, a fixation within limits, and in the other there is a creative expansion into new space. Both expansion and compression bring with them challenges that call forth new responses in the movement that the Chilean biologists Humberto Maturana and Francisco Varela call "natural drift."[4] We need not think of some purpose-laden, teleological process going on here, but simply of a cumulative movement in which each single motion has consequences that open up a new bifurcation. The shift from estrus to menses means that females are secreting the attractive pheromones that serve to keep the males in close association with them at all times. Even if this shift were a genetic freak or mutation of one single female, the primordial Eve from whom the hominids are said to descend, once this change is passed on within a tightly associated cluster of hominids in the savanna, then the accident has consequences and opens up a system of bifurcations that cumulatively takes one group into a culture quite different from the past. For example, if males are attracted at all times to females, and not simply for a mating season, then males are constantly exposed to one another in conditions of maximum sexual excitation. This situation naturally selects for a culture of agonic display, perpetual competition, and a violence that has to be simultaneously sustained and contained. In other words, it selects for just the kind of male warrior culture that we see memorialized in Homer's *Iliad*. So the ancient stories of Eve with her attractive fruit and Helen of Troy with her apple marked "for the fairest," of females who bring about a fall or an enduring war, are mythic intuitions of a biological transformation. As bifurcation branches off bifurcation, one gets the natural history of what one can, by hindsight, call development or evolution. Evolutionary natural drift is, after the title of one of Jorge Luis Borges's short stories, a "Jardin de senderos que se bifurcan."

So the Silvan cultural ecology is our primordial, animal heritage, our garden of Eden, from which we are expelled by the archangel with the flaming sword, the sun, that brings about the general desiccation that shrinks the forest and opens up the savannas. The Silvan cultural ecology can be seen to be the locus of what the cultural philosopher Jean Gebser called the archaic structure of consciousness,[5] although "origin" in Gebser's sense is an everpresent ontological matrix and not simply a linear beginning. The Savannan cultural ecology is, therefore, a loss that opens up a possible gain; it is an expansion into a new space that calls forth a whole new complex of upright posture and bipedal gait, sight over smell, estrus over menses, and male violence. When this male violence is directed at an intruding predator, a shift from the opportunistic robbing of carrion to more organized hunting is brought forth. Imagine a situation in which the hominids are astonished to find that if those who were fighting one another jump on the leopard at the same time, then the tables can be turned and a feared predator can become a prey. None of this takes conscious purpose; it can all be simply gestures of accidental fury in which a bunch of males are screaming, going into display, and picking up anything at hand—such as a branch or a rock—to show off and make a big scene. As the group fighting among themselves is suddenly interrupted and they are attacked, they unthinkingly, in the peak of their own hormonal excitation, turn on the beast and surprise themselves by killing it, or driving it off. So natural drift is not purposive; it is simply a system in which one fork in the road leads to another, and the cumulative pattern of all those bifurcations constellates a developmental history that we call evolution.

A parallel theory of hominization is the aquatic ape theory of Sir Alastair Hardy, one popularized quite wittily by Elaine Morgan.[6] According to this theory, the open savanna is a deadly place and all the fossils found there are of species that became extinct. In the intense desiccation, only the hominids at the coastline who took to the water in shallow coves and bays are able to survive. These are the hominids with the lovely full and floating breasts we human males admire so much; these are our ancestral hominids without hair, except on the head for the protection of the skull; these are the creatures like us, with sea-salt tears and infants who know how to hold their breath and swim at birth. For this narrative of hominization, we have to imagine some prehistoric Atlantis in which we lived in close association with the sea.

Whatever mythic narrative of hominization we choose, the important thing to notice is that the movement from one cultural ecology to another is an accident with consequences, and that the shift to a new environment involves a dynamical pulse between compression and expansion. The forest in which the mammals evolved, under the ferns and under the feet of the lumbering dinosaurs, is a compressive environment. The savanna in which the hominids spread out is an expansive environment. The subsequent Glacial environment is once again a compressive one. Human groups are compressed into new adaptations that require clothing and shelter for survival. In Marshall McLuhan's phrase "the sloughed-off environment becomes a work of art in the new and invisible environment." It is the old animal environment that becomes the literal envelope for the new human. The animal skin becomes clothes, and the stacked skulls and tusks of mammoths become the architecture of the hut, the ribbing of the shelter that becomes covered with hides to form the first human-built structures, such as those of Terra Amata in Iberia or Mezhirich in Ukraine. Within this period of glacial compression, there is a whole new development of fire, engraved tools, and, judging by the endocranial casts that reveal highly developed language centers, fully blown human forms of linguistic communication. The Glacial cultural ecology is the one that sees the movement from Homo erectus to archaic Homo sapiens to Neanderthal and modern Homo sapiens. So we have Ramapithecus for the Silvan cultural ecology, Australopithecus to Homo habilis for the Savannaan cultural ecology, and Homo erectus to archaic Homo sapiens and then modern Homo sapiens for the Glacial cultural ecology. In each case, the cultural way of life of the organisms is so deeply embedded within an environment that it makes no sense to abstract the culture from the ecology that brings it forth.

When the fierce archangel of evolution with its fiery sword, the sun, strikes the earth again, the planetary weather again changes, the ice caps recede, and the rains and the forests return. Thus we encounter the shift from the Glacial cultural ecology to the Riverine. First there are Riverine settlements of fishers and gatherers, such as Lepenski Vir in the Balkans (6000 B.C.E.) or the Ubaid culture (5500 B.C.E.) in the marshes of the Tigris and Euphrates; but then, in the fourth millennium B.C.E., we begin to find the traces of these settlements of gatherers being replaced by agricultural settlements, the first city-states of the Sumerians. The foundational text I shall use for this stage is "How the Goddess Inanna Brought the *me's* from Eridu to Erech."[7] The *me's* are the arts of civilization, not physical objects but something more like the software program for setting up a civilization. The goddess Inanna gets her father, Enki, drunk and tricks him into giving the *me's* to her so that she can carry them back to her human lover, the primitive shepherd Dumuzi. Zecharia Sitchin sees these gods of Father Enki and daughter Inanna as extraterrestrials from the *12th Planet*[8] who have come to earth in rockets and established their base in the alluvial basin of the Tigris and Euphrates. "How Inanna Brought the Me's from Eridu to Erech" is like a southern gothic novel: Enki is the lord of the plantation, Inanna is the beautiful daughter, and Dumuzi is the handsome and sweaty "darkie" brought in from the fields to serve as "the house nigger." Inanna gets the hots for this hunk of a human, then tricks her father by getting him drunk. In his drunken boasting as he lifts his cup, Enki announces each of the arts of civilization that he will give to his daughter, and she exclaims, "I'll take it." Inanna loads them all on her "boat of heaven" to carry them downstream from his city to hers, from Eridu to Erech, or Uruk.

This foundational text of how civilization was transferred from the gods to humans is important from many points of view. One interesting feature is the fascination with lists and enumeration. The arts of civilization are enumerated upon loading and unloading, and whereas for a modern sensibility, long lists of enumeration are boring, for this basic arithmetic mentality, the list is magical and numinous. The poem is my foundational text because it expresses both the foundational mentality of enumeration that is characteristic of the arithmetic mentality and because it preserves the Riverine cultural ecology that is the environment in which human culture shifts from gardening to agriculture, from gathering to food production, from settlement to civilization.

Now that we have reached the point at which we have texts and not simply tools as artifacts of human culture, we can begin to observe, or read, how cultural ecologies are constituted by these textual artifacts. In the development of a cultural ecology, there is a *formative*, a *dominant*, and a *climactic* text. A formative text is the primary or foundational text that articulates the emergence of precisely that new cultural ecology. "How Inanna brought the *me's* from Eridu to Erech" is a formative text. It articulates the new Riverine cultural ecology, and it shows the new mentality, with its fascination with lists and enumeration, with generation and accumulation. For this foundational mathematical mentality of civilization, enumeration is a generative act of how the One becomes two, and how the two, in the sexual act, become One. So the arithmetic mentality is an inherently and naturally sexual mentality. The generation of numbers and beings is a performance of the mystery of cosmic sexuality. So, not surprisingly, our earliest story is a love story, the love cycle of the goddess Inanna and the shepherd Dumuzi. And it is a love story with a zest for sexuality that our Judeo-Christian culture has tried hard to eliminate, so some of the poems may be surprising or shocking, depending upon how deeply captured one is by the Judeo-Christian sensibility. In one work, Inanna composes a poem of praise to her wonderful vulva. And one of the absolutely essential arts of civilization that Inanna steals from Enki and brings to Erech is the art of kissing the penis. The poems that describe the lovemaking of Inanna and Dumuzi are actually the originals for the "Song of Songs" in the Bible, but many ministers could not stand the blatant eroticism of the oral sexuality of "he feedeth among the lilies," so in some versions of the King James Bible there is a marginal gloss for the faithful that says "this indicates the marriage of Christ and his Church." But in these poems, there is no such deceptive priestcraft. The poems celebrate oral sexuality as the mystery of the production of food that sustains life, thus milk, cream, butter, cheese, semen and vaginal secretions are all presented as the wet and riverine landscape of marshes in which humans become touched by the gods to become erotically exalted from savagery to civilization. So the riverine delta of the vulva and the riverine delta of the Tigris both flow with the waters of life.

This primordial mentality of enumeration and generation is an edge of history, the edge between prehistory and history. We now are living at the other edge of history, the edge between history and posthistory, between industrial civilization and whatever is on the other side of the catastrophe bifurcation we find ourselves about to enter. We gain a good deal of insight when we look back to 4000 B.C.E. as a way of trying to come to terms with 2000 C.E. As we move from what Jean Gebser called the mental into the integral, we are in a position to appreciate this other shift from what Gebser called the magical into the mythical. Gebser's archaic structure of consciousness could be even earlier than Dolni Vestonice, but the magical could certainly be applied to Çatal Hüyük, and the mythical would be expressed in the emergence of literate city-states in ancient Sumer. The dying male of Çatal Hüyük is a nameless figure, a nameless figurine. But now, with the clay tablets, we know his name; he is Dumuzi, and his lover is the goddess Inanna.

At this edge between the magical and the mythical, we are right at the point at which folktale is about to become literature. In the early parts of the love cycle of Inanna and Dumuzi, one can still imagine the songs being sung; one can imagine the edge of the settlement that is not yet a great city with a wall and a temple and priests living their elevated and separate lives out of sight of their compatriots. If one goes back imaginatively to the villages of the people coming down from the Zagros mountains to the rivers of the plain, one can hear the songs being sung as worksongs as the women laugh and mimic the motions of coitus as they manipulate the phallic stick inside the churn to transform the cream into butter. One half of the group sings: "Who will plow my vulva?" And in wonderful antiphony, the other half of the group of women sing: "Dumuzi, my Lady, Dumuzi will plow your vulva." Across the road from where the women work and laugh at the men, the shepherds are hanging up balls of curds and whey in their scrotumlike sacks—sacks that drip with the semen that the goddess Inanna declares to be her food. The whole landscape is one of the merging of lovemaking and food making. Sexuality generates life, food sustains life, and lovemaking celebrates both. The language in the early part of the love cycle is very folkloric. The poems are just simple work songs celebrating the beginning of the courtship of the shepherd and the goddess, and in them, one can still feel the closeness between the lady and her shepherd; one can still feel that the society has not yet stratified itself into rigid classes that live in different worlds. The work songs are seasonal; in one season, the ritual may be for the making of cheese and butter, but at another time, it may be for the making of wine, or the making of beer. But in each case, something natural is being turned into something cultural, whether it is milk or cheese or butter or wine or beer. With these work songs, we are right at the beginning of civilization, at the dawn of literature. We are right at the edge at which an oral culture is about to be taken over and written down by a professional caste of scribes, men who will write but not sing and laugh as they move the stylus up and down.

For this folk culture, the celebration is in the production of food. As the temple grows and becomes a storehouse for grain, and as the scribes learn how to use writing to keep records of the stored food, the temple granary becomes the male place, the scrotum where the seed is stored. The goddess is the creature with the vulva; the temple is the place where the male is lifted up to heaven in relationship with the goddess, so to celebrate the continuation of the society, there ia a *hieros gamos*, a sacred intercourse, in the temple. A *hierodule* plays the role of the priestess, and a priest plays the role of the male, and in their sacred intercourse, seed is placed in the vulva, food is stored in the temple, and the life of the whole society is sustained. What is simply a system of metaphors in Sumerian folk culture and folklore, in which semen is equated with butter, scrotum with stored seed, and vulva with sheepfold, becomes architecture and priestcraft in civilization. In the erotic poetry of the folk songs, the goddess promises to watch over and bless Dumuzi's storehouse, and here one should envision the lovers in bed with her hand on his scrotum; but in the evolution of folk culture to civilization, a professional class of priests begins to appropriate that function; it places its hands on the temple granary and says, "We will protect your life. Trust us." So the clay vessel holds the food, the walls of the city hold the civilization, the storehouse holds the clay tablets, and the temple holds the granary. All of these containers are numinous and the mystery of accumulation is sacred.

The poem "Inanna's Descent into the Netherworld" is a very clear expression of the shift from folk culture to civilization. This complex poem is not simply a work song but a cosmological exploration; it probably comes from a time that is a thousand years later than the simple work songs, from 3000 B.C.E. rather than 4000 B.C.E. The text is recited for the ceremony of the new year, so one should imagine the priests moving around the temple and looking up to the stars. When they say that Enlil does not come to the rescue of Inanna, we should understand this to mean that a planet, probably Jupiter, does not appear in the sky, or in a window placed to register this planet's position in time and space. When the poem says that Enki is disturbed by Inanna's descent, that he does move, we should understand this to be the activity of another planet, probably Mercury, in conjunction with Venus. For ancient humanity, the astronomical dimension is never simply an astrophysical description, as it is for us moderns. This ancient cosmology always has implicit within it a psychology; so the architecture of the universe corresponds to the architecture of incarnation. This particular poem is presenting esoteric knowledge for initiates. Inanna passes through seven gates in hell, and at each gate, a jewel is taken away from her. As I explained in *The Time Falling Bodies Take to Light,* this process describes a reversal of time, a movement back from civilization to savagery, an encounter with the terrifying. This encounter with terror, and the specific numerology of seven, signals to us that this is an esoteric text about the experience of initiation.

The spiritual life, like Caesar's Gaul, is divided into three parts: illumination, initiation, and enlightenment. The first stage is illumination and it takes place in the etheric or subtle physical body. It is the awakening of kundalini and the opening of the third eye, the subtle chakra that is in the etheric body, but its functioning is close to and intimately involved with the physical body. Consequently, the first experience of illumination generates a shock wave or recoil in the physical body. The opening of the third eye and the experience of an internal light also generates the illumination of one's darkness, of one's instinctive, hormonal life, of one's unconscious, psychosexual, infantile programs that have shaped one's conscious life and behavior. It is a rocky and difficult period, a period of enormous energy, charismatic instability, and an energizing of one's darkness that exposes one's shadow. The second stage is initiation, and this experience does not occur in the physical plane; it occurs in the intermediate realms of the astral and mental planes. Here, it is a question of a matching grant, for an angel, jinn, or guide is awarded to the aspirant to help him or her through the process of purgation and elevation. In Dante's *Purgatorio,* the guide is a human being, Virgil. In Mohammed's *Night Journey and Ascent,* his *Miraj,* it is an angel, the angel Gabriel. In Inanna's case, the helper is her vizier who goes up to the god Enki on her behalf. This vizier, as it works so closely to the physical plane and brings Inanna "the food of life, and the water of life," is, I think, a jinn. The food of life is the menstrual blood; the water of life is the semen, so what the Vizier is bringing to Inanna is reconception, reincarnation as a way out of the intermediate realm, or the bardo. To this day in *The Tibetan Book of the Dead*, the initiate at death is counseled to unite the red and the white secretions in his spinal column that appear at death to experience initiation and release from the bardo. In Indian Tantric yoga, the red and the white are also considered archetypally numinous and magical, so at the very end of a *maithuna* the yogi has intercourse with the yogini, the *shakti*, during her menstrual period, and the etheric mixing of the two vital fluids ends the period of illumination and ushers in the stage of initiation.

It is important not to confuse illumination with enlightenment, as many people in the psychedelic counterculture do. The elevation of kundalini is illumination; it is very charismatic, dramatic, and unstable. It is the condition of perception and deception that one can observe in many pop gurus, channels, psychics, and mushroom-mullahs. Enlightenment is a stage at which all the noise of psychic transmissions has been eliminated in a stable and integrated state of universal compassion. Enlightened beings are able to have the divine consciousness, the Christ consciousness, as an available background of consciousness to every thought, to every state-waking, dreaming, vision, dreamless sleep, and samadhi. They can—unlike Gilgamesh—watch their minds go through all these changing states and never lose the ground or fundamental consciousness of the divine mind that appears in the gap between our thoughts and dreams—the gap, the bardo, between waking and sleep, death and the afterlife.

"Inanna's Descent into the Netherworld" is an esoteric text about the experience of initiation. In some texts, such as the ancient Nahautl texts that tell of the legends of Quetzalcoatl in Mexico,[9] the initiate sets himself into a coffin, puts his body into a comatose trance, and for three days journeys in the underworld, in the bardo, in the intermediate realms of the astral plane. The Sumerian text is the earliest version we have of this initiatic journey, so it is the archetype for later texts such as Christ's Harrowing of Hell in the Gospel of Nicodemus or Dante's *Divine Comedy*. The inhabitants of this intermediaate realm outside the physical plane— the jinns, angels, and demons—are critical for what one experiences. In this world of pure consciousness, what we get is what we are; so if we have anything inside us of passion or desire, then beings for whom thoughts and feelings are food, beings who feed off these—the way we feed off plants and animals in the physical world—can come in and participate in our existence. We become a symbiotic being, like those spirochetes attached to the protist in Lynn Margulis's films. This demonic world is so confusing and overpowering that a normal human being cannot make it out alone; so out of divine grace in a matching grant for the karma of our deeds and thoughts, a being is sent to us, a guide, a jinn, an angel. Jinns are very effective on the etheric plane, and they, like Alladin's genie, can work very close to the physical plane. Angels work for us in the opposite direction; they go up beyond the astral plane into the higher realms, and come down to us as messengers—the literal meaning of *angelos*—from the Divine. So the vizier of Inanna acts as an intermediary in the intermediate realms and is able to move up from the astral plane into the mental and causal planes of the gods. He brings the red and the white to Inanna, who has been hanging on a nail in hell for three days, sprinkles the water of life on her and revives her. Inanna then can return to reappear on the horizon as Venus, the morning star.

But meanwhile, back on the earth of the physical plane, Dumuzi, the symbol of the ego, has been carrying on as if he were king without Inanna. Inanna, the feminine being, is symbolic of the soul, the psychic being, the being that is the metapersonality of all our incarnations. In forgetting about Inanna, Dumuzi is carrying on like a normal ego, suffering from inflation, pride, and ignorance of the soul and esoteric knowledge. Obviously, he is heading for trouble. The demons that have followed Inanna out of hell, now attach themselves to Dumuzi. Dumuzi flees and returns to his original sheepfold—and remember that in Sumerian sheepfold is a pun for vulva—so this means that Dumuzi is returning to the tomb/womb of the Great Goddess. The ego must die. So the male, whether he is the phallus or the shepherd, must die and be returned to the Great Goddess.

Basically, this is the same initiatic story one encounters in Apuleius's *Golden Ass* or in the ancient Mexican *Anales de Cuauhtitlan*, which describe Quetzalcoatl's descent into the netherworld. Quetzalcoatl is the lord of the dawn; he is the evening star in the West that travels under the earth to appear in the East as the morning star moving close toward the sun, and then disappearing into the greater brilliance of the sun. The union of the morning star in the greater light of the sun thus symbolizes the union of the soul in the Divine. So both of these cosmological journeys serve as a wonderful parable of descent, purgation, illumination, and final integration with the light.

Our Sumerian ritual of descent is a literate text that is memorized and recited; it is a work of astronomical observance and an expression of priestcraft and specialized esoteric knowledge. It is a long way from a simple folk song of women churning butter and sexually joking with the shepherd boys across the way. With the appearance of these literate texts, there arises a split between the literate and illiterate classes, between those who keep, over generations of time, accurate records of star positions and the zodiacal rotation of the Great Year of 25,920 years, and those who are concerned with only the seasonal rhythms of the single year. But in any cultural change, the ancient and archaic is always felt to be numinous, and so for the literate class, the archaic mode of oral culture is set up as a symbol of past time. In the beginning of "Inanna's Descent into the Netherworld," the poem describes how Inanna from the Great Above turned her mind to the Great Below, and in the Sumerian language the metaphor is not of turning one's gaze, but cocking one's ear. Like a robin turning its head to listen for the low and earthly rumble of a worm hidden in the soil, Inanna cocks her ear and listens to the call, the low rumble of the underworld that attracts her.

Folkore is oral, and it is the culture and mystery of the ear. When one shifts into writing and its mythic mentality, one shifts into a visual mode of consciousness, first a syllabic, then an alphabetic script, and eventually the Gutenberg galaxy of lines of print in books and linear perspective in paintings that Marshall McLuhan and Jean Gebser have explored in their books on the evolution of consciousness. For both McLuhan and Gebser, the evolution of folk society into literate civilization is marked by an increasing visualization of consciousness. The oral world is one in which vibrating entities resonate with everything else in the All, but the visual world is one in which the object is singled out in an abstract, containing space. When the abstracted figure, the geometrical figure that stands in place of a sensual object—and this is another version of the abstract written sign that stands for a vibrating word or voice—is returned to the All, it *belongs*. In English, our technical terms tend to be abstractly mediated and refined through another language, Latin or Greek, so we don't often recognize the archaic heritage or experience when we use words like "television" or "manufacture." American English is a modern, stripped-down, analytic language, a technojargon for the computer hackers and Coca-Cola salesmen of a global society. But German is a highly inflected language, a medieval language that is much closer to its archaic roots. German, like Sanskrit, enables us to recover traces of an archaic worldview that linger in its roots and compound words. In German *hören* means to hear, but *gehören* means to *belong*. Belonging, in this sense of communal attachment, is the resonating subject in communion with its society and not the visually detached and abstracted object, alone in a mentalized, Newtonian space. So when Inanna cocks her ear and listens to the underworld, we are being presented with a written text that is reaching out for the archaic mode of consciousness of oral culture. The resonating power of oral culture connects; it takes us back to the folk culture in which we were all children of the Great Mother; it takes us back to the archaic sensorium in which each resonates with All. We feel the need to listen and to go back, because what we see in the sky is disturbing. Mars is no longer in conjunction with Venus; it is off by itself, doing its own thing, shining brightly, and thinking it can get along by itself just fine. Inanna, Venus, is down in hell, in the dark of the underworld, but Mars is still up there shining brightly in the sky, and this process of time, of change, of impermanence is disturbing. Once upon a time Inanna and Dumuzi were lovers, and she was blessing his storehouse and fondling his penis so that it would rise up in exaltation. As the lowly penis that points to earth rises up to become the phallus pointing to heaven, the lowly shepherd is lifted up into kingship. Our narrative is literally a form of time; the fundamental story is the story of change, of the suffering world of impermanence that so disturbed the Lord Gautama. So the story of the male is a story of rise and fall. Dumuzi the phallus was lifted up into his erection into kingship; but all erections are temporary, and now Dumuzi must fall to return to his small and humble state.

Mars may shine up there alone in the sky to forget about Venus in the underworld, but Mercury, or Enki, the busy little planet that goes back and forth in the sky, is more dynamic than Jupiter and will move and seek to rescue Inanna. Because Mercury moves around the earth in a spiraling figure of twenty-eight loops, it is seen as the god of writing, the messenger of the gods. When Enki responds to Inanna and says "my daughter, I am troubled," this represents the relationship between the movement of Mercury and Venus in the sky. Finally Mercury or Enki sends the water of life and the food of life. Enki sends down to Inanna in the bardo world, the underworld, the male and female equivalents of conception, so that down in hell she can reconceive a body and be born again. Out of her entrapment in bardo she can be reborn and return to the Earth. When Inanna rises out of hell, she comes with demons attached to her, looking for compensation, for a substitute. Picture Venus rising with stars that in their helical ascent will be visible briefly at dawn and then fade, perhaps taking Mars, or Dumuzi, with them.

Inanna returns to Earth and finds that everyone is mourning her, is missing her, except her old lover, Dumuzi. Dumuzi has forgotten that he was made a king by virtue of his relationship to Inanna. The erection sticking out by itself has forgotten that the phallus belongs to the Great Goddess. So what is going on in this story is a recapitulation of the basic history of the human being's incarnation into time. Inanna is the psychic being of the human turning toward earth, turning toward incarnation and manifestation, and being drawn down into the world of matter and the whole cycle of incarnation. Inanna brings together the water of life and the food of life. Dumuzi is the ego, this being who has a name and a time, a time of love with the goddess, and a time of death. The ego, the time-bound creature, begins to take himself seriously and thinks he is everything there is; the ego appropriates the all to itself. Dumuzi sits on his throne and forgets that it was the goddess Inanna who raised him to kingship in partnership with her. Mars may shine for a little season, alone in the sky without Venus, but the process of time will force it down below the horizon into the darkness of the netherworld. In the developmental process of the ego, in its growth from humble shepherd to king, it loses sight of its own soul. What our descent into hell is about is the great divorce between body and soul, ego and psyche. Dumuzi is a metaphor for the ego, and the death of the ego is required by all stories of initiation. So "Inanna's Descent into the Netherworld" is not simply a folk song about copulation; it is the fundamental initiatic text that becomes the archetype for all the subsequent descents into the underworld, of Odysseus, of Christ, of Aeneas, of Quetzalcoatl, of Mohammed, of Dante. It is for this reason that I describe this text as the *dominant* text of the Riverine cultural ecology.

The Riverine cultural ecology—the ancient rather than the classical mentality—is the foundational mentality that sets down our basic notions of narrative, of literature and mathematics as they are entwined in myth. This foundational arithmetic mentality is one in which accumulation is the central mystery, a mystery of the Goddess in which enumeration and generation are inseparable. The symbolic form of expression that performs and embodies this central mystery of accumulation is the ritual of the list. For us moderns, lists are boring, monotonous and repetitive, and whenever we come across one of these ancient texts in which the section we have already read is repeated, we become impatient. In fact, in Kramer and Wolkstein's translation, all the repetitions have been eliminated to please the sensibility of a modern audience. We moderns are no longer within the ancient arithmetic mentality; we have passed out of it into a totally different mentality. But for this ancient mentality, the list is delightful. To appreciate how the ancients felt about it, think of coitus and imagine some lover who performed one insertive motion and then stopped to ask: "Was it good for you?" For this ancient arithmetic mentality, the repetitions are delightful and numinous.

The Arithmetic mentality's fascination with the list survives even into the classical period. Think of the Old Testament with its lists of ancestors, of "so and so begat so and so." Genesis and Leviticus are cultural lists, inventories of cultural storage, the list of the ancestors. When one becomes a Zen Buddhist abbot, part of the ceremony that raises a monk to a roshi is the recitation of the list of one's antecedents all the way back to Buddha. Think of Homer's catalogue of the ships in book two of the *Iliad*. In Hesiod's *Theogony*, the gods are born through sexual intercourse, so the act of generation is a performance of enumeration and is considered sacred. It is only when we come to the new geometrical mentality in the pre-Socratics and in Plato that the Hesiodic stories of the sexuality of the gods become an embarrassment. Once we have achieved the sublimation of the world from a cumulative abundance of processive objects to an idealized and abstract geometrical figure, then the carnal and messy world of menstruation, inter-course, and birth becomes degraded and desacralized. So the arithmetic mentality is immanental and an epiphany of the female body, but the geometrical mentality is transcendental and an escape from the carnality of the female into the "higher" perfection of the male "spirit." Plato's *Timaeus* and Aeschylus's *Oresteia* are works that present us with the reconstruction of the natural female body into the perfected cultural male body, from the furies to the law courts of Athens, from the sensible realm to the intelligible realm in the escape of the male soul out of matter in the return to its native star. These two texts are the dominant texts of the geometrical mentality, and it is not till the end of the medieval era that poets, first Sufi, then troubadors, then Dante, seek to recover the cosmic feminine and place Beatrice on high in heaven. Dante is a recapitulation and a literary consum-mation of millennia of human cultural history.

But at this stage, the period of 3000 B.C.E., we are right at the time of the emergence of civilization and of highly individualized personalities, at the time of the great divorce between Inanna and Dumuzi, psyche and ego. Dumuzi inflates to think that he is king through his own power, and so he is destroyed by demons. At this stage of human cultural history, Inanna the goddess is still in power. And precisely because the goddess is still in power, it is appropriate that the world's first writer, a distinct personality with face and name, is a woman and a priestess of Inanna. This personage is Enheduanna, princess and daughter of Sargon of Agade (circa 2300 B.C.E.), priestess to Inanna in the temple of Uruk, and poetess of lyric odes in celebration of Inanna.[10]

In her exaltation of Inanna, Enheduanna composes a lyric that is homologous to the liturgical chant of "Inanna's Descent to the Nether World." She begins with an invocation to Inanna, and then proceeds to a recapitulation of the cosmic evolution in which the contemporary epiphany of Inanna is linked to the temporal progression of the gods in what amounts to an evolution of the world from the ancient gods that are before human civilization to the contemporary aeon of Inanna and her beloved city Uruk. First there is an invocation to the ancient time of the sky god, An, then to the time of the air god, Enlil, who in his gaseous dynamic separated An and Ki, heaven and earth, to create the clear sky in which humanity was able to glimpse the stars. Then we move from the high sky god, Enlil, to the closer sky god of thunder, Iskur. Then the poem proceeds to an invocation of the lesser stars, the Annunaki, that are like little bats that appear at night with the setting of the sun. Then the poem proceeds to move from sky to earth in a celebration of the volcano god, Ebih. We have now in our movement of evolutionary time gone from cosmos to earth. And from this foundation of the earth itself, the poem proceeds to historic time with the founding of civilization and the city of Uruk. Now, having firmly situated Inanna's beloved city of Uruk in cosmic time, Enheduanna proceeds to present the historical crisis of her own time: the revolt and usurpation of Lugalane that has exiled the priestess Enheduanna from her own temple and city. Like her patron goddess Inanna, Enheduanna experiences a descent into the underworld of loss and darkness. In this darkness, not even the moon god, Nanna, is shining. We are situated in the terror of the dark of the moon. *De profundis,* Enheduanna cries out to the goddess to appear as the morning star that prefigures the restoration of light and day. Enheduanna sings out in her twin powers of priestess and poetess, and the goddess responds. The crisis is overcome, cosmic order is restored, and we have the restoration of Enheduanna to her temple and her city.

In this historicizing of myth and mythologizing of history, the arrogant male who will of necessity become the dying male is not Dumuzi, but the rebel Lugalane. Since we are situated within Enheduanna's poem, we naturally read these events from the conservative point of view of the princess. Lugalane is the evil usurper. Were we also to have Lugalane's poems, perhaps the union of the monarch Sargon of Agade and the temple of Inanna might be made to appear like the tyrannical union of Generalissimo Franco and the Catholic church in the Spanish Civil War. From this perspective, Lugalane would be the revolutionary fighting for liberation from the oppressive tyrant. But we have no poetic works of Lugalane, so we cannot write a *Fidelio*-like operatic libretto for the origins of literature. It is Enheduanna who has the first word as the world's first poet, and she has so brilliantly situated her historical crisis within the cosmology of planetary time that she has firmly secured her place in the history of literature. Lugalane remains a mute and unglorious Milton; the Goddess is to have the first and last word.

But when we come forward from 2300 B.C.E. to 2100 B.C.E. and *The Epic of Gilgamesh*, the story is told from the male point of view, and man is now asserting himself and seeking to reject the erotic and deadly embrace of the goddess Ishtar. Gilgamesh says, in effect, "I remember all your lovers, Ishtar, you killed them all, but you aren't going to take me." So the ego will try not only to separate itself in time and space, but also to control time and space by organizing the universe through the power of martial law and institutionalized warfare. In other words, when one is afflicted with something, one tries to gain control of the affliction through an intensification of it. This is what warfare is: a fear of death in which the individual seeks to control death by becoming the agent that inflicts it on others. Because men feel empowered by weapons and warfare, we have children with semiautomatics in our schools and subways, or teenagers with AK-47s in Somalia, Bosnia, and Afghanistan. Take another look at Achilles in Homer's *Iliad*. The hero, half god and half man, reveals himself as he is about to kill Lykaon.[11] Lykaon pleads in vain for mercy, but Achilles says, in effect, "You miserable worm, why should I show you compassion, when I, even I the great Achilles, have to die. So to hell with you!" And so Achilles, insulted by death, becomes the deadly agent of death, the legendary killer who thinks he can master death by inflicting it everywhere around him. Death is an insult to individuated man with a name, and the only way he can eliminate this affront is to shift from being the subject to becoming the subjector. It is like becoming a psychiatrist: you hide your own mental disorders by treating the mental disorders of others.

When we look at the progression of human evolution from hominid to human, we see a progression from silvan to glacial to savannaan to riverine. When we consider the further development of civilization, we see a progression from riverine to transcontinental to oceanic to biospheric. The riverine introduces the polity of the city-state. The expansion of riverine city-states into empires introduces either a transcontinental projection—as was the case in ancient Mesopotamia, India, China, and Mesoamerica—or a maritime projection, as was the case in the Mediterranean with the Minoans, Phoenicians, Greeks, and Romans. In the rise of capitalism, with its emphasis on commerce rather than conquest, there occurs a shift from a concentric empire to world economy. An empire is a simple geometrical formation; there is a center and a periphery, a capital or an imperial court and the outlying provinces. An economy is a more complex dynamical system; it involves a commercial city that has as its phase-space a world economy. In the shift from the military dynamics of empire to the commercial dynamics of a world economy, there also occurs a shift in mathematical mentalities. This is the shift from the geometrical mentality to the Galilean or dynamical mentality in which motion is the quintessential feature. The mathematics of empire is a static one in which the values of an unchanging eternity stand above and behind the political authority; motion and change are looked upon as the evils of a lower, phenomenal world. Whether we are talking about pharaohonic Egypt, or Plato's *Timaeus*, or classical China, Teotihaucan, Tiahuanaco, or the Papacy in Rome, the cultural content may change, but the structure of the mathematical mentality is the same geometrical mentality. The polis for this mentality is the city-state expanded into empire; the class structure is pyramidal in a hierarchy of warriors and priests, and the sexual emphasis is patriarchal. The mental idealization of the geometrical figure, the male *spirit*, is considered higher and more real than the physical and the female. So the ancient arithmetical mentality is immanental, but the classical geometrical mentality is transcendental.

All of this changes in the shift from classical to modern civilization with the rise of capitalism and world trade around the year 1500 C.E. The new trading city has as its phase-space a world economy, not a simple concentric military empire. Florence becomes such a city around 1450, and then Venice becomes an economically dynamic city competing with Genoa for supremacy in the Mediterranean. And then the story is one of a general movement west, from Venice in the sixteenth century, to Antwerp and Amsterdam in the seventeenth, to London in the eighteenth and nineteenth centuries, and finally to New York in the twentieth century. The great economic historian Fernand Braudel says that the sign of the shift of the capital of the world economy from London to New York was the Great Crash of 1929. Now there's a truly dynamical mode of looking at history! Braudel is not tricked by ideological camouflage or the names of famous men; he looks at the dynamics of the system and sees what is really going on. When one stops to consider that the Empire State Building and Rockefeller Center were built in the Great Depression, one begins to get a feel for this dynamical way of looking at history through the development of cultural ecologies.

In this shift from transcontinental empire to world economy, there is the shift from script to print, from classical empire to bourgeois nation-state, and from the geometrical mentality to the dynamical mentality—the new mathematical description of the world as articulated by Galileo, Descartes, and Newton. Naturally, a description of the world is not only a question of mathematics; it is also, as a description, a question of narrative; therefore, literature and mathematics are always inseparably entwined in any mentality. In the new mentality with its focus on motion and change, one sees the shift from the heroic epic to the novel—from Ariosto to Cervantes. The heroic epic is the celebration of the military hero and is quite appropriate for empire, but the novel is about motion, madness, and doubt, as the mind becomes the new focus of attention. The novel is, essentially, the autobiography of the new rising middle class and its dynamical movement is from rags to riches, from the fictional autobiography of *Lazarillo de Tormes* to Defoe's *Moll Flanders* to Dickens's *Great Expectations*. Money, as critics like Dorothy Van Ghent have pointed out, is, in fact, one of the great themes of the bourgeois novel. Money, like the book itself, is an expression of printed paper, of McLuhan's Gutenberg galaxy. This new dynamical movement of money through time generates value or interest.

For the medieval mentality, interest or usury is evil; movement or change in the order of things is evil. So when we come to the great bifurcation that we know as the Renaissance, the fork in the road is profound and leads us into the whole new adaptive landscape we call modernism. On one side of the great divide of 1492 or 1500 is the geometrical mentality in its Mediterranean cultural ecology, its empire of Christendom with its center in Rome. The *climactic* work of this mentality is Dante's *Divine Comedy,* and especially the *Paradiso.* After Dante's sublime Christianization of the Islamic neoplatonic universe of Ibn Arabi,[12] there is nowhere else to go but into Descartes's doubt and Cervantes's brilliant exploration of perception and imagination, madness and mind. The medieval kingdom of King Lear disintegrates; and from the distractions of Prospero's books, the old Italian kingdom is lost and the magus is exiled to the new world of Bermuda, on the other side of the tempest. *The Tempest,* the storm itself, is the presentation of a dynamical system that disrupts the tranquil and unchanging world of the medieval mentality. So we can see that these new works of literature are *formative* texts. Shakespeare's *King Lear* and *The Tempest,* Cervantes's *Don Quixote,* and Descartes's *Discourse on Method* are all *formative* texts of the new mentality in its new cultural ecology, the modern Atlantic rather than the medieval Mediterranean.

The *formative* text for the arithmetic mentality is "How Inanna Brought the *me*'s from Eridu to Erech." The *dominant* text of the arithmetic mentality is "Inanna's Descent into the Nether World," and the *climactic* text is *The Epic of Gilgamesh.* The formative works for the new cultural ecology of the Mediterranean are the Homeric epics, and here I do agree with those scholars who say these two epics are by different authors. The *Iliad* sets out the basic Western conception of tragedy, that tragedy is not a question of having a tragic flaw that can be removed by piety and prayer, the nonsense I was taught in Catholic school. For Homer, it is one's greatness that is one's tragic flaw. It is Achilles's essential greatness that makes him a tragic hero. One's unique excellence, *areté,* is one's tragic flaw, one's *hamartia.* The Athenians are great and daring risk takers, and that saves them with Themistocles and leads them to disaster and doom with Alcibiades. The sailing out of the Syracusan expedition described in Thucydides is another performance of the basic Homeric conception of tragic action, of the movement beyond the limit—as when Patroklos dons the armor of Achilles and goes out beyond the wall to his doom. This Homeric conception of the wall, the container, is a classic example of the geometrical mentality. The *Iliad* establishes our fundamental Western notions of time and action, and the *Odyssey* sets out our fundamental Western notions of space. It is a work that articulates the expanded world of the Mediterranean and expresses the movement away from the female, as the center of the universe, to the male, now experienced not simply as the dynamical principle of vanishing and death, but as dynamical in its discovery of space: from the sea voyage to the voyage to outer space, from one Apollo to another.

Now, one might be tempted to think that Hesiod's *Theogony,* rather than the Homeric epics, is the formative work for the new cultural ecology of the Mediterranean, but Hesiod is a profoundly conservative poet. Farmer-poets, whether they are Hesiod in Boetia or Wendell Berry in Kentucky, are deeply rooted human beings whose minds go down into the soil of the past. Hesiod's *Theogony* is the last light, the sunset effect, of the ancient arithmetic mentality. With its emphasis on the generative power of the gods, it is primarily a list of the gods, a *Who's Who* of who begat whom and how. Its trinity of Chaos, Gaia, and Eros takes us back into the prehistoric culture of Anatolia and the Near East. Hesiod's chaos is the old Apsu from the *Enuma Elish*; Gaia is the Great Goddess, and Eros is the generative power of love and desire, the love story of time in which the male flourishes and dies.

The dominant texts of the geometrical mentality are Aeschylus's *Oresteia* and Plato's *Timaeus*. Both these works express the shift from female dominance to male dominance, from nature to culture, from the Earth of the furies to the city of Athens, from custom to reason. Aeschylus's work of genius sums up more than a millennium of human development, and does so as a way of turning from the prehistoric past to the new democratic institutions of Athens. Originally, tragedy had been a goat-ode, an ode to the sacrificial animal, a dithyrambic chant in which there would be a procession of the women, a contest or agon, then the sacrifice, and finally, the recessional.[13] The roots of this form of sacrifice of the animal, goat or bull, take us back to the dying male of Anatolia. In moving from one actor standing in for the god to three actors and their dramatic interactions, and in transforming the chorus of women attending the sacrifice of the male into the chorus of democratic citizens attending in awe the tragedy of the heroically assertive self, Aeschylus was a literary genius whose profound work expressed the millennia. His work is both radically modern and incredibly ancient, for behind the mask of Aegisthus is the archetypal figure of Kingu from the Babylonian *Enuma Elish*; and behind the trial of Orestes is the New Kingdom text of the trial of Horus.[14] Both the Egyptian trial of Horus and the Athenian trial of Orestes legitimize the shift from ancient mother-right to the rule of the son over the mother and the mother's protector, the mother's brother. For Plato, this process of increasing masculinization reaches its intellectual zenith in the academy's emphasis that the abstract idealization of the geometrical figure is superior to the deceptive world of the senses. If one ascends to this higher reason, one returns to one's native star, but if one fails, then one is reborn as a woman.[15] Woman is the matrix of matter and the receptacle of space, the basin of all attractions; but the Demiurge, the creative artisan who fashions the universe after the perfect geometries of the five platonic solids and the unchanging rotations of perfect spheres, is male. This authoritarian universe of Platonic thought becomes supremely attractive for the medieval church. With Plato, the mind declares its independence of the body, and the transcendent importance of thought over biological life is indicated in *The Statesman*, for there Plato argues that those who persist in their sins of wrong thinking and heresy should be put to death. It is an idea whose time had not yet come, but, thanks to the authoritarian church fathers, the church will take it up. First, there will only be Bishop Irenaeus's denunciation of the Gnostics, but denunciation led to genocide in the Albigensian Crusade, and soon death became a way of life for the church as the Albigensian Crusade was followed by the Inquisition and the slaughter of hundreds of thousands of women in the witch trials.

The final and *climactic* text for the geometrical vision of the universe in the Mediterranean cultural ecology is Dante's *Divine Comedy*, especially the vision in the *Paradiso* of the complex topology of the Primum Mobile, the single point from which depends the topology of the 3-sphere universe.[16] For the geometrical mentality of Plato, motion and change are fallen and sinful, but Galileo is fascinated by motion, and with Newton's calculus of infinitesimals comes the solution for Archimedes' paradoxes of motion. Archimedes's paradoxes of motion represent the way motion appears within the geometrical mentality: a half of a half of a half, ad infinitum. There's simply no understanding motion in this geometrical mentality; one has to shift into a totally new mentality with its calculus of infinitesimals and its concept of the limit before humanity can make any sense of motion. In the medieval mentality, the sky is a blank and perfect celestial vault, the iconic gold background to Madonna and Christ child, but in the new mentality of motion, the sky becomes filled with those agents of motion and transformation, the clouds. So one should think not only of Newton as constitutive of the new mentality, one should think of the paintings of Ruisdael as well.

For this Atlantic or oceanic cultural ecology of modernism, the *formative* texts are those of Descartes, Cervantes, and Shakespeare. The *dominant* text for modern man is, of course, *Faust*. For us Americans, however, the dominant text of our Faustian man is "the great American novel" *Moby Dick*. Ahab is our image of Faustian man who cries out: "Talk not to me of blasphemy, man, I'd strike the sun if it insulted me."[17] The *climactic* text, the one that finishes the Atlantic cultural ecology and its mentality so that there is nowhere to go but into a new planetary mentality is James Joyce's *Finnegans Wake* —the last novel, and almost, in its way, the ultimate book.

Joyce is one of those great literary geniuses, like Aeschylus, whose work consummates the whole process of the development of literature. First he begins with the Riverine stirrings of his vision of life along the shores of the Liffey in his short stories in *Dubliners*; but in "The Dead," the river Liffey becomes another river Lethe. At the shore of the waking and dreaming mind with its edge between life and the bardo realm, Gretta Conroy thinks of her lost dead lover and drifts into sleep while her husband Gabriel looks out toward the west in a meditation on time and death. In *Ulysses*, Joyce sets up the typical day in Dublin against the archetypal journey of Odysseus, and provincial "Dear, Dirty, Dublin" becomes lifted into the larger classical world of the Mediterranean cultural ecology. But the mind of the narrative is Janus-faced, with one side looking toward the streets of Dublin and the other inward toward the stream of consciousness itself. Turning up in a spiral in which he goes both higher and wider, Joyce returns to the theme of the married couple in bed, but reverses the states of consciousness of "The Dead," for now it is the husband Bloom who sleeps and the wife Molly whose mind flows in the riverine stream of consciousness that ends the work. And then again in *Finnegans Wake*, Joyce turns up even higher in his widening gyre to the state of consciousness of a surreal bardo realm in which the waking mind and dreaming mind are situated not simply in the consciousness of a single person, but in the dreaming couple in bed of Anna Livia Plurabelle and Humphrey Chimpden Earwicker, the vast and collective being of the humanity of "Here Comes Everybody"

In "The Dead," Joyce looked westward over Ireland, turning from the Liffey to envision the vast and dark Atlantic of death that surrounds the tiny island of life. In *Ulysses*, Joyce summed up both the modern European world and the classical Mediterranean world of the *Odyssey*; but with the punning, plurisignative language of *Finnegans Wake*, Joyce really summed up the whole flow of Western civilization from Riverine to Mediterranean to Atlantic to Biospheric: from Penelope to Molly Bloom to Anna Livia Plurabelle; from Odysseus to Bloom to Finn again and Humphrey Chimpden Earwicker.

The Atlantic cultural ecology generated not only the European novel, with its focus on character as destiny, as in such classic examples as *Madame Bovary* and *Anna Karenina*, but also the new genre of autobiography with its radical assertion of self. Joyce, in developing his stream of consciousness narrative in *Ulysses*, took this genre to its fullest in making the interiorized self its own kind of landscape; but this development is a climactic one that can go no further, and, in fact, in a classic sort of alchemical *enantiodromia*, it turns into its opposite in *Finnegans Wake*. As the mind of the male flows into dreams, it dissolves, and the hero melts back into a universal self as the publican Humphrey Chimpden Earwicker becomes Here Comes Everybody. Influenced by the Freudian psychology of his day, as well as by the artistic movements of surrealism and the Dadaism of Zurich's Cabaret Voltaire, Joyce chose to situate his narrative in the hypnagogic state of consciousness in which the waking mind shifts into dreaming, but yet is still so bound to the auditory stimuli of the physical world that sounds are transformed into images and images into the little dramas of dreams. Would that Joyce had been a little more of a yogi than a psychoanalyst, for every meditator knows that this sloppy mess of mind is like the noise one picks up as one moves from one station to another on an FM radio band. As soon as one shifts out of the physical through the etheric and into the astral, things begin to become clear and distinct again in the imaginal realm of the astral. And, in fact, in the great sections of *Finnegans Wake*, Joyce does move into the imaginal realm of the Celtic spirit in which folk souls, such as the *Sidhe* of ancient Ireland, appear and sing with a coherence that is musically complex but not the kind of mental linguistic crossword puzzle complications of the other sections. The great section of book one, chapter eight in which the gossipy washerwomen at the ford talk of Anna Livia Plurabelle is, when read aloud, one of the finest parts of the book. When A.E. was being self-consciously Celtic and mystical, he slid down into sentimentality and spiritual kitsch, but Joyce's great sense of humor and his Irish love of bedevilment rescue him from both of those traps, and his fine tenor's ear for music and song takes him up to a language that is a pure joy to hear. If Joyce had been able to carry on with this and take us up to the top of the astral plane and the beginning of the mental—from what yogis would call the *manomayapurusha* to the *vijnanamayapurusha*—then we would have had not simply the *climactic* work of the Atlantic cultural ecology, but the climactic work of the biospheric as well. Joyce would have been Homer and Dante rolled into one. But Joyce left something for the writers of the future to do. Like a Moses on Mt. Pisgah, he sees the promised land of the new culture, but he does not himself enter it. He consummates the entire Atlantic cultural ecology, from Homer to his own time, and then brings us to the threshold of the new biospheric consciousness that is now so much more pronounced in our Gaian era than it was in his.

Joyce's vision of Viconian circularity, of *corso/ricorso*, is an ecological one in which Riverine, Mediterranean, and Atlantic are all taken up into a universal and biospheric celebration of the Great Goddess renamed Anna Livia Plurabelle. The river Liffey flows out to the sea, the sun heats the sea, and the clouds return in rain to recharge the waters that flow down from the Dublin mountains into Phoenix Park and into the river Liffey once again. In the landscape of *Finnegans Wake*, of Howth Castle and environs, with its actual street named the old Vico Road, with its literal Phoenix Park symbolic of the dying and rising phoenix, Joyce has turned the local into the universal, transformed type into archetype. Punning in all the languages he knew, Joyce brought us through his Ireland to the Atlantic edge of Europe and to the edge of a new global, biospheric mentality. So climactic a work is Joyce's that for writers of my generation it was simply not possible to carry on writing middle-class novels about a day in the life of anybody as if James Augustine Joyce had never existed. For an Irish American teenager growing up at that other oceanic edge of history in the Los Angeles of the 1950s and wanting to become a writer—ironically just at the time television was about to take over the culture—Joyce was a tough act to follow. One had to let go of the great genres of Western literature and move up and out of the high European literary mind into the new planetary cultural ecology to explore new genres of *Wissenskunst* in forms of writing that were not simply the mimetic novel or the solipsistic, confessional cry of the suicidal poet.

Like the dynamical mentality before it, this new morphological mentality is both mathematical and literary. It is a shift from the linear causal systems of Galileo, Descartes, and Newton to the new chaos dynamical mathematics in the new sciences of complexity. It is a shift from the linear perspective of modernism to Gebser's integral structure of diaphony; it is a movement beyond mind and the mentalistic structures as we have known them in the modernism of industrial capitalism. It is a movement from the industrial nation-state to the enantiomorphic polity of the biosphere, the Gaia politique. The formative texts for this new biospheric mentality are the parodies of scholarship in Jorge Luis Borges's fictional encyclopedias of nonexistent countries and in Stanislaw Lem's reviews of nonexistent books, both of which signal the shift from the mental to the supramental. Another vision of this shift, from Soviet dialectical industrial materialism to spiritual ecology, is seen in the Tarkovsky-Lem film *Solaris*—the film that prophesied in 1972 the disintegration of the Soviet Union and the shift to a new awareness of Gaia, of the living ocean and the living biosphere. Both the film *Solaris* and James Lovelock's first paper on the Gaia hypothesis appeared in 1972. So, I would point to the year 1972, like the year 1492, as a bifurcation, a fork in the road in which we turned from modernism to planetary culture; 1972 is the year in which Dennis and Donella Meadows published their globally influential book *Limits to Growth*.[18] This book represents one of the first attempts to express planetary dynamics, to represent the interactions of the world economy and the global biosphere in a new way of looking at the world. It expresses the shift from economics to ecology as the governing science of the world.

In 1972, I quit the university and founded the Lindisfarne Association as an attempt to constellate a new group of artists, scientists, and contemplatives who could express and realize the new planetary culture. So, as a writer, I see myself within this planetary dynamical tradition that I am articulating with this analysis of literature and the evolution of consciousness. And I see my own poem and essay cycle, *Imaginary Landscape*[19] as a formative text for this new Biospheric cultural ecology with its new literary and mathematical mentality. Notice that the formative "texts" for this new mentality are duogeneric, science fiction novel and film in the case of Lem and Tarkovsky, or music and film in the case of Stravinsky and Disney's *Fantasia,* or scientific essay and lyrical cycle in my own case. This shift from one mentality to another is thus the shift from *Wissenschaft* to *Wissenskunst* as the literary genre appropriate for this new Biospheric cultural ecology in which information has become our second nature.

In my literary friendship with the chaos mathematician Ralph Abraham, the atmospheric chemist James Lovelock, the microbiologist Lynn Margulis, and the neuroscientist Francisco Varela, I am seeking, as a poet, not to write about the return to nature that one would find in the works of such poets as Gary Snyder or Wendell Berry, but about a much more radical re-visioning of nature—a rearticulation of nature and culture that is coming about in this new epiphany that Aurobindo calls "the Descent of the Supramental." For this manifestation of the supramental, the individual mind, the heroic genius of the age of Newton or Beethoven—which is the essential myth of modernism—the individual mind is insufficient. This new symbiotic consciousness requires a more complex noetic polity, a musical polity, to embody it. So not only are these new art forms, such as *Solaris* or Philip Glass's and Robert Wilson's *Einstein on the Beach,* duogeneric, they are also collaborative. In my own work *Imaginary Landscape,* I crossed two genres, poem and essay, but I also worked in the intellectual chamber music ensemble of the Lindisfarne Fellows. In this ensemble of the Lindisfarne Fellows, there is preserved an integrity of voice that allows the collective pattern to emerge of itself. In *Imaginary Landscape,* the ideas of Lovelock, Margulis, Varela, and Abraham were used to create a moiré of overlapping lines, or, to change metaphors from sight to sound, a fugue of four voices. To their voices, I then added my own in a cycle of cosmological poems that was, for all its scientific surface, very much in the romantic tradition of poems of description and meditation, such as Coleridge's "Frost at Midnight" or Mathew Arnold's "Dover Beach." These duogeneric efforts, experimental and avant garde as they may seem, may, however, be far too conservative to become the *dominant* text of the new biospheric mentality. The new dominant text may not be a text at all, but a hypertext.

In fact, hypertext would seem to be a cultural ecology of its own. The traditional text, quite literally, becomes a pretext for a hypertext: one may start with Homer or Joyce, but as the hypertext cyberspace provides all the commentaries of scholars and the responses of students, the text experiences a meltdown of the integrity of its own membrane.[20] Bacteria, the prokaryotic cells, are said not to be distinct species, but a kind of planetary bioplasm in which cells exchange genes rather promiscuously. Eukaryotic cells, cells with nuclei, by contrast, carry their genes in the discrete package of the nucleus and only exchange genes through the more controlled process of sexual reproduction and mitosis. The cultural ecology of hypertext would seem to be a bacterial world of melting membranes and a global bioplasm of shifting genes. The culture of the text in the literary world in which I was raised is more eukaryotic. There is a nucleus, there is an author. James Joyce, as the last great author of the great era of literature, seems to have ushered in the era of his own demise by conjuring with the spirit of "Here Comes Everybody." The hypertext world is a collective cyberspace in which student papers and Internet chatter are collaged onto the text, and participants can change the text to give it a more personally appealing finish. This sort of cultural development spells the death of the author far more effectively than the merely literary pronouncements of Roland Barthes in the 1960s.

For someone of my generation, this electronic development is frighteningly alien; it is not a literary culture or world that I would care to live in, so in love am I with the integrity of the text and the cult of the genius. It is a culture too much like the Hollywood movie industry, which recently altered classics such as *The Scarlet Letter* and the *Morte d'Arthur.* But when I stop to reflect, I remind myself that the Bible, especially the King James Bible, is a collective expression, that the *Ramayana* is certainly not the exclusive expression of Valmiki, and that the *Iliad* and the *Odyssey* are also probably the works of more than one or two individual bards. The sacredness of the author, as I revere it, is a cultural construction, and a fairly recent one at that, if one looks at literature from the point of view of the millennia, as I am trying to do in this book.

If the *formative* texts for the Biospheric cultural ecology are works like those of Borges and Lem, and if the *dominant* text for the Biospheric is hypertext, then God only knows what wholly "other" formation awaits us as the *climactic.*

When a new mentality comes in, it brings with it an "otherness" in which what was sinful and fallen in the old mentality begins to become the center of attention and even the new medium of communication. For the geometrical mentality, motion is fallen and imperfect, and usury is sinful; but for the new dynamical mentality, the motion of falling objects in space is what the new sciences are all about, and the movement of money that generates value through interest is what the new economy of capitalism is all about. What was hitherto noise is looked upon as interesting information. To get a feeling for this quality of otherness in one mentality and another, think of the way homosexuality is understood, not in New York or San Francisco, where it is more openly accepted, but in Tulsa. For the fundamentalist followers of Oral Roberts, homosexuality is an abomination and the essence of sin. But for the new postmodern mentality, the focus is primarily on the unnatural as the condition of the evolutionary shift out of nature into a purely artificial culture. It is all part and parcel of a technological shift in which artificial intelligence, artificial life, artificial fertilization, thermonuclear fusion, and virtual reality are involved in not simply a fashionable deconstruction of romantic literature, but a complete deconstruction of the whole value system of romanticism's "return to nature."

So a change in mentalities is not simply a change in fashion; it is a cultural transformation in which "evil is the annunciation of the next cultural level of organization." It is a historical tragedy in which both sides are wrong—and right—at the same time. Some homosexuals' commitment to high technology and artifice created a culture in the seventies in which many gay men took "poppers" and antibiotics before going out cruising on Saturday night. Some researchers have claimed that the disintegration of the immune system in AIDS is not simply an HIV infection, but an interior disorganization of the immune system brought forth by a subculture of overuse of antibiotics and recreational drugs. Not surprising, the fundamentalists are delighted and see AIDS as the wrath of God against the Sodom and Gomorrah of New York and San Francisco. Meanwhile, the fundamentalists in their commitment to good old Republican values are breaking down the immune system of the planet as the ozone hole widens and the greenhouse gases accumulate from good old-fashioned industrial development and growth economies. So the candle of our cultural ecology is getting burned at both ends, and there is no way anybody is going to be safe anywhere. All humanity is involved in this bifurcation, or what the chaos dynamicists prefer to call "a catastrophe bifurcation."

Global pollution is another form of the phenomenology in which evil is the annunciation of the next level of organization. Pollution is the membrane between the global economy and the biosphere, and since agriculture and cattle can also be damaging to the biosphere and its global weather patterns, not even an Amish farmer can claim to be innocent. So the only true fundamentalists are the Indians in the Amazon rain forest; small wonder that they are being burned out of their home and eliminated as an option for humanity.

All members of humanity are involved in this evolutionary crisis, no matter at what historical cultural level of development they are, no matter to which mentality they are committed. Humanity is in the grip of a huge obsession—fundamentalists would call it a possession by the Devil—so as we move out of the old cultural ecology of transoceanic capitalism and our once-sustaining biosphere of the physical plane, we find ourselves within a subtle body, a bardo condition, an angelic body politic that is a remorseless description of who we are and who we wish to be. Or think of it this way. Matter and physical reality are a kind of thick insulation, one that protects us from the immediate consequences of our thoughts—that makes us Dumuzi on Earth rather than Inanna in the underworld. When we die and go into bardo, we no longer have that protection, that delayed reaction of the consequences of our thoughts, of our state of consciousness. We become immediately what we are; we are what we think. It is not God's wrath or human justice; it is just is-ness: we are what we are. Now imagine several billion people going into bardo all at once, say, in some gigantic historical catastrophe such as the reversal of the Earth's magnetic field and the wobbling of the poles. Suddenly billions of people are in bardo all at once; they are in the astral plane sharing a common mind, a common noetic polity. Like the quivering spirochetes in Lynn Margulis's films, this pattern of consciousness can become formed enough to allow an emergent state to pattern it sufficiently so that this noetic polity becomes a form of incarnation. "It ain't the meat, it's the motion." So the extended mind of the billions in bardo becomes the incarnational field of other forms of consciousness in the universe. In dynamical theory, you could say that the accumulation of noise draws the system from one attractor to another. The mythological or paranoid forms of narrative for this would be to call it "possession by the devil," for the demonically inclined, or salvation in the mystical body of Christ, for the angelically inclined. The work of art that expresses this catastrophe bifurcation is Hieronymus Bosch's painting *The Last Judgement,* for it shows heaven breaking in on top and all hell breaking loose below.

Now, in chaos dynamical theory, the catastrophe bifurcation brings forth is an acceleration of time, an evolutionary quantum leap. Because the bardo or the astral plane is more pliable to consciousness than matter is, a vividly shared imagination is not simply a shared consensual delusion, but a collective form of incarnation; it is more like a civilization than a fantasy. When a billion people move into this instantaneous civilization in bardo to participate in the galactic consciousness of an archangel, then an enormous leap forward in cosmic evolution becomes possible. The galactic archangel is like an electrical transformer that takes in direct current and steps it down to alternating current so that one can run the domestic appliances without burning up. Only in this case, the domestic appliances are the chakras. If all of this sounds pretty far-out and sci-fi, it is precisely because science fiction was the smuggling past customs of this new mentality. Think of Arthur C. Clarke's novel *Childhood's End* as an intuition of this, or the ending of the film he worked on with Stanley Kubrick, *2001: A Space Odyssey*. From this cosmic point of view, the catastrophe in which billions die and enter bardo all at once may not actually be a catastrophe at all, but a galactic opportunity for accelerated evolution. If humanity simply goes on as usual, we may simply slide down into a Bosnia that lasts for an aeon. For those who require an optimistic outlook on life to get out of bed in the morning, consider the fate of the dinosaurs. The dinosaurs died in the last great collective death of the Cretaceous extinction, but they came back as the birds that we see all around us.

THE HERO VERSUS THE INITIATE IN THE MASCULINE ENCOUNTER WITH DEATH: A COMPARISON OF OSIRIS AND GILGAMESH

The fundamental question of the arithmetic mentality, that mentality that deals with the mysteries of generation and enumeration, is: How is it that the One can become two? The answer is a vision of what the physicist David Bohm called "the implicate order." Time is implicit in space; the male is implicit in the female; the phallus is implicitly contained within the body of the Great Mother. The generation of time is the separation of the phallus from the body of the Great Mother into its own kind of phase-space, into its own phenomenological domain in which it becomes a story, a story of rise and fall. After it has its little season, it is drawn back to the Great Goddess, or to put it in the language of today's chaos dynamical theory, back to that basin of all attractions.

As we move forward in historical time, the ontological domain of the phallus changes—which is simply to say that history is a story. In prehistory, the phallus is deeply embedded in the body of the Great Mother; it is practically the entire back side of the Goddess of Lespugue. As humanity proceeds in its story from hunting to the domestication of animals, stock breeding brings with it an attention to paternity. The Neolithic son-lover of the Great Mother now has his own space to sport with the animals, to flourish for a season before he returns in death. And since stock breeding and agriculture are both part of Neolithic society, the sprouting plant that sticks up, produces seed, and then withers and dies to return to the soil also becomes a phallic story. As we move from the Neolithic culture of Çatal Hüyük to the urban culture of Sumer, we come to a male who has not simply an image but a name. We come to Dumuzi. Here we no longer have to project a story into the imagery of statues, we can read the story of Dumuzi's rise and fall.

The transitional figure between the humble shepherd who is chosen by the goddess Inanna and the great male heroic king Gilgamesh, who rejects the deadly erotic embrace of Ishtar, is Osiris. Dumuzi simply dies, but Osiris becomes lord of the realm of death. The story of Isis and Osiris is a fascinating work for many reasons, because it is, in a way, timeless. It prehends an unimaginably ancient past and it prefigures the future. It is a kind of annunciation of what is going to be the prophetic—avataric is an even better word—the avataric relationship between the male and female as humanity shifts from one zodiacal sign to another, one Platonic month to another. The story of Isis and Osiris is the overture for the story of Jesus and Mary—which is something that D. H. Lawrence recognized when he wrote *The Man Who Died*. The story of Isis and Osiris, as we have it in Plutarch, is like a fossil in the foyer of the Chrysler Building. Plutarch's text is Roman and yet it is describing something ancient, the cultural moment of 2000 B.C.E. But even this story, whenever it first began to be told, is an exploration of the dawn of historical time, because it is presenting the missing link from the prehistoric matristic culture in which the mother's brother is the protector of the female mysteries to a new moment of history in which the father and the son with their patriarchal system of inheritance challenge the rule of the mother's brother. There is a new kingdom text from around 1150 B.C.E. that presents the trial of Horus.[1] This text and the Babylonain *Enuma Elish* are the archetypes behind the trial of Orestes in

Aeschylus's *Oresteia.* The trial is the conflict between past and present. Seth, the brother of Isis, is presented as a conservative figure who uses the ancient flint tools of prehistory; his totem is the boar, and he is all for the culture of human sacrifice that Osiris eliminated in his reforms, in his cultural revolution from hunting to agriculture. Seth is the violent conservative, a Generalissimo Franco of prehistory trying to deny modernism by wedding church and state into a militaristic theocracy. Seth, as the mother's brother, is the protector of the mysteries of the mother, just as Franco was the protector of holy mother church. The new offspring of time, Horus, the son of Isis and Osiris, is proclaiming a new relationship and saying "I am the son of the father and therefore I should rule." So the trial is to determine the legitimacy of this historical novelty, the son. The mother's brother is an adult at the height of his powers and thus represents military force wed to matrilineal inheritance. But a son who is still a child cannot rule, protect society from warring tribes, or really take on the military power of the fully grown and competent mother's brother. The case for Seth is obvious; it is an argument for stability. The case for the son, Horus, is absurd; it is an argument for the introduction of dangerous instability. How can one possibly have a stable order if one is going to have these sons and immature children squabbling with one another. Only the power of the mother's brother can protect the natural order.

But time is also the natural order, and time means change. Once there is a recognition of paternity—and a shift from a culture in which all the children belong to the community to a culture in which there are distinct individuals who are the sons of distinct indvidual fathers—time produces change. Now one has generational time, dynastic time. Matriarchal time is a steady state; all God's children are alike, and life goes on unchangingly. But the shift from hunting and the seasonal round to agriculture and stock breeding introduces the phenomenon of property: herds and land. Land requires water, and irrigation systems, and oxen, and plows; all of this implies a radically new culture. If you have cattle, you can have cattle raids, and the old Mesolithic instrument of the hunt can become the Neolithic instrument for hunting humans. As sporadic, seasonal cattle raiders become replaced by professional defenders and attackers, the cattle raid is transformed into war. To prevent this runaway system of total violence and anarchy, it makes some sense to have human sacrifice as an inoculation against the plague of warfare. And what better candidate for human sacrifice than the king. The king must die, so that the crops can grow. If one has a ritual sacrifice of the king, one can avoid the assertion of the rights to property and the conflict that goes with it in the culture of warring dynasties. So a case can be made for the ancient matristic culture in which the sacrifice of one human protects humanity from genocide. But to hold to the ancient ways of Seth, one would have to go back to the way of life of hunting for men and village gardening for women. And that way of life simply no longer works for cities. With the accumulation of propetry, of herds, fields, irrigation systems, walls, and temples, there can be no going back. Rather than submit to being sacrificed, some kings decide to live and pass on what they have to their sons. Horus wins the trial, and the new era of patriarchy and patrilineal succession takes over.

Mother-right is archaic and inappropriate for the life of the city, whether the city is Marduk's Babylon or Apollo's Athens. The *Oresteia* is a major text in the evolution of consciousness precisely because it plays out these ancient themes from Egypt and Babylon and consolidates the foundation of the patriarchal civilization to come. Behind the personage of Aegisthus stands the mythic and transpersonal figure of the Babylonian Kingu; and behind the personage of Orestes stands the mythic and transpersonal figure of the Egyptian Horus. When one read these texts in this musical way, in which they echo with ancient themes and melodies, then the texts become a historical fugue, an intratextual, polyphonic work of richness and complexity. In Lévi-Strauss's terms, *diachrony* becomes *synchrony*.

When one text is prehending another in this way, the drama is really not just about an author with his conscious intentionality. A modern critic can deconstruct an author's intentionality to try to prove that the celibate is really a lecher or that the lover is really a misogynist, but this kind of deconstruction is only the first and most primitive recognition of complexity. In the new sciences of complexity, linear systems — whether of causation or ideology — are inadequate descriptions of a dynamical system that "surfs at the edge of chaos," to use Stuart Kauffman's term.[2] A text is a complex system; it is like a fossil that is embedded both in an ecology and in a culture of narrative explication, such as Darwinian evolution. A text is, therefore, a performance of a cultural ecology in which the storyteller or bard or critic is re-presenting the text in an explication that is really a new kind of storytelling in a radically new kind of informational cultural ecology, the noetic polity of our own posthistorical era. This narrative of literature and the evolution of consciousness is intended to be something like an exhibition in the spiral of Frank Lloyd Wright's Guggenheim Museum: one can look and become lost in an individual work, or one can look up and down and across the space to envision the synchronic spiral in which the trial of Horus, the *Enuma Elish,* and the *Oresteia* are all in the same position inside a metaculture in which information has become our second nature.

A journalistic critic is concerned with making judgments from within his accepted culture, so he speaks for his culture with arrogant confidence and says that this is good and that is bad. An academic deconstructionist critic tries to challenge these bourgeois pieties with a Nietzschean nihilism that tries to prove that although *x* pretends to be *x*, it is really *y*. I am not performing either of these social functions, for both of these are simply the flip sides of the same worldview.

When one steps out of line from the academy's concerns with deconstruction or genderbased discourse, and tries to think about the larger story of the evolution of consciousness, then a different sort of criticism is called for. The essay becomes not simply an analysis of the mythic text but another performance of the archetypal myth itself. A fairy tale or a fragment, like the one we find in Plutarch, can be enormously inspiring. An artist can come along and make another artistic work out of it. Think of Faust, which is not just Goethe's *Faust* but an entire tradition from Marlowe to Goethe to Gounod to Thomas Mann. If Faustian man is the quintessentially modern man, selling his soul to the devil to have a Hollywood face-lift into eternal youth and technological power over nature, then Gilgamesh is the quintessential ancient man, trying to create an ego through slaying the spirit of the forest, rejecting the deadly embrace of the goddess, and seeking through travel in space to find an escape from time and death.

Archetypal figures such as Faust and Gilgamesh endure for centuries because they capture and express the spirit of an age. Spirit of an age, the German *Zeitgeist,* is an expression that we pass around among ourselves without much thought as to what it really means. In much the same way, we pass dollars or pesos back and forth in economic exchange, but rarely do individuals have any esoteric knowledge of what the images of the eye at the top of the pyramid or the eagle on top the cactus with the serpent in its mouth really mean. The idea of the spirit of an age is one that we can neither do without nor begin to understand. The myth of Osiris in particular is a performance of this essential mystery of time. Osiris is about nothing if not about time. Seth takes his measure, constructs a coffin to fit Osiris, throws a great party for his 72 conspirators, and tricks Osiris into trying on the coffin for size. Once Osiris is in the coffin, Seth and his conspirators lock it and cast it into the river. The key to this narrative is the number 72. It is a number one will find popping up in many circumstances, for 72 is the number of the Sumerian *annunaki,* the number of

Cabalistic names of God, and the number of the disciples of Christ. This mystical number is about time. The time it takes, in the precession of the equinox, to make one complete rotation through the signs of the zodiac is 25,920 years. This is known as the Great Year, the "Magnus Annus" referred to in Yeats's famous poem about the Second Coming. The 360 days of the idealized year, without the five festival days of the sacred intercalary adjustment, is the perfect circle. 25,920 divided by 360 equals 72, so 72 is the basic unit of the Great Year, a moment of cosmic time, the length of a normal human life. Seth is this frightful archangel of evolution who is tricking the free-ranging spirit into a physical body, into a specific modality of time. Once Osiris's spirit is captured in the coffin of the body—and I would ask you to remember that in the Orphic tradition in Greece that follows this Egyptian tradition, the word for the body is "tomb"—he is cast onto the river of time where the currents of the river carry him to a tree into which he becomes embedded. William Blake expressed this esoteric knowledge in his poem "The Human Abstract."

> The Gods of the earth and sea
> sought thr' Nature to find this Tree
> But their search was all in vain:
> There grows one in the Human Brain.[3]

The natural drift of evolution carries the spirit into the tree, the central nervous system with its spinal cord, brain stem, and cortex. It is there that the male spirit becomes embedded and lost in time. Its female twin, the part of the human soul that has not incarnated in time, must find it and seek to resurrect it so that the divine child, Horus, may be born. And this divine child carries the real meaning of human evolution in time, the goal that awaits us at the end of a dozen Great Years.

The myth is all about time, and if 72 is the basic number of the ordinary typical life, 2160 is the basic number for the archetypal life, the life of the avatar of an age, the spirit of an epoch. In popular hippie mythology, this is now an idea that everybody knows in the words of the song from the musical *Hair*, "This is the dawning of the Age of Aquarius." We are now coming out of the age of Pisces, the age of the avatar of Jesus. So, in the words of W. B. Yeats's most famous poem, "The Second Coming," "Surely some revelation is at hand;/Surely the Second Coming is at hand."[4] So we look to a new cosmic figure that will embody the new story of the new aeon. Inanna and Dumuzi are the archetypal Near Eastern couple for the period beginning around 4000 B.C.E., and Isis and Osiris are the archetypal Near Eastern couple for the aeon of transition from matriarchal to patriarchal culture, for the period of 2000 B.C.E. And Jesus and Mary are the archetypal Near Eastern couple for the period of 1 to 2000 A.D. It remains to be seen whether Sri Aurobindo and Mother Mira Richard are the archetypal couple for the Aquarian age.

Now it used to be thought by scholars that the religious tradition of the Great Year, the astronomical precession of the equinox, was only known in classical times and celebrated in the Roman Mithraic mysteries.[5] Recently, however, scholars, such as Martin Bernal in his book *Black Athena*,[6] have begun to suggest that this astronomical knowledge may be much more ancient. The issue is highly controversial, and scholars have no way of proving the case one way or another, but I would suggest that the image of father Abraham finding the ram caught in the bushy tree is a symbol of the transition from Taurus to Aries, or the Great Month of 4000 to 2000 B.C.E., and that the imagery of the twinned female body and the bull on the wall paintings of Catal Huyuk express the transition from Gemini to Taurus, or 6000 to 4000 B.C.E. Basically, I believe, but have no way of proving, that this mythological iconography of the zodiac goes all the way back to Paleolithic, Ice Age culture.

When the 72 conspirators of Seth lock Osiris in the coffin, the number is a signal that this is an esoteric narrative; this would be recognized immediately by all esoteric initiates. The myth is not primitive gibberish but a cosmological narrative that is describing the evolution of the solar system and all those gods, Seth, Isis, and Osiris, are actually the planets emerging in the evolution of the solar system. When Isis and Osiris are described as making love inside the womb, one should understand this image as presenting the gods as both planets, Earth and moon, and, as well, distinct beings who will take on a personal life on Earth. Osiris is a moon god that is cut up into the fourteen pieces of the waxing and waning moon by Seth. Isis is, of course, Mother Earth, and the love affair of Isis and Osiris is their primordial embeddedness before the Earth and moon evolve into distinct planetary entities. Many of the stories of the relationship of the gods and their love affairs, their conjunctions, often have to do with the juxtaposition of the position of the planets in the sky. In *Imaginary Landscape* I made an analysis of the fairy tale *Rapunzel* to show that the story is about the conjunctions of Mars and Venus and that the flower that is put forth by the plant, Rapunzel, has the same shape that the planet Venus makes in its motion in the sky.[7]

One can see that these archetypal stories, whether myth or fairy tale, are never simply narratives with one level of meaning. There is a good story for the masses, and there is an esoteric cosmology for the initiates.[8] For the Egyptian temple initiates, our story of Isis and Osiris is about the nature of time and evolution on four levels simultaneously. The first level is the *cosmological,* and it is the story of the evolution of the solar system and the planets. The second level is the *sociological* and it is about the evolution of society from matriarchy to patriarchy. The third level is the *psychological* and it is about the evolution of consciousness through the various vehicles of the subtle bodies, the *ka* and *ba.* The fourth level is the *spiritual* and it expresses the evolution of the human spirit through time and the limitations of the aeon in which Osiris cannot progress beyond the position of serving as lord of the dead. It will take another solar month of 2160 years and another avatar for a new aeon before humanity can take up the matter of life and death once again and carry the spirit of humanity another step forward in its cosmic journey.

So Seth is not simply an evil and reactionary figure; he is a cosmological principle of manifestation working in collaboration with a subtler divine purpose. Seth is the principle of limitation, and he is at the heart of the very mystery of form, of incarnation. He binds the infinite and divine spirit into finite time; he breaks up the higher spirit into distinct subtle bodies of incarnation. Seth dismembers the spiritual body of Osiris into the fourteen phases of the moon from waxing to waning. Once there was a vast and indefinite dust cloud, but as the solar system evolved, it broke up into distinct, corpuscular fragments, and the Earth and the moon took on form. But in the brilliance of mythic stories, the narrative is multiple, so one level is symbolic of another, and the shift from the old order to the new is both cosmological and sociological. Seth is also a symbolic expression of the ancient prehistoric society; he is associated with flint tools and the boar, which is probably another astrological symbol and one that involves human sacrifice. There is obviously some profound astronomical symbolism in the boar that we have lost, for the boar kills Attis and Adonis, and one will find images of the boar carved in stone on Malta.

Seth, as the mother's brother, is the protector of mother-right. The Great Mother as the basin of all attractions demands that the king must die, that there must be human sacrifice to return the body literally to the Great Mother. Osiris as a culture hero celebrates a new level of society, not the hunt with its Paleolithic flint tools, but agriculture. He is a cultural hero bringing a change in the human order, a change in society, but also a change in values because he eliminates human sacrifice. This, of course, brings him into immediate conflict with the old order that Seth protects. If one eliminates human sacrifice (*sacri-fecere*, which literally means to make sacred), then one is claiming that the individual is more valuable than the collective. One is giving a new value to the individual and his story. This conflict between Seth and Osiris is like today's conflict between the United States and China over human rights. We emphasize the right of the individual and are willing to accept an intolerably high level of noise, crime, and disorder as the price of individuation. China insists on the stability of the collective order and is willing to accept cruelty in the punishment of criminals and a loss of individual freedom as the price of collective order and stability. The conflict between these two gigantic countries is now becoming archetypal, and we will have to be careful so that it does not express itself in the form of a war to see who is going to be the world power for the Pacific Rim culture of the twenty-first century. In the case of Seth and Osiris, the conflict leads to a final resolution in which Seth becomes the prow on the ship of the sun god Ra, which is a symbolic expression that the point of limitation is the point of the entire evolution of the solar system.

Seth can never be defeated, but times do change, and Horus, the son, is enthroned. The old order must give way to the new, so there is a story to time. Individuation is achieved. History, that narrative of names, of dynasties and dynastic succession, has come forward with its acceleration of time. The old steady-state order of the nameless phallus being sacrificed and returned to the Great Mother went on unchanged for tens of thousands of years, but now with the introduction of historic, literate civilizations, time will begins to play itself out in centuries for the ancients and decades for the moderns.

So when the male-bonding pair of Gilgamesh and Enkidu defy the goddess Ishtar and seek to slay the spirit of the forest to make a name for themselves, they are declaring a war on death that is at the heart of the paradox of individuation. Osiris, who is at the threshold of the transition from prehistoric culture to historic civilization, is clearly a more ancient and transitional figure than Gilgamesh, for he is not the distinct and highly individuated personality that Gilgamesh is. Osiris is simply the man who dies, the male who loses his phallus. Isis is much more real — even in this tiny fragment from Plutarch. She laments, she travels, she explodes in rage, she yearns and sorrows. Osiris just dies; he is a function and not a person, a phallus and not an individual man. Although we have moved forward in the story from the Great Mother of the Ice Age to this sister-lover Isis with her brother-lover Osiris, we have not yet reached the point of the takeoff of individuation and personality. Osiris cannot create a dynastic son without the more dynamic help of Isis, and Osiris cannot become more than the lord of the dead. His realm is the bardo, the astral plane. Physical matter remains beyond his reach, and that confrontation with matter and death, with the crossing of spirit and matter, will take the work of another aeon and another avatar.

Because Isis is so much more powerful than Osiris, even though she is the young sister, we can still recognize in her activity an epiphany of the Great Goddess. Osiris founds civilization and eliminates human sacrifice but himself becomes the sacrifice; so although he is, perhaps, more than the dying male of Çatal Hüyük, he is still very close to a Neolithic phallic figure. Osiris is an epiphany of the male performing the mysteries of definite incarnation, the temporal body with its mystery of the phallus, but the story is precisely about whatever happened to the phallus of Osiris. It is swallowed by a fish, swallowed by the great waters of the deep. Like the archaic iconography of Seth as the boar, this association of fish and phallus is also incredibly ancient, for Alexander Marshack has traced this association of moon, phallus, and fish all the way back to engraved bones from the Magdallenian culture of 13,000-14,000 B.C.E.

What all this iconography means is almost impossible for us to decipher, but we can at least suspect that it probably has something to do with configurations of stars and planets in the sky. For whatever reason, Osiris in his aeon cannot become an independant male; he cannot keep his phallus. In rituals of sacrifice, even up to historical times in Anatolia and Lydia, the genitals of the priest would be offered up on the altar of the Great Goddess. The third century theologian Origen castrated himself to achieve a state of purity, and even in the twentieth century, among the Aborigines of Australia, the purpose of initiatic subincision was to cut open the bottom of the penis to make it look like the labia majora of the female. So this cult of sacrifice in which the male is made to look like the female is another version of the sacrifice that requires the return of the phallus to the Great Mother. The phallus has to be returned. It is on loan. It is not one's own; it belongs to nature, to the nature of reproduction and generation. It is really the property of the Great Goddess, Mother Nature. So one has to give *back*. In the *dawn time*, it is literally the back, the back side of the Goddess of Lespugue.

When the male gives back the phallus, then the customary order is restored. So the story of how Osiris loses his phallus is what the myth concentrates on. Even without life, Osiris is able, with the help of Isis hovering above his body, to inseminate and impregnate her to give her a son, Horus. Out of rage for this outrageous act of generation at the threshold of death, Seth returns to the story and cuts up the corpse of Osiris into fourteen pieces — which symbolizes the dismemberment of the moon into its phases — and scatters the pieces of his body all over the world. The grieving Isis has to go to all these places to gather them together. The archetype of the Great Goddess who grieves over the male and yet at the same time is responsible for his death and dismemberment is at the heart of our story, the story of time. What Seth is doing is at the command and behest of the Great Goddess and the matrilineal order.

Now with the myth of Osiris, we are, in the Magnus Annus of the 25,920-year cycle, in the aeon of roughly 4000 to 2000 B.C.E. There is a severe limitation to this aeon, and to time in general or what Anaximander will later call "Necessity and the arrangement of time." Osiris cannot recover the phallus and become physically reconstituted to conquer death and rule in the physical plane. He has lost his phallus to the fish, which probably means that it can only be in the aeon of Pisces that the avatar will be able to conquer matter and return from the dead. Osiris can only become lord of the dead world. He becomes the lord of the astral plane, the bardo.

Osiris, the green god, becomes the lord of growing things. He is the crescent moon. (In Latin *crescere* means to grow.) In the astral realm, there is a generative power behind things. In twentieth-century biodynamic gardening, Rudolf Steiner insists that one should not go out to plant until the crescent moon is in its waxing phase. If there is a waning moon rather than a waxing moon, Steiner maintains that the plants will lose their energy; therefore it is an unpropitious time to plant. This ancient cosmology in which there is a subtle relationship between the forces of the moon and the forces of plants was reintroduced in the anthroposophical movement in agriculture and in homeopathic medicine by Rudolf Steiner. As lord of the moon, Osiris is the lord of growing things, he is a culture hero of agriculture, but as the lord of the dead he cannot return to the physical world. He cannot recover his phallus. The story requires that a new condition be embodied in the deferred phallus called the son. So the resolution to the dilemma of what it means to be a dying male is to create a son, and then try to control time and deny the power of the ancient goddess by generating the rights of the son, the rights of property and dynastic inheritance.

In the old matrilineal order, no one had names, everyone was buried impersonally. The bones were placed, higgledy-piggledy, in the megalithic tumulus, the great vault that is the womb/tomb of the Great Mother. When we come to the heroic age, the Bronze Age of militarism and patriarchy, then we encounter the graves of heroes with names. And then we come upon the passing on from one generation to another, from one male to another, from father to son. This system of property and inheritance is a real threat to the matrilineal order. "Property is theft," as Marx said. Property is the thief of eternity. The second law of thermodynamics says that the world is moving remorselessly toward entropy, and here one should see entropy as another epiphany of the Great Goddess, the basin of attraction, the black hole composting the light of stars. The whole world is running down, everything is going to go to heat-death, and all the stars will have to distribute their light and power equitably throughout all space. Space itself is another form of a matrix, the receptacle of Plato's *Timaeus*, and is the Great Goddess, longing to end form and return to her primordial rest. So the dynamical career of individual agents of form, of individuals, is a threat to the slow, vast, conservative order, the longer wave of time. To name individualized things, to have property, is to try to steal time from eternity in the form of monumentality. But in the grave of the hero, one doesn't simply toss in the anonymous bones; one names the king and kills all his servants and wives as they take their place in the tomb of the great man. This shared death is, for example, what we find in the burials of the third dynasty of Ur. Perhaps this archetypal pattern is behind the pattern of criminal or psychotic behavior today in which a depressed male seeks to kill himself along with his wife and children or coworkers. The failed ego seeks its final monument. In the historical civilizations, the males try to create big things, to inscribe names on monuments, to write that in such and such a battle King Big High Mucky-Muck conquered and took control of life from the goddess by having the power to kill so many. For the ontologically lost male, peace is boring; it is the long wave of time, the enduring pattern of the goddess; but war is sharp, an intensification of the feeling of time as the thrilling instant, as *now*. It will take forty years for a teenager to become wise, but put a fast car or a Kalashnikov machine gun in his hands and there's no stopping him. If a sixteen-year-old in the south Bronx can have a Porsche and an Uzi *now* by dealing drugs, no one is going to be able to talk him in to going to school, studying hard, and waiting to become a suit with a life in the burbs. We will never get beyond all this contemporary violence unless we begin to understand where it is coming from, and just how deeply rooted in human culture it really is.

Osiris expresses one attempt of the male to eliminate violence, to eliminate human sacrifice, to transform the mysteries of time, but he could not resolve the problem; the best that he could do in 2000 B.C.E. was to become lord of the astral plane. But Isis and Osiris, the avatars of one aeon, are an overture to the next aeon, and Mary and Jesus will pick up the problem where Isis and Osiris left it.

The story of Mary and Jesus is deeply embedded in the culture of the Near East with its mythology of the dying male, and also with its ancient esoteric mysteries of time. Mary is another epiphany of the goddess figures in the images of the great goddess of the crescent moon, from the Goddess of Laussel to the Virgin of Guadeloupe. In the passage from one aeon to the next, Isis becomes Mary, and Osiris becomes Jesus. The ambiguity of Isis as mother goddess and sister-lover is also reflected in Christian myth in the fact that there are two Marys. There is Mother Mary, and there is Mary Magdalene, the shadowy initiatic consort to Jesus. Mary Magdalene, the temple-prostitute turned disciple, is such a wonderful archetypal figure that she has served throughout the ages as a screen for numerous artistic projections such as those of Nikos Kazantsakas and D. H. Lawrence. Recently there has been a blossoming of new books like Clysta Kinstler's *The Moon Under Her Feet*,[9] in which Mary Magdalene figures as importantly as Jesus. In paintings such as Grünewald's *Crucifixion*, the two Marys at the cross are brought together. But unlike Osiris, Jesus on the cross, about to peform his harrowing of hell, is not going to be content to be lord of the realm of the dead. He intends to be the lord triumphant, Christ the King, lord of the material world. Christ is out to take hold of matter and return from the dead in a physical body. The echo of Isis gathering up the pieces of the body of Osiris is heard in the gospels when it is Mary Magdalene who is the first to see the resurrected body of the Christ in the cemetery. The mystery of Jesus and Mary is a retelling of the story of Isis and Osiris; it is the attempt, from one avatar to another, to deal with the initiatic mysteries of time. The story is important because *story* in its very nature is a performance of time, and history is critical, because there is an evolution of consciousness with each crisis. We have made spiritual progress in the movement from Osiris to Jesus.

The story of Isis and Osiris looks forward to the story of Jesus and Mary, or one can say that Jesus, as an initiate, is consciously working out these individual esoteric themes of life and death. Notice in the New Testament that Jesus is always taking great pains to repeat a mythic pattern. He goes into Jerusalem on an ass because it is required by the story. He is always at work to fulfill the prophecies. He is out to fulfill the prophetic mission of Israel as it was established by Melchizedek in giving the grail to father Abraham.

Osiris is the avatar of an aeon; he is the initiate of the esoteric mysteries of time. He plays his part in the cosmic drama, and in so doing performs the sacrifice, the act of making time sacred, of making time or the aeon serve the larger purpose of the Great Year of 25,920 years. Gilgamesh is not an avatar, he is a hero.[10] He sums up the qualities of his age, with no knowledge whatsoever of the larger cycle or the meaning of human existence. He defies time, rejects the goddess, seeks to make a name for himself, and vigorously objects to death. The hero is the ego writ large. If Osiris is a mythological figure that enables us to glimpse the transition from matriarchy to patriarchy, Gilgamesh expresses the time when patriarchy has consolidated its power and is deeply entrenched.

There is an earlier fragment of the Sumerian story of Gilgamesh, Enkidu, and Inanna[11]—one that I discussed at length in *The Time Falling Bodies Take to Light*—that takes us back to the landscape of the riverine marshes before the rise of the Sumerian cities. Inanna is walking and sees the *hulupu* tree and is attracted to it and decides that she wants to make a bed out of it. To transform wild nature into divine culture, to make a bed that will fit her form, certain things have to be done. The tree is not yet in a position to be used by Inanna because the serpent that knows no charm is rooted in the base of the tree, in the roots; Lilith is in the trunk, and Imdugud, the thunderbird, has made its nest for its young at the top. (In this iconography of bird-tree-snake one should recognize an emblem of the spinal cord, limbic ring, and cerebral cortex of the human brain.) What is really being talked about in this story of making a bed for the goddess is how to prepare a vehicle of incarnation for the human spirit. This task requires a cooperation between male and female. Some heroic figure needs to appear and cut the tree. And the hero who can do this is the great Gilgamesh. Imagine this prehistoric landscape as the planet before human incarnation, not just the world of the marshes before the establishment of cities. From the esoteric point of view, it is not really appropriate to look at one's body as the singular form of one's incarnation; we all take our incarnation in the natural history of the planet, so the planet is actually part of our subtle body. It makes no sense to talk about life or the evolution of consciousness unless one is talking about planetary dynamics and the unfolding of the entire story of our Earth: the lithosphere, the atmosphere, the biosphere. In many esoteric traditions—Steiner goes into this quite extensively in his *Occult Science*—consciousness, the human spirit, is said to predate the evolution of the solar system. The reason we get this kind of split between body and mind is because we didn't evolve simply on this planet. The paranoid inkling of this gets expressed in literalist narratives that state that we came from outer space in rockets or flying saucers. The scientific narrative for this intuition is the theory of panspermism of Francis Crick in which the meteorites brought in the organic molecules from outer space and seeded the prebiotic soup of the ocean, and out of that life evolved. So one takes one's choice in how one can interpret this myth of the extraterrestrial origins of life and humanity. In the case of either the scientific or the paranoid narrative, if one looks at the deep structure, the story is saying that life does not evolve simply by itself on our isolated planet, that something has to come in and impregnate the matrix, Mother Earth.

In Theosophy, the faithful claim that the impulse for human incarnation came from the lords of Venus, and so Inanna as the goddess Venus looking at the earth and wanting to make a place for herself, is the story of the lords of Venus looking at the earth and waiting for it to evolve to the point where it can receive the divine body. When Gilgamesh comes on the scene, then something dramatic happens to the *hulupu* tree. The serpent is killed, and the force is released from its rootedness and spread throughout the area; Lilith takes off to haunt ruins and make love to demons. In other words, Lilith is expelled to the astral plane. She is reduced to a life of haunting ruins and making love to demons. The thunderbird, expelled from the tree, flies off to live in the mountains. Lilith is confined to the astral realm, but the Thunderbird is confined to the etheric, the realm of lightning and elemental power. What the story is saying is that there are forms of consciousness on the Earth that antedate human beings. The elementals of Earth and the demons of the moon are very deceptive creatures and are angry at human beings for displacing them. They wish to reinhabit the physical plane, the domain that has been established for the human physical body. Our hero the Sumerian Gilgamesh has his ax of the road, his tool for clearing the path of evolution, and this tool of the physical plane has the power to separate and keep things in their place: Lilith to the astral plane, and the thunderbird to the etheric. The thunderbird, the power of lightening and thunder, the elemental power of the Earth, removes itself to the mountains. Notice that our hero Gilgamesh is not a shaman trying to commune with Lilith or Imdugud the thunderbird; he is trying to push them out of the tree so that it can be made fit for the descent of the body of the goddess. In other words, humans want the physical plane for themselves; everyone else, except the animals, are expelled into the etheric and astral planes. We will encounter this story again when we come to look at the *Ramayana*.

Once the Earth has been prepared for human consciousness, then the bed of Inanna is made. But out of the wood of the tree, the *miku* and *puku* are made, the stick and hockey puck of a new cosmological game. Out of the wood of the tree, the goddess Inanna creates the ring and the rod, the stick and the ball, the male and the female. In other words, out of nature, the game of culture is created. But in playing the game created by the goddess, men forget that it is about the balancing of male and female forces, for in this sodality of the game only men are allowed to play. And so this little girl appears and is upset that she is not part of the game. She pronounces the sacred name of the sun god and causes the puck to fall into the underworld. Gilgamesh's great friend Enkidu offers to descend into hell to get it back. The instructions given to Enkidu to prepare him for his descent into hell sound like a Buddhist text for initiation or going into bardo: be non-attached, do not identify with the wraiths, lest one be captured in hell.

> Kiss not the wife you love,
> Strike not the child you hate,
> Lest the cry of the nether world hold you fast—[12]

This journey into the underworld becomes a pattern for the millennia, of Innana, Enkidu, Odysseus, Er, Aeneas, Christ, Mohammed, and Dante's journey from hell to heaven. When one lines them all up, one notices an evolutionary progression that describes an increasing densification of the ego in which the spiritual world no longer functions within the culture as a parallel world of gods and demons but becomes instead a psychological state of possession. One can see this rather clearly in the *Aeneid*, but that is another story for another time. This story of Enkidu's descent, however, is about the heroic encounter with death in which the underworld is a clear and distinct parallel world. It is about the attempt of the heroic male to reject the female, to assert himself in space and kill the cycles of nature in slaying the spirit of the forest. Here we encounter the historical roots of our ecological crisis, the very beginning of the conquest of space and the industrialization of the biosphere. Here is the fundamental pattern that Mother Nature is ecology, is this eternal recycling in the Eternal Round. The male principle of the hero is the untraditional and historically radical assertion of a private agenda. The big man wants to make a name for himself, but a name is a label for the part that dies. So the best that one can hope for is that the name will survive us in fame. The name is a kind of spiritual son in place of a physical son, for this male-bonding couple does not have sons. The male-bonding couple tries to separate itself from Mother Nature to create a new all-male artificial culture in art. Here we can see the historical foundations of the gay culture of today. The genius of gay culture is deeply wedded to art, to the attempt to replace nature with artifice—whether one is talking about fashion or literature, about Giorgio Armani, Jean Genet, or Marcel Proust. This sort of cultural project in which one does not reproduce oneself in a son but seeks to create a name for oneself in a great work of art is present here at the dawn of history, in this mystery-drama of male love and male bonding. But when Gilgamesh and Enkidu try to develop their male bond, they are inevitably brought into conflict with the goddess of love and war, of birth and death. These heroes are trying to create an artificial culture beyond her natural world of birth and death, and so the goddess is outraged. She sends down the bull of heaven to destroy the heroes, but the cowboys make short work of it, kill it, and, in mocking her rituals of male sacrifice, fling the bull's genitals in her face. The female priestesses of the goddess react instinctively and go into their traditional ritual to sing the song of the dead male over the severed phallus of the bull; however, our heroes are saying, in effect, that you can have this displaced phallus of the bull, but you can't have us. The heroes have their own agenda. They are going to go out and make a name for themselves, kill the forest, and upset the whole world of nature. And so the goddess says, "You think you can escape nature to create your own private culture, then take this." She sends a degenerative disease, and Enkidu dies, not like a hero in battle, but rotting in pieces on his bed. Sound familiar? Gilgamesh has to watch his best friend die in pieces, confronting death and mortality in all its unheroic ugliness of disease. So AIDS, in one form or another, is also back here with the story of the first male-bonding pair at the dawn of civilized history. The male attempt to escape the feminine is an attempt of culture to escape nature, and as such it is doomed to live out the tragedy of dissolution.

That was one world of 2000, and here we are at another world of 2000. In our beginning is our end. We at the end of civilization are still playing out the themes that are laid down at the beginnings of civilization in the Gilgamesh epic. The Gilgamesh epic is the fundamental text of Western civilization. Gilgamesh is the hero, he is not, like Osiris, the initiate of the aeon; he is not the yogi, the wise old man of the mountains, Utnapishtim. He cannot master the challenge of Ishtar, or the challenge of Utnapishtim, the challenge of conquering death, or the challenge of conquering sleep. The extroverted hero, being neither initiate nor yogi, only knows the world of action, of travel in physical space, of making names and fighting wars, of building walls around cities with empires that won't last all that long. Being neither shaman nor yogi, the hero returns to his city. He goes back, sadder and wiser, and the poem ends the way it began, in a beautiful *aria ∂a capo* that celebrates the walls of the city, the tragedy of form, the impermanent nature of the container, body or body politic, of human life.

THE PATRIARCHAL CONSTRUCTION OF CULTURE AND THE REIMAGINATION OF THE FEMALE BODY: A COMPARISON OF THE *ENUMA ELISH* AND THE *RIG VEDA*

In Paleolithic and Neolithic iconography the emphasis is on the vulva as the source of emergence, as the magical wound that heals itself. In a celebration of cyclicity and eternal return, the menstrual blood is an epiphany of the numinous. So in Paleolithic burials, red ochre is smeared on the dead to suggest their revival in the spiritual world, and the statue of the Goddess of Laussel is covered with red ochre. Only in the new patriarchal cultures does menstrual blood become a symbol of shame and a reason to exclude women from the mysteries. Before, it was *the* central mystery. But if one is going to appropriate women's mysteries and take them over, then one has to appropriate their symbols and language and reconstruct them in a whole new way that legitimizes men and delegitimizes women. This cultural transition is supported by the shift from gardening to stock breeding and is expressed in the shift from the vulva to the phallus as the primordial icon. When we come to the time of the *Rig Veda*, the language and culture is intensely masculine. The translator Wendy Donniger O'Flaherty describes the text in the following way: "The *Rig Veda* is a book by men about male concerns in a world dominated by men. One of these concerns is women, who appear throughout the hymns as objects, though seldom as subjects."[1]

In this new masculine culture, we encounter a symbolic shift of emphasis from menstrual blood to semen. Now *the* central mystery becomes semen, semen seen as butter in the churning of cream. Recall that we saw this metaphor in the cycle of poems about Inanna and Dumuzi. Notice how appropriate it is, because milk comes from the cow—the celestial cow—but the cultural act of churning, the phallic dance of intercourse in the churn, turns it into butter, and this expresses a movement from nature to culture. Semen becomes more valuable than milk in its raw, primitive, and female state. So in this shift of emphasis from milk to butter there is expressed an appropriation of the breast by the phallus. Recall the Neolithic statues of the Great Goddess with phallic neck and with breasts shaped like the glans penis, and consider that there the homology worked with the opposite emphasis—the phallus was the property of the Great Goddess—and you will appreciate just how far we have come with these prehistoric cowboys of Central Asia.

Butter is created with a phallic stick inside a churn, a female vessel, and so is the magical *soma*, the psychedelic elixir that is ingested in the sacred rituals celebrated in the *Rig Veda*.[2] *Soma* is created with phallic pestle and thunderbolt stones, so, not surprisingly, *soma* is called the semen of the cosmic horse; the discharge of white electricity in the sky is an ejaculation of the semen of the cosmic horse.

The transformation of cream into butter is an exoteric cultural process, but there is also another stage, one that is more of an alchemical process, and that is the transformation of butter into ghee. This process requires fire, for the butter must be boiled, and as it is boiled, it breaks apart into globules of fat and a clear, golden elixir. When the fat is removed and set to the side, the clear and golden elixir remains. Butter is symbolic of the normal cultural personality, the human being with its mixture of illumined and neurotic traits; but ghee is symbolic of the purified, illumined, and clarified personality, one with all its neurotic traits removed.

Since the production of ghee requires fire, it is not surprising that fire is another important symbolic mystery presented in the *Rig Veda*; it is presented as an epiphany of the god Agni in his fire ritual. Here too the metaphoric imagery is pointing to the ordinary body, the material wood, and the illuminated body moving upward from Earth to heaven in fire. The esoteric dimension of this imagery, one understood by initiates only, is that this fire is contained within the human body in the form of the vital energy and heat of the kundalini. When the semen of the male initiate is heated with this mystical fire, then it is boiled and transformed into the golden elixir of ghee and moves upward through the spinal column from the base of the spine to the head. Here the interior elixir, the *soma* as semen of the cosmic horse, is no longer an exoteric process of ingestion in public rituals, but an interior process for the solitary initiate, the yogi. This process is secret and initiatic because if it becomes public, it becomes distorted into a group neurotic process. One ends up with the mushroom-chewing hippie trying to pretend he is a yogi, but what he really is a psychically inflated personality whose ego has gone through a process of magnification and explosion rather than purification. In the media magnifications of the 1960s—a culture that still hangs on in California—these people became self-proclaimed gurus and psychedelic prophets, but a look into their eyes reveals the gleam of the fanatic, the psychedelic fundamentalist, the Mushroom Mullah on the lecture circuit, with all of the dissonance of a charismatic but nevertheless disturbed and unstable personality.

As we move forward in time from the prehistoric cultures in which we have only iconography to the historical cultures in which we have texts, the whole question of the translation of the metaphoric systems embedded in language becomes critical. There are indeed as many different *Rig Vedas* as there are translations. Since I am not a pandit, I worked with three different translations in an effort to escape the narrowness of a single translator and approximate the complexity of the original text. I used Aurobindo's *Secret of the Veda,* Wendy Donniger O'Flaherty's *Rig Veda,* and Antonio de Nicolas's *Meditations on the Rig Veda.*[3] Each of these translations is very different and uses the text to put forward a very different cosmology. Aurobindo's is yogic and esoteric, de Nicolas's is philosophical and aesthetic, and O'Flaherty's is sociological and anthropological in a straightforwardly exoteric way. Which one is the true *Rig Veda?* Which one is closest to the cultural reality of "the Other," and not simply an expression of the agenda of its editor?

The question is hermeneutically naive, for we are in the same position with texts that Heisenberg said we were with electrons: to observe an electron is to disturb it; any observation or measurement is a description of the historical condition of the observer. What to do? To avoid simplicity and simplemindedness, I would suggest that we avoid any single, linear, fundamentalist hermeneutics, be it Freudian, Marxist, Derridean, or hippie, and, instead, allow an ecology of consciousness to emerge by creating an imaginary hyperspace in which multiple readings are seen together. If we accept at one and the same time the esoteric, yogic reading, the philosophical-aesthetic reading, and the strict, sociological, linguistic reading, then we begin to have an artifact of the evolution of consciousness and not simply the ruts made by an author riding his hobby horse.

O'Flaherty's *Rig Veda* is very close to the literal level of the individual words; it gives us a feeling for the archaic world view — of what is physically going on with the words being used for metaphors, of what is happening in terms of butter and semen, of cows and sacrifice, and of wealth and property. In O'Flaherty's linguistic focus, one can get a feeling for the landscape, with its vast open steppes and infinite sky. This is not a landscape of architecture and enclosures, of palaces and fortresses. It is the prepalace world, the prearchitectural level of consciousness. It is an expression of the arithmetic mentality in its full articulation, with its fascination with lists, enumeration, and generation. Here repetition is not boring, as it is for us, but is rather the performance of a central mystery. Repetition is numinous. Lines are repeated no matter how long they are, again and again and again, because there is this fascination with the list as a mystery of generation and accumulation. In many ways, the genius of the arithmetic mentality stamped Indian culture for all time. One sees this trait expressed in the *Upanishads*, the *Mahabharata*, the *Dhamapadha*. Indians in their religious formation are in love with lists, with four noble truths, five *skandas*, an eightfold path, ten boomies, a twelvefold cycle of dependant origination, twenty derivative unwholesome factors, and a partridge in a pear tree. The list provides a sense of empowerment, and so to memorize a list is to empower oneself against the forces of chaos and darkness. And this still carries on in modern India. I'll never forget how astonished I was in graduate school at Cornell — in Robert Martin Adams's seminar on James Joyce — when an Indian student began to recite a list that he had been taught of the *bad* novelists of the nineteenth century. The notion that education is a gaining control of the incoherent through order in the memorization of the list still carries on in modern India.

When we shift from the linear sentence of Sanskrit to the more ideographic form of Chinese, then we begin to get more of a feeling for the geometrical configuration — consciousness registered in the ideogram, in the hieroglyphic complexity condensed into a spatial form. The geometrical mentality stamps the Chinese for all time, from An Yang to the Forbidden City, and their sense of themselves as being at the center of the world and the alien foreigners at the periphery still influences their foreign policy and politics to this day.

The Babylonian *Enuma Elish* is fascinating precisely because it enables us to see this transition from the arithmetic to the geometric mentality. The *Enuma Elish* appears around 1750 B.C.E. and ends up in its final codification in the library of Ashurbanipal in the seventh century B.C.E. The text starts out with the usual sort of enumeration of the generations of the gods, and it has the typical lists and repetitiveness, but the conclusion of the text celebrates the achievement of form in the construction of the city of Babylon. Marduk builds Babylon out of the dismembered remains of the goddess Tiamat. The form of the city is an expression of the power of geometry to repel chaos, and it reveals the triumph of mind over matter, male over female.

The Babylonians are also credited with inventing algebra,[4] and since algebra is a shift from concrete enumeration to an abstract idealization of numerical functions, it represents a miniaturization of the arithmetic mentality, a shift that comes at this period of the development of the new geometrical mentality. In the ancient arithmetic mentality, the central mystery is how can the One become many? How can the Great Mother generate her children? The answer to this question is expressed in the entwined mysteries of generation and enumeration, and, therefore, sexuality, especially female sexuality, is at the heart, or womb, of this mystery. Thus we see in the early Sumerian mythos of Inanna and Dumuzi an emphasis on sexual intercourse and the accumulation of food in the storehouse. Over time, however, there is a shift away from the stored seed to abstract value. Coins replace cows in trade, and the abstract signs of writing replace the vibrating sound of the human voice. Semitic Akkadian is still a syllabic script, but that other Semitic people, the Phoenicians, take the syllabic reproduction of speech further in inventing the alphabet, which was more efficient for their transcultural trade in the Mediterranean. When coinage and the alphabet interact in this new geometrical mentality that has its cultural ecology in the Mediterranean, one crosses the great divide between the ancient and the classical worlds, the arithmetic and the geometrical mentalities. And so the ancient experience of number and enumeration, this sexual power of generating multiplicity, is replaced by the classical number theory of algebra. Let x = any number. As algebra miniaturizes the arithmetic mentality, it reduces it and surrounds it with the new geometrical form, the abstract idealization of the concrete object. The female body, the primordial chaos, is dismembered and out of its pieces is reconstructed a new universe of male order in which the city of Babylon is built. Out of the blood of the mother's brother, Kingu, the male that served the Great Mother and the prehistoric matristic culture, human beings are created. Notice the double bind: we as human beings are created to serve the gods so that they can withdraw from the manifest universe into the epiphanic universe, but we are made to serve with the blood of a rebel. And so human beings are fundamentally caught in a contradiction. The whole story of the *Enuma Elish* is one of the mother's brother losing power to the father. The mother's body, matter as literally *Mater*, is torn apart to construct the cultural artifact of the city. So we can see that this movement from nature to culture is homeomorphic to the *Rig Veda's* movement from female to male, from milk to semen.

The text of the *Enuma Elish*, as a cultural artifact, expresses the major evolutionary transition from the arithmetic to the geometrical mentality. In the cultural achievement of the geometrical form of the city is the celebration of rationality, kingship, and male power. The story is an evolutionary one of the movement from chaos to order and its recitation in the temple as a new year's ritual performs the historical transition from one mentality to another. What we also see going on in the story of chaos threatening at the gate is the story of the political evolution of society from the assembly of elders to the militaristic monarchy. The invaders surround the city, and the charismatic warlord says to the weak old men of the assembly: "The barbarians are at the gate. You have got to give me absolute power and the tablet of the destinies if I am going to repel them." Clearly, what we are seeing in the story of the old gods who are too weak to deal with the crisis is a Feurbachian projection into heaven of a political evolution on Earth, the evolution of kingship. Where there was once a steward, an *Ensi*, who might have been simply *primus inter pares*, one among many, there now arises the supreme military dictator. When we read between the lines of the text, we can make out two transitions: one from matrilineal succession with its power of the mother's brother, and the other the evolution of *ensi* and assembly to monarchy. Patriarchy has arrived and is digging in with pure military power to stay for a long time to come.

The evolution of kingship expresses the sociological level of the text, and the evolution from matristic to patriarchal culture expresses the anthropological level; but there is also a cosmological level, and this level has to do with the more fundamental relations between chaos and order in the evolution of the solar system. What we see in the text is one of the first articulations of what we would now call the second law of thermodynamics. *Absu* is the primordial abyss; it is the intuitive vision of the solar system as a dust cloud before it began to swirl and congeal into distinct planetary entities, into planetary divinities with names. The cream congeals into butter, distinct curds begin to separate from whey to congeal into cheese, so these ancient activities of producing food are homey metaphors for the transformation of the raw into the cooked, nature into culture, chaos into order. The production of butter and cheese becomes a kind of *participation mystique* in a cosmological process.

The old gods in the *Enuma Elish* are characterized as ones who love rest, who are slow and sluggish and want to resist change and go back to their primordial state. The new gods, however, are disturbing them by throwing noisy parties; they are dynamic and are constantly moving and violating the peace of the ancient ones. Evidently, the rock concert has a long and ancient history. To protect the new gods from the anger of the old gods, Ea places a magic ring around the newly emergent activity. In other words, in order to create a *form* against the forces of disintegration and decay, one has to have a magical membrane. Whether one is talking about the evolution of the planet in the solar dust cloud, or the evolution of the cell in the prebiotic soup, one has to have a magical membrane that resists equilibrium, that keeps the form from scattering its molecules equitably throughout space in the heat-death called entropy. Thermodynamic disequilibrium is a violation of the old order. One can see that the story being told in the *Enuma Elish* is not mythological gibberish; it is an archetypal description of the movement from chaos to order and novel emergent states. The reactionary gods are very much against this process of inverse entropy and wish to pull the universe back to its primordial condition.

Most scholars never pass from the sociological and anthropological levels of a mythic text to the cosmological level because it upsets their whole notion of scientific progress. They see themselves at the top of history and at the top of society, looking down at the ignorant and precivilized worlds of myth and transforming these geological ores into the polished jewelry of scholarship that earns them tenure in their universities. But myth is not raw matter waiting to be transformed into the precious metal of science; it is already a metal, a refined and complex technical language of an initiatic elite.

These ancient Mesopotamian mythic narratives set up the structures of consciousness that we inherited through Greek mythology and philosophy.[5] The pre-Socratic philosophers rationalized mythic images into physical concepts for individually speculative cosmologies. The Great Mother of prehistory became the *apeireon*, the unlimited, of Anaximander. For example, think back on your high school reading of Homer's *Iliad* and recall book twelve in which Homer says that as long as Achilles and the gods are angry, the wall stands; just so long does the battle rage. Book twelve opens with a long celebration of the wall on the shore that protects the Greeks from the Trojans. Homer goes on to say that later, in the fullness of time, the gods will wear down the wall and tumble all the swords and daggers and helmets into the mud where they will become archaeological artifacts for Homer's time—a good four centuries later than the Trojan war itself. Poseidon and the gods, as expressions of the forces of entropy and erosion, will wear away the wall and wash it down with the waves of the sea. But as long as Achilles is angry, the battle rages. As long as *form*—that membrane between order and chaos, time and eternity, men and gods—endures, then history carries on. The battle will continue. Part of the tragedy for Patrochlos, the friend of Achilles who is going out to his doom, is that he does not understand the temporal phenomenology of form, the nature of the limit. He is warned by Achilles not to go out beyond the wall, the ditch on the beach that defines the space of encounter between warring parties, but he is distracted by donning the armor of Achilles. He literally mis-takes himself, and this confusion in identity leads immediately to his dissolution in death. If one goes beyond the wall, one exceeds one's limit and encounters dissolution. Like the magical circle that Ea sets around the younger gods to protect them, the wall is set on to the beach to protect the new and invading force of the Greeks from the ancient power of Asiatic Troy. So when Patrocholus dons the armor of Achilles, he becomes entranced and thinks: "Now don't I look grand—just like Achilles." And in his distraction is his doom. He loses a sense of his true self and his true identity and goes beyond the limit to his own death.

Myth precedes math. The concept of the limit, which much later gets rearticulated for us by Newton into calculus, is basic to the mythological mentality we see expressed in the *Iliad* and the *Enuma Elish*. What we have in the *Iliad* is another version of the cosmological relationship between order and chaos that is expressed in the *Enuma Elish*. The distance between the two texts and the two cultures is not as great as one might think, for we need to remember that many of the architects and stonemasons who worked on the Persian temples of Persepolis were international craftsmen and went back and forth between Athens and Persia. The Persian War was, as all wars are, whether in the case of the Crusades or World War II—a two-way street, a form of cultural exchange. Whether we are talking about Aryan and Dravidian India with the text of the *Rig Veda,* or Akkadian Babylon and ancient Sumeria with the text of the *Enuma Elish,* or ancient Anatolian Troy and Homeric Greek Ionia with the text of the *Iliad,* or Andalusian Spain and

Provence in the new Arabic-influenced poetry of the Troubadours—poetry that leads to the *dolce stil nuovo* of Dante and on into what becomes the Renaissance—we are talking about a process in which passionate conflict generates an exchange of cultural characteristics. We saw it ourselves in World War II. We gave the Japanese Detroit and we took their Zen monasteries into California.

The kind of cultural exchange that we are considering in Vedic India and Akkadian Babylon is one in which the conscious agenda is of control through military invasion, but the hidden agenda is one of cultural possession through the unconscious. One invades a country to control it, but then, most often through the conquered women who sing the old lullabies during nursing and tell the old myths and legends to the children of the conquerors, the oppressed begin to take possession of the oppressors souls. The ancient horsemen of the steppes invade agrarian, matristic society to take control of its religion and appropriate its symbols, but then the power of the conquered culture reconstitutes itself through music and art and one encounters the shift from woman celebrating her power as reproduction to woman celebrating her power as seduction. The literary figure is no longer the Great Mother as the passage into life and death, but woman as the sexy destroyer of men, the femme fatale: Ishtar and Delilah.

The transitional figure from the Great Mother of Anatolian Çatal Hüyük to Akkadian Ishtar, the goddess of love and war, is the Sumerian Inanna. Inanna is no longer the Great Goddess of cosmic creativity and procreativity but is the young maiden of erotic poetry celebrating her vulva and awaiting Dumuzi's entrance to her marriage bed. But still the relationship with Inanna is dangerous for Dumuzi, and he becomes the dying god. Inanna is the one who endures beyond the descent into hell. So even in her sexy garb as the young maiden of the lover's bed, Inanna is an epiphany of the Great Goddess with her eternal power. Death is not for her. She will resurrect and rise out of hell; it is the male who must die. This archetypal pattern is underlying many different stories. Biology, the power of life and death, is under the governance of the goddess, and when Dr. Frankenstein tries to conquer death with the new science of electricity, he only creates another tragedy, and it is the female, in her epiphany as the artist Mary Shelley, who observes his rise and fall from the side of time. Whether as prehistoric horseman or posthistoric scientist, man rides in proudly to conquer and becomes taken over by all he is not thinking of and does not understand. Science is the conscious content, but myth is the unconscious structure. We may try to translate these myths into scientific laws in order

to move from ideas about chaos and form to the second law of thermodynamics and think we are being very scientific, but our scientific laws and
ideas are really workings out of deep archetypal structures that have their
roots in myth.

In this move that I am making to reverse the rationalization of myth
that the Greeks effected, I am just about the mirror opposite of Anaximander. If one takes Anaximander's description of the unlimited (the *apeiron*)
and the arising of the limited thing that must pay back to the unlimited
according to necessity and the arrangement of time for the crime, the act of
theft of its existence, to return to the unlimited, all one has to do is translate
the two words of the unlimited and the limited back into the Great Mother
and her son-lover to recover the primordial universal religion that extended
from Iberia to Siberia in the prehistoric Glacial cultural ecology.

Strangely, in his book on the origins of geometry, the French philosopher Michel Serres goes into great detail about Anaximander and the
apeiron, but he never sees that the unlimited is really the Great Goddess, the
basin of all attractions. In *Les origines de la geometrie,*[6] there is no recognition
of this prehistoric cosmology that is influences how rational philosophy
emerges and develops. What the Greek physiologists in Iona do is to take
the ancient mythic constructs of Anatolia and secularize them, change the
poetic and imagistic language into single concepts. In this development, the
phallic quality of *physis* —the arising—is transformed into physics. The
Great Mother becomes the unlimited or matter. The prehistoric cosmology
of the dynamical, time-bound male and the enduring, eternal female is
refined into a "pure" and sexless abstraction. In this shift toward rationality,
there is a movement away from plurisignative language and ambiguity
toward a linear, conceptual code for specialists. Small wonder that geometry
and mathematics begin to take over and that Plato wishes to banish all the
poets from his perfect state. Now this use of language is just about the
opposite of what we have in the case of the *Rig Veda.* In the polysemic world
of Sanskrit roots, and in the tonal systems in which these ancient chants are
embedded, we have the arithmetic world with its fascination with generative
number and sexuality and not the sexless world of pure abstractions that
hover aloft in the empyrean.

One way to recover a sense of poetic complexity is to consider the
wonderful ancient, transitional texts such as the *Rig Veda.* But in this effort
to jump over Anaximander back into the imagination of prehistory, we do
not land on solid ground but find ourselves over a cliff in wordless free fall.
The problem of translation becomes immense. Sanskrit is almost untrans-

latable into modern Americanized English because each of the Sanskrit roots has multiple meanings. The *Rig Veda* is a prehistoric kind of *Finnegans Wake*. Here is an example of how difficult things can become in translation. This is Aurobindo's translation of the first hymn to Agni, a hymn of the morning sacrifice:

> Strength is awake by kindling of the peoples and he fronts the dawn that comes to him as the Cow that fosters; like mightinesses that rush upward to their expanding his lustres advancing mount toward the heavenly level.
>
> The priest of our oblation has awakened for sacrifice to the gods; with right mentality in him Strength stands up exalted in our mornings; he is entirely kindled, red flushing the mass of him is seen; a great godhead that has been delivered out of the darkness.[7]

And here is de Nicolas's:

> I Sing to Agni, the Priest and God,
> The Chanter, The Source of Wealth.
>
> Sung by ancient Rsis, Agni
> is sung by new ones too; he will bring the gods here.
>
> Agni gives man prosperity and growth
> From day to day, He gives glory and heroes for sons too.[8]

So, you see, they are scarcely the same text. Aurobindo's refined, Edwardian language does not allow us to enter the concrete world of the senses, for he immediately takes us up into a rarified world of polite symbolism for psychological states of ritual and religious awe. We need to remember that Aurobindo, before he became the yogi "Sri Aurobindo," was a revolutionary nationalist. In the racist scholarship of his day, Aurobindo encountered the racial theory of the Aryan invasion of the dark, Dravidian plain. As he began to learn various Indian languages, he found this neat division between dark and white simplistic and unacceptable. There were the great "White gods" of the mountainous North who came down and conquered the "darkies" of the plain, and the *Rig Veda* was supposed to be the story of their invasion. Even Wendy Donniger O'Flaherty says that that story, so beloved of nineteenth-century scholarship, is overly simplistic. It is all much more complicated than that. Twentieth-century Fascists took this nineteenth-century theory of race and developed it into the notion of *Blut und Boden,* blood and soil, as if certain races were rooted to their corner of the Earth. But this is historical and prehistorical nonsense; there are two races present in the burials of Çatal Hüyük, the dolichocephalic and the brachycephalic, and there are now some indications that even Neanderthal and Cro-magnon were mixed in some settlements. Humans have been on the move long before they were even human. The doctrine of *Blut and Boden* leads to what we see going on in Bosnia today. Aurobindo became suspicious of these simplistic notions of race and primitive religion. Since he found examples of all sorts of Aryan elements in Tamil and Tamil elements in Aryan and Bengali, it made no sense to him to divide things in that particular way.

If one goes back to Mohenjo-Daro, to the ancient cultures of the Dravidan plain, one finds seals that picture gods or shamans in yogic postures; therefore, the esoteric system of yoga is not a cosmology brought in by the Aryan invaders of the North.[9] The whole story of the Aryan invasions is a racist rationalization for the caste structure. It is another version of the British myth of the Norman invasion of Ireland, put forth by David Hume, according to which there was no culture in Ireland before the British invaded it. This in face of the fact that when Charlemagne wished to end the Dark Ages and encourage higher education on the Continent, it was to monks from Irish monasteries that he had to turn to find people with a knowledge of classical Greek. The British in India and Ireland were fond of this invasion myth for obvious reasons, and, for equally obvious reasons, Aurobindo, as a revolutionary nationalist, began to distrust it. When he read the translations and then went back to the *Rig Veda* in the original language, he began to see that the work wasn't simply about cows, wealth, and primitive superstitions. For him it was a psychological document, and *soma* was seen as the ambrosial wine of enlightenment and not a psychedelic mushroom or plant. There is no concrete suggestion in Aurobindo's psychological yogic reading that there is any physical basis for this experience of illumination.

Everything for Aurobindo is a psychological metaphor. So we end up with a sociology that is not an expression of the ruling class but an assertion that the chants are a secret code, a metaphoric system that is the technical language of an initiatic school of *rishis.* But Aurobindo's translation is so Tennysonian and puritanical that one cannot get any concrete sense of the archaic mind of the *Rig Veda.* So an attempt to understand the evolution of consciousness is thwarted. If we turn to a more literal text such as Wendy Donniger O'Flaherty's, we get a much better feeling for the concreteness of the language and the physicality of the imagery.

Aurobindo suggests in one of the concluding chapters in his *The Secret of the Veda* that there is a mystery to this yoga that cannot be spoken of and will not likely be recovered. This statement seems to come at a time when Aurobindo was between two experiences of illumination — the early one he had in prison in 1909 and the major experience of enlightenment in 1926. Aurobindo was at work on these translations of the Veda from 1914 to 1920. By 1926, it seems as if all the other yogas come together and he begins to understand the Vedic tradition in a new way.

Aurobindo could have explicated what the technical language really means in terms of the esoteric physiology of tantric transformation, but he shied away from it. I assume that he did so because as a revolutionary he did not want to play into the Victorian British prejudice that Indians were savages unfit to rule themselves. For the Victorian British, lingams and yonis were visible proof that the Indians were still down at the primitive level of a savage religion of mere fertility. If one were to go beyond lingams to begin talking about semen and *soma* as the semen of the cosmic horse, of churning cream into butter and transforming butter into ghee, then it would be really just too much. It would certainly play into the idea that Indians were disgusting savages, for, clearly, English gentlemen would never talk about such things. Such vulgarity would prove that they were not fit to rule themselves and that Christianity was needed to purge out all this primitive magic so that the Indians could be made to fit to serve in the industrial world of British civilization. Aurobindo had a low opinion of Christianity. He was educated by Irish nuns in India, went to boarding school in England, and then on to Cambridge, where he encountered the Church of England in the most boring Edwardian period of its life. When he came back to India and began to learn Indian languages and literatures, he became convinced that Jesus was nothing compared to Krishna. Krishna had this vast cosmic consciousness, but Jesus was simply a good man, a local prophet within a not very enlightened tradition, since the esoteric knowledge of the ancient Indian *rishis* is not exactly to be found in the Old Testament. Aurobindo's feelings for Christianity were weak to begin with, but as he developed his integral yoga, Christianity just drops out of the picture. And his appreciation of Buddhism was a typically Hindu one too. He saw Nirvana as simply an extreme nihilistic variation of the Adwaita Vedanta that dismisses the physical world.

When Aurobindo wrote *The Secret of the Veda* he was, ironically, unwilling to discuss its secrets. He himself was not working within the tantric tradition, and later when he went on to articulate his integral yoga, he would say that it was a mistake to try to awaken the force of kundalini from the bottom of the spinal column because that process of instinctive energization would generate all kinds of states of instability and madness. And I would certainly say amen to that. Aurobindo's yoga works from the top down, from the center above the head and from behind the heart. In the goodness of time, these centers will reorchestrate the lower centers at their own appropriate moment of spiritual development and, therefore, will not precipitate the kind of psychotic instabilities that occur when one tries to work from the instinctive level up to the intuitive. If one tries to crack open the spinal column and seek to force the kundalini upward, then one is in for a very bumpy instinctive ride through the evolution of consciousness.

The Tantric path of illumination is a much more shamanic and wild process of instinctive transformation. In a seal from Mohenjo-Daro, a figure has his heels jammed up against his perineum, has an erection, and has horns growing out of the top of his head. Perhaps we can appreciate the ideas that Freud put forth in his essay "Wit and the Unconscious," that even jokes are palimpsests with many cultures layered over one another. So when we say, "I am feeling horny," there is an archaic cosmology lingering on in our contemporary slang. Aurobindo was totally against sex, and it was absolutely forbidden in his ashram. Since he was separated from his parents as a tiny child, raised by nuns, and sent way from India to boarding school in England at the age of seven, I doubt if anyone ever touched him in life, except to inflict the pain and punishment that is typical in English boarding schools. So it is small wonder that Aurobindo has no use for sexual love or the affectionate touching of the human body.

But the *Rig Veda* is fascinating precisely because it gives us a way of getting into a mind that is older even perhaps than the texts we were considering in the Sumerian love cycle of Inanna and Dumuzi. Try to picture what comes forth in your mind in the *Rig Veda's* imagery of the cosmic cow and the cosmic horse coming forth in the cave of dawn. Dawn is described as the pinkness of the cow, or the horses of the storm god riding through the sky. What springs immediately into my mind is the imagery of Lascaux. Think of the walls of Lascaux: the cow in the vault over the sign of the lattice and the line of the small horses running together. The archaic ritual being presented in the Veda seems itself to be an act of recovery through the power of chant of an archaic mind that is probably ten thousand years old. The ritual chants of the *Rig Veda* celebrate the primordial qualities of what it means to be human. In the hymn to Agni and fire there is a wonderful symbol of the difference between inert matter and fire, a dense body that is not illumined and an illuminated being whose auric radiance transforms his flesh and unites it with the colors of the sky. The difference between wood and fire becomes the difference between the ordinary and the illuminated body, or the corpse and the living being. Fire, of course, is the primordial techno-logical innovation of human culture, from somewhere around 300,000 B.C.E. It is the primary discovery, the Promethean gift that makes us human.

Along with the celebration of Agni, fire, is the celebration through chant of the power of the word, or *vac*. Language is the other mystery that makes us human. When we come to consider the cosmology of language and the power of the chant, we really need to shift from Aurobindo and O'Flaherty's translations to de Nicholas's. In his work at the State Univer-sity of New York at Stony Brook, de Nicholas was working closely with the musicologist Ernest McClain from Brooklyn College. Both de Nicholas's *Meditations on the Rig Veda* and Ernst McLain's *The Myth of Invariance*[10] were part of the scholarship of the 1970s with its focus on what I have called "the planetization of the esoteric." De Nicholas enables us to understand that the *Rig Veda* is basically music more than poetry. Consider his remarks:

> Since multiplication and division by 2 produce the octave matrix, 2 is essentially "female." By itself 2 can generate only "cycles of barren-ness." (2:4:8:16, etc., numbers 2 to the nth power). The original unity, 1, which is subdivided to produce the "octave double" 2, requires divinity to be conceived as "hermaphrodite," and apparently accounts for the Rig Vedic statements of the daughter (2) being produced from the father, 1, without benefit of a mother. God = 1, and his virgin daughter = 2, and they must be coupled in divine incest to produce the prime number 3, "the divine male number," from which brahman tones (or angels), and "citizens of the highest property class" (Socrates' metaphor), are generated. The musical function of 3 probably gives rise to the later notion of a "demiurge" or subordinate god who actually creates the phenomenal world; from this the demiurge = 3 and the virgin daughter = 2, the "human male number 5" emerges as 3 + 2, in a statement widely appreciated in ancient times, but one quite myste-rious once the musical origins of culture have been forgotten. (The prime number 3 appears to have been deified by Ea-Enki in the

Sumerian-Babylonian pantheon and by Thoth = Thrice Greatest Hermes in Egyptian-Greek pantheons.)[11]

So the proportional system of tones — of two going into three, or one going into two, and one generating complexity and one generating just a simple geometric progression — is at the heart of the harmonic structure of the chant. The ritual is a performance of a cosmology. In this threefold cosmology, there is the fire, *agni*, and there is the power of speech, *vac*, and there is the sacrifice in which the two are brought together in the One. These are not poems meant for the eye on a page, but chants meant for the ear within a resonanting space. And these chants would have to be intoned in a particular way so that the musical structure could be heard to be recapitulating the cosmic structure. One has to imagine that the sacrifice is probably some musical resolution to a harmony or dissonance in which unity is being sacrificed to create complexity and multiplicity. Through the complexity and dissonance comes the resolution achieved by the sacrifice. We can imagine, then, that this sacrifice is a musical performance of how the universe was created when God sacrificed himself/herself in order to create time and space. So this Pythagorean system of ratios and proportions, the system that Pythagoras learned when he was a prisoner of war in Mesopotamia, a system that he got from the Chaldeans, is not an invention of Pythagoras but something that goes back into the darkness of prehistory, back to the *rishis* of the Veda, and perhaps even all the way back to Lascaux. Imagine oneself in that cave: one hears, resonating in that vault, a chant, and as its dissonances resolve, suddenly there is the light of torches, and one sees on the walls the cow of dawn and the galloping horses of the god of thunder.

There is fire, there is the word, there is the sacrifice, but where is the fourth? As it says in the opening of the *Timaeus*: "One, two, three, but where, my dear Timaeus is the fourth?"[12] The fourth is *soma*. Wood vibrates in combustion into fire, into Agni. And the word, *vac*, vibrates in space, in the vault of the dawn. When the word, the mantram, vibrates inside one's spinal column — and this is part of the practice of kriya yoga in which I was initiated — then *soma*, as the semen of the cosmic horse, becomes symbolic of an interior physiological process as a new consciousness dawns in the sudden opening of the third eye in an ecstatic experience of illumination. In the sacrifice, the four come together through ritual chant before the fire. For the exoteric practitioner, there is the ingestion of the elixir of the plant, *soma*; the white, seminal-appearing liquid of internal regeneration; for the esoteric practitioner, there is the silent interior chanting that sets the whole spinal chord into resonance and transforms the seminal essence into an energetic ascent in which the eyeballs roll up and an interior third eye opens in a state of ecstatic cognitive bliss.

Unfortunately, the California-hippie way to understand *soma* is to become the typical American consumer and think that the way to enlightenment is through consuming mushrooms and enjoying illumination without all the hard work of yogic *sadhana*. The way to really dig the *Rig Veda* is to get stoned. The *soma* plant or mushroom is certainly part of the exoteric ritual, and I do think that Aurobindo is being a bit too Edwardian and refined when he looks upon it solely as a metaphor for the ambrosial wine of illumination. But I do agree with him that for the few esoteric initiates, there is another interior experience that is being alluded to in the imagery of the chants. Scholars now maintain that, in the case of the later Eleusinian mysteries, when the initiates went down into the darkness of the cave and had this experience of "seeing the sun at noon" that the cereal beverage the mystae were given to drink came from a certain Macedonian grain that, even to this day, has an argot fungus that grows on it, and this fungus is as psychedelic as the mushroom *amanita muscaria*.[13] Even skeptics who were initiated in the mysteries reported having an overwhelming and undeniable religious experience —as is described in Apuleius's *Golden Ass*. So there is no doubt, in my mind, that there is a psychedelic dimension to these rituals and that the countercultural emphasis on mushrooms has a certain value in balancing the very refined views of Aurobindo on *soma* or of Rudolf Steiner on initiation in the ancient mysteries, but one has to put these countercultural readings alongside the other three or four levels that we have encountered through O'Flaherty, de Nicolas, and Aurobindo.

Now I know that no scholar would ever be willing to be so wild as to try to connect Lascaux with the *Rig Veda*. They are millennia apart in time and as far apart in space as India is from France. However, when I read: "Lord of Madra, thunderbolt, you burst the cave of Valla, open and release the cows," Lascaux flashes into my mind. This cosmology is incredibly archaic. It is a musical cosmology of a system of proportions and relationships that are being embodied in the singing. The sacrifice expressed mathematically is also being expressed materially in the sacrifice of raw matter being transformed into fire. The material world is recapitulated in the animal world of sacrifice, in the cultural world of the transformation of milk into butter, and in the human world of the transformation of the ordinary human through *soma*; and it is also recapitulated in the posthuman world, in the yogic transformation of the initiate through the transformation of butter into ghee, semen into the prana of illumination. All these levels are going on at once, and there is not one single level that is the correct, linear interpretation. These chants are imagistically and aurally poly-phonic, polyvisual.

For the male initiate, in the experience of the awakening of kundalini, the seminal fluid is transformed and the individual in trance goes into a state of erection. What we see in a seal from Mohenjo Daro is the shaman with the cow horns on his head, appropriating the cosmic cow of dawn. If one takes the horns and put strings across it, then one will have Orpheus's lyre in the shape of the Greek letter omega, the symbol of the womb. If one sets the strings to vibrating, in other words, if one vibrates the word into the womb, then one gets the resonant space of creation, birth, emergence from the womb of all things, and the male principle inseminating. Recall Lynn Margulis's films of the slow and sluggish protist and the vibrating string of the spirochete. Now open all these windows at once in the hypertext space of the imagination to see the horns on the head, the Orphic lyre, the Greek letter omega, the vulva and the semen, the space and the sound, and in all of these instances notice the androgynous quality of the Orphic shaman in which the male appropriates the power of the female body to himself. The horns of the cow are his helmet. The sign of the vulva as the wound that miraculously heals itself is appropriated by the male in the new all-male mysteries. To appropriate the ancient female mysteries, the shaman must be the male that is female. Whether one is talking about a Plains Indian in female clothes or Jesus revealing to the doubting Thomas the labial wound made by the phallic spear of the Roman soldier, one is talking about a male empowered through the appropriation of the female body.

All of these elements are in an ancient seal from Mohenjo-Daro from 2400 B.C.E. The figure in the seal is not sitting in *sidhasana* (full lotus posture). He is sitting in a very difficult fakir position, balanced on his toes with the heels right up under the perineum. His ithyphallic condition indicates that he is in trance, for in dreams the phallus becomes erect. When the yogi is withholding his seed from the female, he is shifting from sexual reproduction to self-reproduction in the birth of the higher self. In moving away from the female body to give birth to himself, he is appropriating the female mystery of birth in a new male mystery of rebirth. "No women allowed in this club," whether it is the ashram, or the academy of Plato, or the hunt described by Faulkner in *The Bear*, in which the men get away from women to go out into the wild to drink whiskey. The making of whiskey, with its pots and distilling tubes, is itself another symbol of this Indo-European archaic ritual of transformation. From the thunderstones and pestle of lunar *soma* to the tubs and tubes of moonshine, one has a system in which the seed of the grain is transformed into spirit, then moved up through its spinal tube to become the elixir, and then taken into the brain to produce an altered state of conscious. Remember that whiskey is a Gaelic word, *ouiskebaugh*, that means "the water of life," and you will realize that we have not come all that far away from *soma* and the semen of the cosmic horse. This is one reason why the alcoholic is a kind of failed mystic and why many great artists, such as William Faulkner or Dylan Thomas, became caught by alcoholism. They are mystics manqué, just as the hippies are mystics manqué, but the true mystic is not the alcoholic or the drug-crazed huckster of consumerism.

What we have in the ancient Vedic metaphoric complexes is not simply a single system, but a technical language for initiates. In Aurobindo's post-Victorian culture, one could not discuss, as we now can, matters as gross as menstrual blood and semen. The metaphoric system was meant for those who had been initiated and had the internal experience. Just as today when physicists talk about "fields" and "solar winds," they don't mean simply dirt and breezes, when these yogis talked about *soma* and the horses of dawn, they didn't mean simply mushrooms and rodeos. We need to keep in mind the culture of the time, and Wendy Donniger O'Flaherty certainly helps us there, for if we only read Aurobindo's translations, we end up with a psychologizing away from the actual culture of the time and a gentrification of the archaic tantric practice. We cannot perceive the evolution of culture from the archaic mind of the Indo-European because the artifact has been turned into Victorian prudery in Tennysonian verse, without the benefit of Tennyson's slick metrical prosody. One won't recover the archaic mind of the Indo-European with Aurobindo's verse, but if one looks only at O'Flaherty's translations, one won't get a sense of the tantric practice that is at the heart of the metaphoric complex. And if one looks only at de Nicolas, one will get a wonderful scholarly reconstruction by someone who is sympathetic and is trying to recover the whole mathematical system of proportion and harmonics, but one will end up with an intellectual's and not a yogi's experience of vibration.

So we have to read all three of these translations simultaneously, and maybe even four or five other translations that I don't know about, in order to put together something that can take us back through ten thousand years of human experience. The numinosity of the sacred is often created through an evocation of the past; after all, we don't have fluorescent tube lighting on the altar in a cathedral; we have candles.

Neanderthal humans buried their dead with the ancient Acheulean fist-hatchets they no longer used, so this pattern of sacralizing an old technology goes as far back as we can trace it.

The *Rig Veda* invokes the most ancient world of the cave of dawn, but when we take a closer look, we can see just how different this new culture of the cowboys of the steppes is from the Magdalenian cave. The Great Goddess of Laussel marks the entrance to the cave sanctuary. She holds aloft the lunar crescent of the horn, the cornucopia of her abundant womb, and is covered with red ochre, with the magical menstrual blood of lunar renewal. Throughout the iconography of the cave sanctuaries, according to the deciphering of the signs by the prehistorian Andre Leroi Gourhan, there is a dyadic code of male and female signs, a balancing of cosmological forces like yin and yang. The dominance of the Great Goddess is still in evidence at Neolithic Çatal Hüyük, but when we come to the world view of the *Rig Veda* we have passed over from the archaic matristic culture to the new world of patriarchy. Although the *Rig Veda* invokes the imagery of the pink cow and the cave of the dawn, it does so only to appropriate these ancient powers to the new culture of the priest of the sacrifice, much in the same way that the Pope will talk about "Holy Mother Church," but will not allow women to become priests.

This process of male appropriation creates a new condition of strained metaphors for the proportional system explicated by de Nicolas. The father-daughter incest motif probably comes about through a sexual substitution; originally, I suspect it was not the divine father but the divine mother and her daughter, the matron and maiden complex we see sculpted as one body on the walls of Çatal Hüyük. This matron-maiden complex continues on down in time from prehistoric Anatolia to historic Greece to become Demeter and Persephone. In trying to re-create, reconstitute, and reappropriate the ancient image of the divine mother and child, the priests of the fire sacrifice had to translate the image into father and daughter and so they got caught up in a contradiction and had to generate an incest mystery to achieve the unity of the one flesh that had been expressed before. This is the kind of mentalistic approach of allegory that priestcraft often introduces to the symbolic structures it inherits from artists. You see the same process of allegory going on in the medieval literature of the Holy Grail, when rationalization by Christian orthodoxy turns literary works into emblematic collections and allegorical codes. (Compare the medieval French works, the emblematic *La Queste de Sanct Graal* and the more artistic and symbolic *La Morte le Roi Artú.*) The early Vedas seem wild, tonally complex, and richly symbolic, but as priestcraft takes over, they become rationalized routines for rituals controlled by a managerial class. The same thing happens in the later *Upanishads* and in the *Mahabharata,* when priests stick in a lot of homilies and sermons to transform the poem into a pandit's library. And the same sort of thing goes on in Leviticus in the Bible.

In the transition from a tradition of matristic custom to militaristic power, archaic imagery becomes institutionally codified. Look at Athena. According to Maria Gimbutas, Athena was originally the owl goddess of death, a symbol of the third aspect of the Great Goddess, the three being the matron, the maiden, and the crone. When the owl goddess of Old Europe is turned into Athena, she has to be appropriated by the patriarchy and born of the brain of the male. She bursts forth from the head of Zeus. Athena is then turned into a warrior and given warrior's instruments and armor. So we end up with an amalgam of imagery that is ridiculous. The more one retraces the prehistory of Athena as the owl goddess of death—the goddess of wisdom that flies in the twilight—the less Athena as the male patriarchal construction of the daughter that we see in Aeschylus's *Oresteia* makes any sense.

This transition from matristic custom to patriarchal power is no mere local event, but a general consequence of the evolution of culture from sporadic cattle raids to organized warfare. Here is a poem from *The Book of Songs* from China around 600 B.C.E. The first stanzas describe the building of the village, the constructions of the settlement, the communal way of life. Toward the end, the poem comes to family life:

So he bears a son,
and puts him to sleep upon a bed,
clothes him in robes,
gives him a jade scepter to play with.
The child's howling is very lusty.
In red greaves shall he flare,
be lord and king of house and home.
Then he bears a daughter,
and puts her upon the ground,
clothes her in swaddling-clothes,
gives her a loom whorl to play with.
For her no decorations, no emblems;
Her only care, the wine and food,
and how to give no trouble to father and mother.[14]

So this is China 600 B.C.E., the *Rig Veda* is India circa 800 B.C.E., and the final redaction of the *Enuma Elish* is Mesopotamia circa 750 B.C.E.. We know the stories of Greece and the story of Adam and Eve in the Old Testament. The more we seem to learn about the gentle Maya in Mesoamerica, the more they too seem to express the culture of the warrior in a condition of runaway competition and generalized violence in battle, in the ball game, and in rituals of human sacrifice. This transformation of human culture is remorselessly universal. Somewhere around 2000 B.C.E. the remnants of the prehistoric matristic cultures begin to be eliminated in new religions, new cosmologies, new ritualistic works of literature. And now, as we approach the year 2000, it seems that everything is in conspiracy to end patriarchy and our traditional sexual culture. The warrior culture is in trouble because artificial intelligence and smart weapons mean that one has to play war so fast that humans can't play the game as well as machines anymore: so good-bye to noble warriors and hello to sadistic gangs. I am of the generation that can remember the G.I. Joes of World War II, the common citizen-soldier going off to war; but today's army is a professional force, a global SWAT team and a staff of experts playing video games inside tanks. Now electronics has its own speed and needs that bring us to the point at which these technologies are in a condition of runaway and positive feedback. Smart weapons mean that war can't be played in real time because warriors can't respond appropriately and quickly enough, so warriors are no longer going to be a heroic class. Warfare is beginning to displace itself into other subcultures and supracultural domains. First, it displaces itself into teenage gangs, soccer matches and riots, and retribalized genocide in Bosnia and Rwanda. Second, it displaces itself into states of psychic possession. As the astral and etheric planes invade the physical plane through electronic virtual reality technologies and the ingestion of neuroreceptor drugs, the physical structure of patriarchy and warfare is being pushed out of the physical plane and into the etheric and astral—right at the same time that the astral and etheric planes are breaking into the physical through these mediations of virtual reality technologies. One can see this process being prophesied in popular films such as *Terminator II, Flatliners* and *Mortal Kombat*. Electronic culture literally begins to become a video game of demons and dragons, or William Gibson's blend of voodoo and cyberpunk, and we end up with a reconstruction of reality that naive materialists are not really prepared for.

So patriarchy is on its way out from the sheer development of our patriarchal technologies. It is also on its way out from the gay shift in the cultural spectrum from two traditional sexes to eight postmodern sexes. (Mom and Pop, yin and yang Lesbians, yin and yang gays, yin and yang bisexuals.) And it is on its way out from the feminist reconstruction of culture and identity. Now, of course, patriarchy is not going to go out blowing kisses at the feminists. There will be more groups like Aryan Nation, Ku Klux Klan, skinheads, et alia. We will probably have some sort of sexual Bosnia in which gays lobby to have pictures of homosexual love and marriage in elementary school textbooks and fundamentalists react violently and become underground terrorists. But if we look at it from the larger perspective of the millennia, I don't think there is any way that our patriarchal culture is going to survive. It will perish from its own violent contradictions. Sons will not inherit the values of their fathers, and warfare will become a self-destructive balkanization of civilization. So in a hundred years, I don't think we are going to have patriarchy around anymore.

But as patriarchy breaks up, it releases all the old unconscious programs and so we encounter the return of the Neolithic Great Goddess with her consort of the dying male. Today a lot of males are attracted to living out this myth by becoming martyrs. They seek to suffer and are willing to immolate themselves or castrate themselves on the altar of the Great Goddess. So this gives us our New Age culture in which the New Age women may "run with the wolves" but the New Age men bleat with the lambs. The weakened sons of a dying patriarchy do not inherit the power of their fathers but are attracted to martyrdom in the mysteries of the Neolithic goddess. This cultural pattern is very pronounced in New Age communities and communes. But that, I think, is deadly and a cultural dead end. What is further on down the line in the turn of the spiral is, I assume, something much more interesting and complex than a simple return to the dying male of prehistory.

And what is true for war is also true for that other side of Ishtar, human sexuality. Aurobindo and the Mother write sex off as an evolutionary loss and eliminate it from the future evolution of consciousness in the manifestation of the supramental body. Science and medibusiness are hard at work to take over reproductive technologies to do to the family what agribusiness did to the family farm. They are being helped by the chemical pollution that is, poetically enough, lowering male sperm counts. Nature is having its revenge against macho industrial man's assault on the biosphere. Just as Ishtar struck down Enkidu, Nature now seems to have industrial man by the balls. And for the dwindling traditionalists who are still holding on to the myth of romantic love, feminism and feminist rage are working hard to eliminate courtship and romance, feminine glamour, and the beauty myth in merchandising the female body. Meanwhile, their colleagues in feminist literary criticism are aiding them by deconstructing the traditions of authorial wisdom, so an undergraduate would be embarrassed now to admit to "reading Greats," as once students of the patriarchy did in another era at Oxford. If McLuhan was right when he said that "the sloughed-off environment becomes a work of art in the new and invisible environment," and I think he was, then the electronic and nanotechnological transformation of human biology means that for the many, traditional sexuality is ending, but for the few, it is being retrieved as a new Tantric mystery school. Looking back over all my books, and this study of literature and the evolution of consciousness, my life's work seems to me to express the sunset effect of romanticism as well as the dawn of a new Tantric mystery school of heterosexuality. The uniqueness of our time is that in the writer's imagination he or she now seems to enjoy the position of an astronaut for whom dusk and dawn are a single horizon.

THE SHIFT FROM THE ARITHMETIC TO THE GEOMETRIC MENTALITY: ANOTHER LOOK AT THE BIBLICAL STORY OF SAMSON AND DELILAH

The story of Samson in Judges 13-16 sticks out in the Bible with an integrity all its own. It reads like a folktale or folk song that found its way into a rabbinical recension of various sacred texts. Because it shows the evils of concourse with foreign women, it was kept as a homily of the virtues of ethnic purity and is not reworked and refined into more theological material. It still rings out with all the primitivity of a folk song about a folk hero. Like an ancient fossil in a stone used for a refined temple, this little story takes us back to a time before cultural identity was established in and by temples. This folktale about the heroic Samson helps us to see that the

Bible is not a single unified text written by God Almighty himself, but a mishmash of historical materials assembled by many generations and then whitewashed with a thin plaster by schools of priests supported by the palace. As apologists for the class in power, the priests were trying to hold on to cultural identity in an impossible place. The Palestine of Samson's time, like the Balkans of today, was a crossroads, a rural halfway house between more advanced civilizations. At a crossroads between Egypt and Mesopotamia, Palestine was a difficult place to live if one wished to have ethnic purity instead of cultural diversity. Precisely because these crossroads between civilizations are often passed over and more primitive, they can be sullen, resentful, paranoid, and violent; they can explode with a savage commitment to "ethnic cleansing" that the more sophisticated, cosmopolitan, and multicultural centers of civilization can neither understand nor accept.

The religiously sanctified violence in Bosnia today is both repulsive and inconceivable to someone living in the new planetary culture of the late twentieth century. One part of humanity has shifted into the musical and noetic polities of the next millennium at the very same historical time that the rest of humanity is tearing itself to pieces in seizures of religious hatred and violence. There is, of course, a very good chance that this violence may become universal and that what is happening in the Balkans could spread throughout the world. Serbia could, recalling the Middle Ages, reclaim Kosovo in Macedonia, and this could signal the explosion of ethnic warfare as the nativistic reaction to global electronic integration. We could have the Serbs fighting the Albanians and the Macedonians, the Greeks fighting the Serbs and the Turks, the Turks fighting the Greeks and the Kurds, the Kurds fighting the Turks and the Iraqis, the Armenians fighting the Azeris, the Israelis fighting the Iranians, the Chechnyans fighting the Russians, and on, and on, across Russia, Tibet, and China. But we Americans would not be safe from these seizures of ethnic violence, for within our multicultural society, groups such as Aryan nation would attack African Americans, Asians, and Hispanics. To our north, the Quebecois of the rural areas would seek to burn out the Asian grocers of Montreal, those ethnics who denied them sovereignty in the last referendum on Canadian nationhood, and North America would become as crazy as the Balkans or the Middle East.

If we wish to awaken from what James Joyce called "the nightmare of history," then we need to understand this linkage between an electronic technology that brings humanity together in a World Wide Web and the disintegrations of human identity that explode in desperate seizures of illusory ethnic purity. Serbia today, having never achieved the cultural expression of the adjacent Ottoman and Hapsburg empires, explodes in seizures of paranoid violence, delusionary victimization, and hysterical rage for self-expression that for us Americans appear to be lunatic forms of defensiveness in fantasies of martyrdom. But this cultural explosion is no different in kind from the bombing of the Federal building in Oklahoma City. If we are going to avoid the complete balkanization of the planet, we need to understand that the spiritual evolution of humanity to a higher level of consciousness—what Sri Aurobindo called "the Supramental Manifestation"—has turned religion into an evolutionary backwater of violence and sullen dissolution. Here again, we need to remember that whenever a cultural form is about to disappear it has its most intense expressions. The biggest pyramids are built during the Mayan collapse; the tallest totem poles are carved at the end of that Pacific Northwest culture, and the largest "superchurches" are to be found today in Atlanta and Dallas.

There is, of course, a very good chance that humanity simply will not advance into a new planetary culture, and that the prophecies of Sri Aurobindo will have to be put off for another time, or another species. The triple assault of global pollution, universal violence, and technological transformation may simply prove too much for humanity to bear. But since my life's work has been devoted to going against the mainstreams of American culture—by seeking to articulate this new planetary culture in an age of ethnic violence, seeking to embody a postreligious spirituality in an age of repopularized, Superbowl religions, and seeking to establish educational alternatives such as Lindisfarne right at the time when giant communications corporations were consolidating publishing, bookstore chains, and the electronic media into the absorption of education into the entertainment industry of celebrity management—I shall carry on to finish what I started. As Bishop Berkeley said in going against the stream of the scientific materialism of his day, "We Irish think otherwise."

So, thinking otherwise, I want to turn to "the Good Book," not to add to the evangelical banalities that flood the satellite dish in my rural Colorado backyard, but as a way of understanding the bad in religion in an effort to avoid it.

The little fragment of Judges 13:16 is the lesson for today. It stands out perfectly by itself and reads like an archetypal folk story, be it of Jack the Giant-Killer or Paul Bunyan. It has all the typical motifs of folklore: the formulaic repetitions, the three questions, the repetition of patterns in which the wife tries to entice the husband and then Delilah tries to entice Samson, as well as the magical folklore motif of the angel of God who appears and announces to the woman who is barren that she is to bear a special child. In folklore, the hero must always have a special conception, and so his mother is often barren until late in life, or impregnated by magical means. And this folk wisdom has a certain basis in fact, because we know now that women who give birth quite late in life have a higher incidence of bearing either geniuses or idiots. Symbolically, the motif of "barren until late in life" means that the normal generation of individuals through time is not adequate to the production and birth of the hero or savior. The avatar or messiah comes to, but not out of, the society he is to save.

These formulaic qualities, and the briefness of the story, show us that we could take the whole story of Samson and turn it into a folk song or a tall tale. Exaggerations are part of the charm and zest of the tall tale of the folk story. The ballad of Samson the strong is full of all the wonderful exaggerations of the folk imagination. With a single jaw bone of an ass, Samson is able to slay 3,000 people. Since 3,000 people are on the roof of the Philistines when Samson brings it down, we can begin to suspect that for the primitive mentality of the times, numbers are a vital quality and not an abstract quantity. For our civilized, urban, and abstract mentality, a lot of things in the narrative don't make much sense rationally, but they do make sense as a celebration of good storytelling. They just make a better story, and since stories are a form of cultural storage, a better story makes for a fuller culture. The exaggerations of the archetypal encounter of the hero against enormous odds make the tale of Samson easier to remember and sing.

So with the story as we have it in Judges 13:16 we are really dealing with a fragment that sticks out of the Bible, like a fossil skull in the exposed strata of a cliff. Other fragments and folk material, for example, the Midrash, were not so fortunate; they were kicked out of the sacred texts by the priests in the temple at work on the recension for King Solomon. But because the story of Samson is such a good story and is one that teaches a lesson that is vital for survival in a crossroads of cultural diversity—stay away from foreign women—the priests kept it in the sacred canon. If a text reinforces the power of the ruling class, if it celebrates cultural identity and the divine power of Israel against its Philistine neighbors, it is useful in the work of shifting from a tribal amphictyony to a unified nation, and so it is kept. In Judges, we have warring clans; in the Book of Samuel, we have moved to the amphictyony of warring tribes; and in the Book of Kings, we have evolved into the nation of King Solomon, a nation unified around the temple, with its rabbinical school that produces the unified and unifying sacred text.

So in the evolution of society from the oral culture of the tribal settlement to the literate culture of the kingdom, there is an evolution from folklore to literature. This is the same kind of cultural evolution that we saw in the evolution of the work songs about the love of Inanna and Dumuzi, sung by maids churning butter, to the more complex and astronomical liturgical chant about "Inanna's Descent into the Netherworld," sung by priests in a temple observing the positions of the planets. Folklore is told or sung by the people among themselves, but sacred texts are produced by priests or pandits who are serving to preserve and reinforce the interests of a ruling military class. Just as there is an evolution from work song to liturgical chant, there is an evolution from shaman to prophet to high priest. Nathan as a prophet to King David is what Henry Kissinger was to President Nixon. He is an advisor inside the palace and not a prophet in the wilderness.

If one considers the process of cultural evolution from Judges to Samuel to Kings in the Bible, one will see the changing structure of society and the changing role of the prophet. For the mentality of a priest in the temple at work in rationalizing the culture, all the crazy stuff we see in the apocryphal *Book of Enoch* — all that sci-fi lore about flying saucers and Atlantis-like civilizations before the flood — all that stuff is just too far-out and wild. It takes the follower of a religion away from the center of power to a universe that is vast and unstable, and so it is not the sort of thing that rulers need to keep the people happy at their work. But if one is a member of a wild and wacky cult out in the desert, be it Essene or Merkabah, Gnostic, or whatever, works such as the *Book of Enoch* are just the sort of apocalyptic vision that confirms one's suspicions about the rabbis or pharisees who have sold out to the palace. And so it goes, from one edge of history to another.

But meanwhile, back in the temple, the wild and wacky stuff gets kicked out of the official Bible. What gets accepted is what reinforces the world view of the temple and the palace, and so the high priests labor to produce a canonical and unified Bible. But anybody can see it is a patchwork job. When fundamentalists refer to the Bible as the word of God, they have a political mission in mind and are trying to turn Jefferson's deistic republic into a Near Eastern theocracy. Anyone with a mind alive to world literature recognizes in the story of Samson and Delilah the very rich and *human* world of folklore.

Now, in the "politically correct" MLA (Modern Language Association) language that is in fashion in American universities at the moment, this establishment of a canon of revered and sacred texts is known as "the construction of discourse by a ruling elite." My generation was raised with a construct called "Western civilization," and I was trained to look upon the Jews and Greeks as the creators of the triumphant greatness of our postwar dominant Western civilization. The Jews gave us the higher moral ethos of monotheism, which, supposedly, rescued us from sinking into the dark earth of a pagan animism, and the Greeks gave us philosophy and Western science, which rescued us from sinking down into the murky passions of Near Eastern emotionality. To pass on the greatness of Western civilization from one generation to the next, scholars such as doctors Hutchins and Adler at the University of Chicago created courses on the "Great Books" and even published a "Synopticon of the Great Ideas." Liberal arts colleges from William and Mary to Pomona—where I went—passed on "the Tradition." Actually, the whole thing worked rather well, and the liberal arts college was a great American institution, and Pomona in particular was a wonderful college. But one generation is never satisfied with the other, and so, way back in the 1950s, I challenged my teachers, insisted on adding anthropology to the English curriculum, and confused my English teachers by asserting that Piaget should be read alongside Wordsworth. And so I shifted from the construct of English as a major to Anthrophilit—Anthropology-Philosophy-Literature—as a triple major. The difference between this shift from English to cultural history and today's academic shift from English to cultural studies is that my shift was based on an interior experience of gnosis. For my generation of the 1960s, the essential experience was a yogic or psychedelic one of illumination. Thus began our worldwide search for texts outside "the discourse of the West" that gave voice to this mystical experience of gnosis. And so we shifted from our teachers' emphases on Plato and Aristotle, Niebuhr and Tillich, to the poems of Rumi, the *Tibetan Book of the Dead*, the *Zohar*, the *Bhagavad Gita*, the *Tao Te Ching*, the *Gnostic Gospels*, the *Book of Enoch*, and the *Book of the Hopi*—any text that recovered, preserved, and held aloft this essential experience of illumination and "cosmic consciousness."

And that, obviously, is quite a different cultural project from the one animating the hearts and minds of the "politically correct" generation in the universities today. The cultural project of the 1990s is one of anger and revenge: blacks getting even with whites, women getting even with men, gays getting even with straights, Hispanics getting even with gringos, postcolonials getting even with colonials. Each group is possessed by a certain animus, a kind of folksoul or collective ego. Now when one takes a folksoul or collective ego, the kind of emotional plasma that flows over and through crowds, rock concerts, football matches in England, wars, cults, ideological movements, and the like, what one gets is a gross caricature of an individual ego. And what one gets is violence. If one takes a folksoul and promotes it to a cultural deity or God Almighty, what one gets is precisely what we see in the Old Testament. One gets Jahweh, a war god screaming for the annihilation of the uncircumcised, as we see in Judges 14:19: "and the Spirit of the Lord came upon him, and he went down to Ashkelon, and slew thirty men of them. . . ."

This apotheosis of the human ego leads to the state of possession, of Islamic *jihað* against Jewish *herrem*. It leads to a form of cultural entropy in which no cultural connections are possible as all human bonds break down in what Rudolf Steiner predicted would be the nature of our time, a Hobbesian "war of all against all."[1] The political cleansing in the universities leads to a Balkanization of the spirit, an ethnic cleansing in Bosnia, or Israel, or Northern Ireland, or Kashmir, or Sri Lanka, or the Aryan nation's Idaho. When education is not based on gnosis, on illumination and compassion, when education does not literally lead one out —*exðucere* — of the ego, it can only lead to the violent collision of all the equally empowered egos. So the construction of a cultural identity built upon sacred texts is not merely an academic matter. Knowledge of the sacred text is empowerment; it separates the educated from the philistines.

Now, thanks to the sacred text of the Old Testament, we have all been raised to look down upon the uneducated and repulsive "Philistine." But here we encounter a problem, one that causes real cognitive dissonance for those who have been raised in "the discourse of the West," to think of our progenitors as the Greeks. For it now turns out that the Philistines and the Sea Peoples were actually Greek-speaking Minoan people. This general period was a dark age, one of the volcanic explosion of Thera, the collapse of Minoan civilization, the Mycennean wars, widespread folk wanderings and migrations, as well as the particular Israelite invasion of Canaan. It now appears that many of the Greek-speaking peoples were also in migration, and that some made it over from Crete and Cyprus to invade Canaan along with the migrating Israelites. So the Philistines are not philistines, they are civilized Greeks! Things have been reversed by the biblical narrative, and actually the real Philistines are the Israelites. They are the primitive, raggle-taggle group of tribes that have just come out of slavery in Egypt and have straggled into the more developed and sophisticated settlements of Canaan. The Israelites don't have cities. They don't have architecture; they don't have court poets; they don't really have much of a culture except for this mini-malist religion that is their faith in their single tribal war god, Jahweh. The Philistines, by contrast, are cultured and have built great architectural temples for their god of the sea that protected them during their voyage to safety.

This whole period of Judges is a historically fascinating one because it seems very much like the kind of dark age we are about to enter: a period of natural catastrophes and civilizational disintegration. It is a period of flights of refugees, of wandering peoples, of huge volcanic explosions with their disruption of weather patterns and their dependant crops and harvests. Imagine the impact on our global economy if we lost one whole year's harvest because of the change in the weather from the volcanic ash in the atmosphere. Think of an America in which catastrophe is not a rare event, but is seasonal like winter storms, and not just one catastrophe, but a cluster of interacting ones occur: hurricanes, earthquakes, floods, and tornadoes. And imagine their impact on insurance pension funds, government bonds, futures markets, and on, and on in an interlocking chain, "the cascade of accumulating differences" that in chaos dynamical theory leads to a new "catastrophe bifurcation." This is the preclassical world of the Eastern Mediterranean from around 1350 to 800 B.C.E. And it feels as if it is going to be the postmodern world again around 2000 C.E.

Imagine that all those Edgar Cayce mystical prophecies about the destruction of Los Angeles and Tokyo by earthquakes were to come true. Imagine the economic impact of these events coming at a time when the greenhouse effect was melting ice caps and causing the flooding of the coastal cities. And imagine what people in the twenty-first century will be trying to do to restructure global civilization as one volcano after another blows up and changes the weather so that we lose one or two summers' harvests. Imagine a summer in which there is no new food at all. We don't have enough food reserves for our global population to make it through such a crisis. Lest one accuse me of being too fanciful, consider a recent article in the *New York Times* that reported on the discovery of more than three thousand volcanoes under the ocean that are exploding under the waters around Easter Island and Tahiti. Most of that volcanic material is now going into the ocean, but remember the impact on global weather patterns when just Mount Pinatubo exploded, when merely one volcano went up in smoke. Then imagine Mount Pelée, Mount Saint Helens, Vesuvius, and Etna going off all at once. And that will give you a feeling for what is going on behind the text of Judges 13:16. We have a dark age with a loss of culture. If one looks at the earlier Egyptian or Minoan civilizations, or even the Megalithic cultures of Malta, Newgrange, Avebury, and Stonehenge, one sees a high level of culture, of astronomical knowledge and cosmic ritual. But in the *Iliad* and Judges and Samuel, that cosmic knowledge is missing, and what is center stage are the warlords with their emphasis on violence and destruction. Such is the cultural background of Samson.

In church and Sunday school, the words of the Bible can often lull one into a comforting sense of goodness, but what does "And the Spirit of the Lord came upon him, and he went down to Ashkelon, and slew thirty men of them. . . ." really mean? It doesn't sound like a description of the descent of the Holy Spirit in the form of the white dove of peace and love. It sounds more as if the hero had become possessed by the folk-soul of the group, and in a warrior's trance-like seizure of violence, gone out to slay in order to protect his tribe. (This concept of "folk-soul" that I am using is explained in the books of Rudolf Steiner.[2]) When one is "channeling," or being seized in an altered state of consciousness, one becomes exalted, more than oneself. In my ancestral tribal tradition, that of the Irish, the ancient Celtic warriors would go into battle stark naked. This completely freaked out the Romans, who were all armored and trying to behave rationally as a fighting machine, in the kind of precise movements that one sees displayed in the Hollywood epic with Kirk Douglas, *Spartacus*. Celtic warfare is primitive and shamanic; it works very well for people whose ego formation is so labile that they can easily shift into trance and live more in their astral body than their physical body. For highly individuated and urban people, those densely situated in their egos and their physical bodies, this talent has been lost. For them, warfare is simply frightful and frightening, and they need the togetherness of the mechanized movements with shield and armor to keep them from running away in fear. But for the barbaric warrior in the state of seizure with his daimon, fear was not a problem. Like a self-impaling dervish, this sort of warrior would not feel fear or the pain of the arrows sticking in his flesh and would charge and kill people long after the point a rational and civilized person would be dead and out of action. So my ancestral Celts were at a more primitive level than the Romans, and they fought randomly and wildly in a display of individualistic mania and power. The Celtic warrior was really a shamanistic warrior. Picture the naked, screaming Celts confronting the machine of interlocking shields of the Romans, and you have a picture of what it was like when Samson confronted the Philistines, or David confronted Goliath in his Greek armor. The shamanic warrior feels "the Spirit of the Lord" come upon him, and in that altered state, he can do what no ordinary soldier could ever do. So the exaggerations of the story of Samson are actually telling another kind of truth.

If one wishes to know more about these altered states, one should read Michael Murphy's book *The Future of the Body*.[3] The book is a thousand-page compendium of both religious and sports literature on altered states in which people are taken over and begin to operate in a supernormal or paranormal manner. So when we encounter these folk exaggerations in the text of the story, we shouldn't think that the storyteller is simply lying for the sake of the story.

In these traditions, whether it is of Samson in Israel, or Arjuna in India, or Cuchulain in Ireland, battle has a sense of excitement to it precisely because it precipitates the warrior into this altered state. The shamanic warrior, the sacred warrior, becomes more than himself as he goes into battle. So battle itself begins to be a kind of ritual that, literally, separates the men from the boys. This quality of entry into the barbaric mind is what is so richly given in the text. We are glimpsing something really quite ancient, something older than the civilized, rational mind.

Perhaps it is easy to see why I wanted to move in this narrative from the *Rig Veda* to Judges. Both texts take us back into an archaic masculine mind. Both texts are full of the celebration of male power, of the notion that a man really comes into himself when he guards his power, when he stores his seed. Samson's hair is what Freud would call "a displacement upwards," a symbol of "as above, so below." The ancient Indo-European notion was that "loss of semen is loss of soul." Women were like succubi, they sucked your soul out while you slept, so wet dreams were dangerous. In the case of the *Rig Veda*, what one sees is a much more sophisticated and worked out praxis of *soma* and semen. In the less esoterically or yogically developed folk psychology we encounter in the story of Samson, we find the more common association of hair, head, and vital essence or magical power that the classicist R. B. Onians explored in his study of the origins of European thought.[4] According to this ancient psychophysiology, there is a relationship between the base of the spine and the top, between the seminal fluid and the cerebral-spinal fluid. This folk psychology still survives in the modern superstition that it is bad luck for an athlete to have sex before the big game. Notice how archetypal this athletic subculture is. The heroic quarterback can have the great-chested cheerleader as consort, but before the game he has to be with the boys in the locker room. Women are a threat to his magical power. So this notion of male mysteries still lingers in the athleticism of today, or in military culture, for there, too, on the night before the great battle, one is counseled to abstain from sex.

Women are a threat. When Samson is described as lying in the lap of Delilah, he is put into a position of perverse rebirth. The hero should guard his seed and give birth to himself through the birth canal of his own spinal column. The lap of the woman was originally the vulva of the Great Goddess who brought us forth in birth and takes us back into her womb of earth in death. This cyclicity is all well and good for the natural man, for the Neolithic son-lover of the Goddess, but for the solar hero, for the man like Gilgamesh who wishes to make a name for himself that can outlast the repetitive cycles of lunar female time, for the man who wishes to have an enduring and permanent erection, the lap of the woman is a deadly trap. Notice once again—as we saw in the conflict of Gilgamesh with Ishtar—that the female is now presented as having seductive rather than reproductive power. Delilah's power is not as the mother of sons but as the destroyer of men. As a foreign woman, she begins to stand for the whole culture of the foreigners, with their worship of the goddess and their Canaanitic matrilocal customs that keep men under the control of women.

The Great Goddess is demoted by the Israelites, and Eve is made to be not the mother of us all with her cosmic reproductive power, but this seductive little housewife who comes to Adam and says "dear, wouldn't you like to have this nice apple?" And then the whole world goes to hell, all because of her. Eve is the primordial seductive temptress, and Delilah is her copy. And even Samson's wife entices the secret of his riddle out of him. Women can entice because the only power that they now have is erotic power—seductive and not reproductive power. Man now controls the means of production through the invention of warfare, the way of death that becomes a way of life. Against this new militaristically organized society, the prehistoric agricultural matristic society hasn't got a chance. The culture of custom and authority gives way to the new culture of power; it is another variant of the story of the *Enuma Elish*.

For the Israelites, surrounded by the matrilocal cultures of Canaan, women are a literal threat to patriarchy, for in marriage the husband is expected to go to live with the family of the wife. Notice in our story that when Samson takes a Philistine wife, he is presented as going to live with his father-in-law. So this Philistine culture, whether it is Minoan, Anatolian, or Cypriot, is clearly a matristic culture and not the patriarchy of father Abraham. The Philistines are a double threat; they take up good land and, through intermarriage, lure the Hebrew sons away from the culture of their fathers. The Israelite solution was not simply warfare *with* the enemy, but cultural annihilation *of* the enemy. Notice in the story that the narrator justifies Samson's living with the Philistines and taking a Philistine wife by saying that this came from the Spirit of the Lord moving within him, for it enabled Samson to move among the Philistines and kill them all the more easily.

Samson's father complains, "why do you have to go down with the uncircumcised," why do you have to have a wife with the Philistines? Aren't Jewish girls good enough? Here is the archetypal attraction that the *shiksa* holds for the good Jewish boy. Delilah is Greek; since the ancient Greeks were cousins to the Celts and often blue-eyed and blond, let's imagine her along Hollywood lines. Let's succumb to politically incorrect cultural stereotypes to envision Samson as a brown-eyed, dark-haired Semite under the pull of fascination to a trashy blond with blue eyes. This sexual pull of "the Other" is the problem built into diploid sexual reproduction. Delilah, we can be sure, is no mere peasant girl, milking goats, but a civilized and refined Cypriot Greek. Since she, too, has a fascination for "the Other," she has the hots for this hunk of savage. It is a situation we encountered before in the Goddess Inanna's attraction to the lowlife of the ordinary human being, the shepherd Dumuzi. So this is a very old story, an archetypal story that survives into our Southern gothic novels in which the daughter of the plantation owner gets the hots for the "darkie" sweating in the field.

Since this fascination with the Other is a two-way street, the stories can also present powerful men attracted to women of inferior station. The powerful man who runs the financial empire in Wall Street is attracted to the chorus girl. Recall in all those black-and-white B movies made during the Depression that it is always the man of power, be he gangster or banker, and the chorus girl. She is the bitch goddess in disguise who does a number on him and begins to lead him to his destruction. In the masculinization of culture, a split occurs, so the man of power has power in the conscious world of muscle or money, but he is subject to the attractive pull of unconscious power, of the foreign and the feminine. The unconscious gets projected onto the feminine. We see this pattern with Aeneas and Dido in the *Aeneid*. Dido is the Semitic princess of Africa. She is different, enchanting, sexy and attractive, and full of ancient mysteries. But our hero Aeneas has an empire to found, so duty calls and he sails off and leaves Dido to perish on her funeral pyre. In Purcell's opera, Dido's lament is a very beautiful aria. Aeneas doesn't get trapped in Dido's lap the way Samson becomes ensnared by Delilah. In the *Aeneid*, woman is the victim and in Judges, the man. Dido perishes; she is the old Phoenician, African, Semitic culture that dies to give way for the Roman. Although the Phoenicians were the first to create the cultural ecology of the Mediterranean, they were not fated to become its masters. In Dido's lament, we hear not only the pathos of the movement of Aeneas to found Rome, but also the return of the Romans to Carthage in the Punic Wars, when the last remnants of Phoenician culture were destroyed and salt was sown so that nothing would ever again grow in its soil. The conflict of the Romans and the Phoenicians is at one end of Mediterranean history, and the conflict between the Israelites and the Canaanites and Philistines is at the other, but in both cases, the conflict is between male and female, patriarchy and the matristic civilization of the goddess.

In this conflict between the Israelites and the Philistines, between male and female, savage and civilized, architecture plays a very important role. Since the most dramatic image of the story is that of blind Samson bringing down the enormous building of the Philistines, it will be worth taking a closer look at this building and its pillars. The storyteller pictures this Philistine building as a flat-roofed colossus, for he speaks of three thousand people gathering on the roof. The indigenous architectural style for the Mediterranean area is one of flat roofs and common walls used to carry the load of the roof. The Minoan style of the Palace of Knossos of 1500 B.C.E. can be traced all the way back to Çatal Hüyük at 6500 B.C.E. To picture what Çatal Hüyük look liked, see it as another version of Taos Pueblo in New Mexico. Now the architectural style of the Mycenaean Greeks from the rainy north was of sloping roofs supported by tree-trunk pillars. The north, having more rainfall and abundant forests, has an architectural idiom that is entirely different from the mud walls of the goddess culture of the south. In the north, the tribal warlord has a free-standing big house called a *megaron*. It has sloping roof and tree-trunk pillars. The famous Parthenon in Athens is a later translation from wood into stone of this original form of the big house of the big man. A free-standing big house asserting itself in space is appropriate for the military hero, but the architecture of the goddess culture of the south is the opposite. The architecture is communal; the walls are shared, the load is distributed throughout, and the roofs are flat and offer a patio space for entry and socializing. When the storyteller presents us with the image of three thousand people on the roof, he is presenting us with a typical Mediterranean cluster, a pueblo form of structure that would be very much like that of Çatal Hüyük, but when he presents us with Samson between two pillars that when shifted can bring the whole building down, he is describing a structural feature than could only work for the Mycenaean *megaron.* There are indeed pillars in the Minoan palace, but shifting two out of place would certainly not bring the house down, so it seems as if the storyteller is conflating the foreign structures of his enemies, the Greek Philistines and the Canaanites, into one. Or perhaps the story is conflating the time of the death of Samson and the closely related time of another devastating earthquake, one that destroyed the palaces of the Philistines but spared the humbler houses of the Israelites. Either way, the poetry of the situation works very powerfully, for the image of the savage oppressed and contained by an architectural form represents precisely the archetypal conflict of savagery versus civilization that the folktale is all about.

But here the savages are the good guys, and the civilized are the bad guys. The containing form is Greek, but Samson is this divine savage whose wild sexual power, symbolized by his hair, explodes and destroys the containing, civilized, architectural structure. This archetypal image of primitive, sexual power contained and constrained within architectural form is a beautiful description of the pain of humanity caught in the confusion of the transition from the arithmetic to the geometric mentality.

Samson is presented to us as a man always in pursuit of prostitutes, lovers, and wives. In the culture of sexuality as described in the story, the Philistine wife of Samson is nothing more than a sex object. When his father-in-law gives Samson's wife away to another and Samson complains, his father-in-law says, in effect, "Oh forget about her; her younger sister is prettier, anyway, so take her." In this culture of men, women are seen as merely a commodity of exchange; if one gives them too much power or tries to please them, whether they are Eve or Delilah, it always leads to trouble.

Samson is a folk hero rather than a tragic hero, but like a figure of tragedy, he is presented as a man whose unique excellence (*areté*) is also his tragic flaw (*hamartia*). Samson is larger than life and endowed with greater strength and greater virility than the average man. He is presented as an extremely sexual being, and it is his sexual drive that gets him into trouble. The great man in the lap of the seductress is presented to us as a male vision of abomination, and the end result of this extreme situation is another extreme situation: castration. So Samson is shorn of his hair, his auric radiance, and his eyes are put out. As Milton put it in one of his memorable lines in "Samson Agonistes," "Eyeless in Gaza, at the mill with slaves." And, of course, the shearing of the hair and the removal of the eyes is another Freudian "displacement upwards" for castration. So we look upon Samson with awe and with terror, and, like the ordinary man in the Greek chorus, we recoil from the tragedy and pray to the gods to be spared the heroic condition that generates the tragedy, be it Samson of the Bible or the Agamemnon of Aeschylus.

Because of the extremity of his stature and drives, the path of moderation is not open to Samson, so he can only destroy his enemies through destroying himself. He becomes a sacrifice, and in his act of sacrifice offers his whole nature to the work of the Lord. Now in extremity, there is a reversal of fate; the flaw of Samson, his attraction to Philistine women, was a necessary agency to destroy the enemies of the Israelites. Even Samson's sins and flaws are part of the mysterious ways of the Lord. Here is the *felix culpa* of Milton, the fortunate fall or necessary sin, that brings about redemption. Samson, the slayer of thousands, must himself become a victim of sacrifice, and in moving toward his tragic fate, he inspires in us that sense of awe that is at the heart of tragedy. He becomes sublime, impersonal, or metapersonal, as all his faults become purified in the refiner's fire of his tragic death.

The image of Samson between the pillars bringing down the gigantic structure is an archetypal vision of crucifixion. Samson is the victim, the dumb savage at the mercy of his sexual drives who becomes destroyed by women and caught in the geometrical containers of civilization. At one level, this is the eternal story of the innocent country boy who is destroyed by women and the big city. Think of Bernard Malamud's novel *The Natural* as another example of this story. At another level, this is an archetypal story performing the archetypal pattern of "redemption through the primitive." Samson brings down the superior civilization to make way for the next civilization. Rome falls to the Goths to destroy classical civilization and make way for medieval Christendom. And at yet another level, the tragedy is symbolic of a more interior process of purification and mystical transformation. Personality is presented in all its giantism, and yet it is personality that must be offered up, sacrificed to and for the divine. "Let the Seer slay reality, then slay the slayer" is an aphorism of the yogic seer Patanjali. This sacrifice of the personality through and with the personal is something we will encounter again when we consider the *Bhagavad Gita,* in which Krishna encourages Arjuna to carry on with the battle and not seek to escape the conflict in the quietistic nihilism of the world-denying *sanyasin.* It is only through the personal that the personality is transformed. Samson without his strength and sexuality is not Samson; without them, there would be no story at all.

And the story is a very good one indeed. The image of Samson between the pillars, bringing down the architectural edifice is a powerfully haunting image because it captures an important moment in the human story, in the story of the "evolution of consciousness." It dramatizes the end of the arithmetic mentality and the transition to the new geometric mentality. The arithmetic mentality is one filled with the numinosity and power of generation; it is a world of sexuality, of immanence rather than transcendence. It is a world of propagation and accumulation. But the geometric mentality is a world in which the ideal is transcendent, the mental geometrization of the world picture replaces the concrete and sensuous, the *Bruderbund* replaces women's mysteries. In the arithmetic mentality, number is generative and reproductive, as the One, the Great Goddess, becomes the many of her children. Reproduction and enumeration are entwined mysteries, and sexuality is natural, sacred, and divinely feminine. But in the geometric mentality, the idealized mental form, the geometrical figure, the spirit and not the flesh, begins to take over. As sexuality is brought under containment, the container no longer is the womb or the storehouse of seeds and grains; the container of male power becomes the fortress, the big house of the warlord, the palace of the king. In the Babylonian *Enuma Elish*, we saw the body of the Great Mother dismembered so that the military hero Marduk could construct the ultimate architectural container of the city of Babylon. The *Enuma Elish*, like Judges 13-16 is a transitional text that is showing us the contradictions and tensions of humanity in the evolution from one mentality to another. With the *Rig Veda*, we are in the prepalatial landscape; we are still back there in the arithmetic mentality in which male sexuality still contains the mystery of self-regeneration. But in the case of Samson, we have the landscape of the palace and the temple with its conflict between savagery and civilization, and here sexuality leads to self-destruction.

Samson is the primitive man of the past. The men of the future are King David with his palace prophet-advisor Nathan, and King Solomon with his Canaanitic architect Hiram of Tyre. Samson destroys the temple, but David and Nathan plan it, and King Solomon and Hiram construct it. The Jahweh of tents is about to be cajoled into the temple, as stated in 2 Samuel 7:6: "Whereas I have not dwelt in any house since the time that I brought up the children of Israel out of Egypt, even to this day, but have walked in a tent and a tabernacle." Jahweh enters this new fangled Canaanitic container only on condition that Solomon be a good Jew, and Solomon promises anything to get Jahweh into this new "Holy of Holies," so that he can pull off a palace coup in the moral order and force all the tribes to look toward Jerusalem and his temple when they pray. No longer will the shepherd look up to the stars; he must look toward the city, toward the world of the palace of the king and the temple of the high priest.

For humanity in the fullness of the arithmetic mentality with Inanna and Dumuzi, sexual intercourse was sacred and numinous, but for the new humanity, substituting the geometrized description for the sensuous encounter, the vulva is a trap. Only by escaping from women and the body of the senses can men be free in the new and idealized mental world. Whether it is the temple, the academy, the university, the church, the space colony, or the contemporary boys' club hacker mysteries of artificial intelligence and artificial life, this new world is all male and mental, and the old world female, menstrual, and dirty. Plato inscribes over his all male club of the academy, "Let no one ignorant of geometry enter here."

The story of Samson is a folktale from the dark age that seems to come in the shift from one mentality to another. Now as we move from the mentality of linear systems of description and control of Gutenberg and Galileo to the chaos dynamics of the new sciences of complexity, we look out again at a dark age of religious violence and a new mathematical mentality we are just too primitive to understand. It is not hard to feel for Samson. He was the end of an age; Solomon with his Canaanitic temple will take over Israel, so the edifice that Samson brings down is as much Hebrew as Philistine.

10

THE ALLIANCE OF THE ANIMAL AND THE HUMAN IN THE EXPULSION OF THE DEMONIC FROM THE PHYSICAL WORLD: A CONSIDERATION OF THE *RAMAYANA*

The *Ramayana*,[1] as a work of poetry, is in a class by itself in world literature, because from India to Bali it probably has had the largest audience of any single literary work in the history of humanity. It is a supremely populist work and has been turned into puppet plays, comic books, and recently even a television soap opera in India. Although the *Upanishads* are chronologically earlier than the *Ramayana* — the earliest *Upanishad* coming from around 800 B.C.E. while the *Ramayana* is thought to come from 500 B.C.E. — I want to begin with the *Ramayana* because I think that, in its own way, it is a more archaic document, one that really is about the emanation of divinity into human form as a way of stabilizing the physical plane and making it the incarnational vehicle and domain for human beings. Beneath us is the hell realm, above us is the heavenly realm, but mediating between matter and spirit is the intermediate realm of psyche, of what Jung called the collective unconscious, or what the Theosophists called the astral plane. This is the disincarnate realm of dead humans, demons, and spirits of nature and mind. It is a busy intersection of other dimensions and parallel worlds, a booming and buzzing confusion in which psychic channels get lost when they go hitchhiking with truckers on the astral interstate and can't tell whether they've been picked up by angels, demons, or dead religious sociopaths. The *Ramayana* is, however, a good map, a sort of yogic Rand McNally that can help us get through this wild terrain so that we can find our way home and become more enlightened human beings.

So let's begin with a map of all the kinds of creatures we are going to run into in the cosmology of the *Ramayana*.

1. *Pretas* — Ghosts.
2. *Yakshas* — House spirits; fertility spirits (these are servants of Shiva and therefore pre-Aryan).
3. *Rakshasas* — Demons (these beings are animal- and man-eating).
4. *Asuras* — The equivalent of Titans from Hesiod's *Theogeny*; "Former Gods of Old"; opponents of the new gods or Devas.
5. *Kumbhandas* — Gnomes; earth elementals.
6. *Nagas* — Underwater elemental spirits; serpents; salamanders.
7. *Garudas* — Elemental spirits of air.
8. *Gandharvas* — Heavenly musicians.
9. *Apsaras* — Paradisal maidens of extreme beauty (like the houris of Islam.)
10. *Devas* — The gods, headed by Indra (these are like the Olympian gods of the Greeks, headed by Zeus.)[2]

Now for a good, red-blooded American, all these beings are just so much mythological nonsense. We think that they simply don't exist. Like leprechauns, fairies, angels, or Santa Claus, all these creatures are supposed to be from a prescientific time when most people were peasants and, therefore, superstitious, or just plain stupid. Now we have science, so now we know better. Thanks to Jungian psychology, we can call these beings "projections" and feel safe and secure that everything in the universe comes from our own great human collective unconscious. This is the Swiss Küsnacht or American suburban worldview—the lily-white suburbs in which there are no Blacks, no Jews, no angels, and certainly no demons. Everything out there is "us."

The world of psychology and science is a comfort to us because it gives us a way of denying or explaining away the ontology of evil, the ontology of the demonic. The trouble is that when we move into the world of big science, we encounter a weird world of superstitious beliefs in which all kinds of stuff we never see is said to exist. High priests tell us that quarks and bosons exist, and we have to take their word for it. Something that only exists as a nanosecond blip on a meter is said to be more real than actual human experiences of artistic and religious enlightenment experienced by yogis, saints, and artists in many different cultures throughout the ages. When the high priests of physics tell us about their world of invisible particles, things begin to get pretty weird. Let me give you chapter and verse from Paul Davies's *Other Worlds: Space, Superspace, and the Quantum Universe.* "If accepted completely literally, it [the quantum theory] leads to the conclusion that the world of our experience — the universe that we actually perceive — is not the only universe. Co-existing alongside it are countless billions of others, some almost identical to ours, others wildly different, inhabited by myriads of near carbon-copies of ourselves in a gigantic, multifoliate reality of parallel worlds."[3]

So Big Science gives us permission to believe in parallel worlds and other dimensions — as long as these beliefs and ideas have absolutely nothing to do with our experience and have absolutely no moral or aesthetic implications for how we live our lives. We may take it on faith that quarks or antimatter exist, because the high priest tells us so; but we may not believe in *gandharvas* or leprechauns. I don't accept the comfortable Jungian Küsnacht cosmology in which every form of consciousness in the universe is a projection from the human collective unconscious. Creatures of parallel worlds, whether Asuras or Rakshasas, are real and they are not under our control; but they do like the fact that we don't believe in them because this allows them to gloat over our heads as they take possession of us in Bosnia and Rwanda.

A cosmology kicked out the front door of a culture has a way of sneaking in the back door. Such is the case with Grimm's fairy tales in the nineteenth century, and comic books in the twentieth century. Superman, for example, is a wonderful New York Jewish response to Nietzsche's *Übermensch.* Created by Jerome Siegel and Joe Shuster in 1938, Superman presents us with an ironic Woody Allen vision of the bespectacled, dark-haired nerd who becomes the savior of truth and the American way.

Demonic evil is complex, European, and mental, but truth is simple, extroverted, innocent, and American. Right at the time of the Depression, when the economic capital of the world was shifting from stodgy London to New York's Gotham City and America was about to take on the dark and twisted mental powers of European philosophy turned into German Fascism, the comic book heroes of Superman and Flash Gordon appeared and began to play out for the imaginations of the children of a new scientific world, the return of the gods and demons of the prescientific world. Alex Raymond's Flash Gordon,[4] in fact, is a pop American version of the cosmology of Rudolf Steiner. Steiner claims that Lucifer actually had a human incarnation in China in about 3000 B.C.E., so you can look upon the villain Ming as a Luciferian Lord of the fallen angels and the whole sequence of battles as taking place on the astral plane. Dale is the classic Jungian anima projection and consort to the extroverted hero Flash Gordon, and the whole archetypal battle, which takes place on the astral plane, is a turn on the spiral that replays Atlantis as a recapitulation of America's coming battle with the demonic forces that use Nazi Germany as their historical puppet.

And in a similar way, *The Wizard of Oz* is a Sufi parable of individuation. Dorothy's companions on the way to the Emerald City are really personifications of the subtle bodies—the etheric, astral, and mental bodies. If you look at the medieval illuminated manuscript *King René's Book of Love*,[5] you will see a knight with the winged heart on his helmet. The winged heart is a Sufi emblem; it symbolizes the opening and uplifting of the heart chakra through the practice of prayer and *zikr*. The Tin Man who has achieved his quest and wears a heart on his armor is another version of the knight on his quest to do a great work for his lady. The Emerald City is also a technical term used in Iranian Sufism.[6] We Americans, who are so intent on creating a culture of technological materialism, cannot take in esoteric lore directly; it has to find another way in, and so comic books, science fiction, and movies are the back door.

The *Ramayana* should be looked upon as the mythological popular art of its time, as a story in which Rama is the Superman and Flash Gordon of his day. And in this prehistoric comic book cosmology, we encounter a rich and complex ontology in which there are not only human beings. There are gods and demons galore. In this intermediate world of dream, imagination, and spiritual vision, gods and demons are not simply, as we like to think they are, projections from the human collective unconscious.

This intermediate realm, or *Kama loka*, is located between the human, material realm and the higher, formless realm of *Brahma loka*. *Kama loka* means "desire realm," so it is a world of attraction and repulsion that keeps the wheel of karma and rebirth spinning. It is not the higher spiritual world of the Brahman delineated in the *Upanishads* or of the Buddhist's emptiness. The *Upanishads* are elitist works written by yogis for the students who were sitting at their feet—which is the literal meaning of an *Upanishad*. But the *Ramayana* is a supremely populist work about the world of love and hate, gods and demons, loyalty and treachery. Rama is the archetypal hero, Lakshmana is the archetypal faithful brother, and Sita is the archetypal faithful wife. If we look upon the *Ramayana* as high literature, then these characters are all a little too good to be true. Rama is the supreme goody-goody; he is not a Homeric figure like Achilles whose unique excellence (*areté*) is also his tragic flaw (*hamartia*).

Like the Homeric epics or the Arthurian cycle, the *Ramayana* is an accretive work of the centuries to which many poets and singers of tales have contributed. The core of the work may be Valmiki's, but he most likely did not invent the figure of Rama, and he certainly did not artistically control the shifting characterizations of Rama that are to be found in the heroic cycle. For Valmiki, Rama is a symbol of perfection *in* society, rather than in Buddhist abandonment of the palace; for the later bardic contributors, Rama is an incarnation of Vishnu. Toward the end of the epic, Rama becomes the tragic figure of a king so controlled by rumor and the opinion of others that he abandons his pregnant Sita to the wilderness where she gives birth to twins—a folk motif that is picked up and played out again in the Grimms's fairy tale *Rapunzel.*[7] In the later tellings of the traditional stories, one can begin to see that the poets are beginning to be attracted to ideas of the *felix culpa,* the fortunate fall, the idea that the exile in the wilderness was necessary to end the epoch of demons, or that the abandonment of Sita was necessary for the birth of poetry, an art that Rama's children will bring back to him when they return and recite the epic of the *Ramayana* they have learned from Valmiki in their exile. Here we can detect the esoteric motif of the lost or prodigal son returning to the embrace of his father, and here we can detect the esoteric belief that we are all exiles in this world, that our true kingdom is in another world, and that poetry can help us reclaim our majestic spiritual identity.

Although the *Ramayana* is often described as a love story, it is really not a love story at all. Romantic love is a medieval chapter in the story of the evolution of consciousness; it comes later on down in the line of time, and will, in fact, be added as a new element in the medieval Tamil version of the *Ramayana.* But Valmiki's *Ramayana* is a premedieval story about the loving father, King Dasaratha, who, constrained to honor a vow to one of his conniving wives, is forced to send his eldest and favorite son into exile. Rama, the absolutely perfect and obedient son, willingly accepts his sentence of fourteen years of exile in the desert and departs, accompanied only by his faithful wife, Sita, and his even more faithful brother, Lakshmana. The epic is a story about the patriarchally preeminent relationship of the loving father and the faithful son, the son and his faithful brother, and the problems that come to men because of women: from Kaikeyi, the conniving wife of King Dasaratha, to Sita, the foolish wife of Rama who does not listen to the instructions of her husband or the good advice of her brother-in-law and so is kidnapped by Ravana, the lord of the demons. It is all about structural social relationships. It is not about passion, romantic love, and the transcendental yearning of the feminine soul that brings it into conflict with patriarchal warrior society. We will see this story later in *Tristan and Iseult* or *La Morte Le Roi Artu,* but the *Ramayana* is decidedly not a medieval story, and it certainly is not a modern story about adultery. If we stop to reflect on the nature of adultery in *Madame Bovary* and *Anna Karenina,* we observe a split in which the ego is bound in time to society and the husband, but the psyche is calling the soul to a world of longing and belonging beyond society. If Sita had fallen in love with Ravana, and had wanted to stay on his magical island of enchantment—the beautiful Ceylon of rubies and moonstones—then we might have a medieval or modern love story. But the *Ramayana* is definitely not such a love story. It is a cosmological fairy tale and a parable about the dutiful son and the faithful wife, both seen from a point of view that affirms the traditional male social structure. Sita is an example to all women, and the one time she acts like a silly, irrational woman and does not listen to her brother-in-law, she gets herself and everybody else into a lot of trouble. Eve is captured by the devil, and Sita is captured by the lord of the demons, Ravana. So whether we are ancient Hebrews or Indians, the mess of history is all woman's fault.

Another traditional way of looking at the *Ramayana* is to read it as a historical document about the Epic Period of India, about the Aryan invasion from the north, and the conquest of the dark races of the Tamil south. My take on this poem is, however, quite different from all the interpretations I have encountered. There is an invasion south, all right, but it is the movement of the divine human spirit down south into the biology of the evolutionary animal body. I see the *Ramayana* as a mythological vision of the hominization of the primates, and so, not surprising, the monkey Hanuman is its real hero.

Before the descent of the human soul into the stream of planetary evolution, we were floating about in the realm of indeterminate consciousness—of consciousness without an object. Then we drifted down into dream and fantasy, and as these dreams became more fascinating and vivid, they became worlds of projected incarnation—wet dreams of a sort. The problem was that in this realm of projected desire, we were subject to being consumed by demons—immaterial beings of unlimited and caricatured desire. Now, these beings of uncontrollable desire, the *rakshasas*, eat thoughts and desires the way we humans now eat plants and animals. To get a feeling for these *rakshasas*, call to mind the two paintings, one by Hieronymus Bosch, the other by Matthias Grünewald, entitled *The Temptation of St. Anthony in the Desert*. When humans slip out of the determinacy of their physical bodies in dream or sloppy meditation, the demons appear to consume these hermits and psychedelic fakirs.

The ruler of these demonic *rakshasas* was Ravana, and his psychic realm was unlimited within its own level of existence. Through profound meditation and yogic practice, Ravana accumulated such great merit that Brahma himself was drawn to him and had to offer Ravana great rewards. Ravana asks for unlimited powers in the manifest universe, power even over the gods; but because humans and animals were so lowly and insignificant, he does not think to ask for power over men and animals, and this will prove to be his undoing and lead to his defeat by Hanuman and Rama.

As you can see, the cosmology of the *Ramayana* is an earlier version of the relationship of men and demons presented in the Cabala and the Koran. In these Semitic myths, the devil, made from God's immortal light, is appalled when God creates Adam out of mud. When God asks Lucifer or Iblis to fall down on his knees to honor his latest creation, the devil is disgusted and proudly refuses. Evidently, the creation of humanity disrupts the steady state of the universe of light and introduces the new creative disequilibrium of matter. The devil as Lucifer-Iblis will have no part of an evolutionary process that displaces him and his kind, and so the war in heaven is really all about the emergence of humanity in the evolution of the universe. The *Ramayana* is another vision of the cosmological relationship between creatures made of light and creatures made out of matter. But in this earlier version, Ravana does not even notice men and animals, for he is intent only on gaining infinite power in the universe of the gods. Brahma is constrained to honor Ravana's wish, and so the lord of the *rakshasas* does gain cosmic ascendancy and even Indra is captive and subject to Ravana.

What to do? God as Vishnu decides to project into a human body, to take on a human incarnation. Vishnu becomes Rama. Vishnu's female consort Lakshmi becomes Sita, the future wife of Rama. But since humanity is now in the age of patriarchy, the vision of Sita is somewhat ambivalent. She is beautiful, yes. She is faithful, yes. But she is willful and has no good sense and will not listen to the perfect brother, Lakshmana. And so she becomes seen and then captured by Ravana. The female and psychic half of humanity represented by Sita becomes captured by Ravana, the lord of the demons. And this expresses how characteristically the feminine side of humanity, the psychic channel, the sibyl or the poetic man, can become captured by the astral plane. Psychic individuals become caught in things such as LSD, Scientology, *The Urantia Book, Seth Speaks*, or cults organized around the channelled messages of a medium. The only thing that can rescue a poor soul that has become an enchanted wraith lost in the astral plane of drugs and demons is a good, normal, healthy, physical body—a definite, limited, and concrete body of animal evolution. The body we so desperately try to ignore or escape is actually a divine gift, an act of divine grace given to protect us from the illusions and terrors of the astral plane.

So into our story come the wonderful animals. Enter Jambavan the lord of the bears and Hanuman the crafty and wonderful monkey. The mammals, with their more highly developed central nervous systems, are to have their day in triumphing over the demons and wraiths of the astral plane. Notice that man alone, the great hero Rama, is not able to defeat the demonic armies of Ravana by himself; he needs the help of the animals. The feminine side of humanity, in concert and love with the animals, is released from its capture by the demonic, and the demons are slain. In other words, they are pushed out of the physical plane and restricted to the astral plane, and the collaboration of animal body and human spirit creates the new domain for the evolution of humanity.

Bears and monkeys are mammals, and the unique excellence of mammals is their mammary glands, which create the bonding and intimacy of love for infants and lovers. The *Ramayana* dwells on the beauty of Sita—on her tiny waist and large breasts—and we should too. To get a healthy sense of the ancient Indian understanding of breasts, do a little homework. Take a field trip to the newly opened Indian court at the Metropolitan Museum of Art in New York. Take a long and loving look at the statue of one of the *apsaras*, the paradisal maidens of heavenly beauty. This statue focuses on the thrust of the breasts, and gives such an incredible torque to the spinal axis that it makes it obvious for all to see that breasts are the leaders of human evolution. They are what we are all about. Recall D. Michael Stoddard's *Scented Ape*[8] and remember that the infant recognizes its mother because of the pheromones that are secreted in the areola of the nipple. In mammalian nursing, the synesthesia of smell, taste, and touch come together in an orchestration of the sensorium that creates the essence of the high human consciousness we know as love. It lays down the foundation in consciousness for what the act of love will be for adults. Take away the mammalian bonding of animal, carnal love, and raise children without parents on MTV, gangsta rap, and the technology of fast cars and guns, and you will get a new race of demonic humans who become killers at the age of eleven. Our contemporary shift from flesh to electronics is precisely a shift from the human to the demonic and is a rewinding of the tape of human history that takes us back to Ravana's capture of Sita and his effort to hold her captive on his beautiful and magical island of Sri Lanka.

Without the help of the bears and monkeys, Rama cannot cross the sea to the magical island to rescue Sita. But with them, he can build a bridge. Middle Earth becomes the realm that will now mediate between hell and heaven. The physical plane has been stabilized by Vishnu working through Rama and Sita, and the human story can now begin on Earth. The cosmic age of gods and demons is at an end, and the age of humanity has begun.

The *Ramayana* is a wonderful fossil that tells the story of the evolution of consciousness. It is extremely important for our time because I believe we are at the end of Rama's period of the stabilization of the physical plane for human beings. The evolutionary crisis of our time is the disintegration of the physical plane and the animal body as the vehicle for the incarnation of human beings. This is happening through declining fertility caused by chemical pollution in the environment and from all kinds of electromagnetic pollution from the invisible electromagnetic fields that surround us and erode the integrity of our biological immune systems and break down the animal integrity of the our old evolutionary mammalian body. So now we have all forms of cancers, leukemias, and immune system diseases and don't yet understand through big science what is really happening to us; but we do intuitively sense our evolutionary crisis and are expressing the catastrophe bifurcation through art—primarily through science fiction.

The spiritually repressed or unrecognized reality of our condition is unconsciously being precipitated into our world in the societal form of technology, but in the psychological mode of the demonic. When we cannot create our destiny through enlightenment, our fate is inflicted upon us through ignorance. Ravana is back and the astral plane is leaking into the threadbare and worn-out physical plane through the help of drugs, virtual reality helmets, and body sheaths, and a generally pervasive saturation of our bodies in invisible oceans of electromagnetic fields of noise. From electronic watches strapped to our heart meridians to microwave ovens to cellular phones to television transmission towers, the old mammalian body of Hanuman and Jambavan is just so much meat cooking in a global mulligan stew of electromagnetic noise.

Through esoterically naive uses of drugs and technology, the subtle bodies are being appropriated and degraded. In the 1960s, LSD appropriated the astral body and precipitated the astral plane into the commons of the electronic media. Now the appropriation is moving closer on down to taking over the physical body as the etheric body is becoming appropriated through the uses of virtual reality helmets, gloves, and full body sheaths. A generation of preteens will be taken over—just as television took over the previous generation—by virtual reality helmets and coin-operated rides in shopping malls. Kids trip out on gangsta rap, play *Mortal Kombat* in helmets, and then play with reality by spraying the subways and freeways with semiautomatics pistols. Demons are riding piggyback on human minds and laughing in delight as scientists insist that they don't exist. Just read the ads in *Mondo 2000* or *Wired* to get a feel for this other brave new world. Or think about cyberpunk fiction or the great battle between "the Borg" and Captain Jean Luc Picard in *Star Trek: The Next Generation*.

When I was doing some fieldwork for my book *The American Replacement of Nature*, I went to the Human Technology Interface Laboratory at the University of Washington in Seattle. I went with an open mind and a sense of excitement that I was going to see some new, cutting-edge science. It was cutting edge, all right, but it was more like a frontal lobotomy or castration of the subtle bodies. I went to the lab with my spiritual buddy David Spangler; both David and I felt a sense of massive electromagnetic invasion into our subtle bodies, and it took us an hour after we left the lab to get our etheric and astral bodies back into their proper alignment. I think that people who practice yoga of one sort or another are more sensitive to the fields of electromagnetic noise than are people who have been raised on MTV and heavy metal music. The sense of acute dislocation and psychic violation that we both felt in the brain on coming out of the trip into cyberspace was really morally disconcerting, and we both had strong feelings that this new technology was going to be very bad for the all the eleven-year-olds who were going to be putting on the virtual reality helmets in shopping malls all across the country. The experience of putting on the helmet and glove reminded me of the X-ray machines that used to be in shoe stores when I was a kid in the 1940s.

You need to understand that in order for the computer to read your movements and gestures and translate them into cartoon landscapes in the Liquid Crystal Display television monitors in front of your eyeballs, you have to wear a strong magnetic field in the form of a glove or a full-body sheath. So the virtual reality sheath is really a kind of appropriation of the etheric sheath—the *pranamayakosa*. Now when you appropriate something, you actually take and degrade the cultural integrity of its original context. It is like White hippies going Indian and doing sweat lodges and sun dances, or men appropriating women's mysteries into the militaristic structures of patriarchal priestcraft. In our contemporary situation, culture becomes cultural shoplifting and theme park consumerism. This literalization of the esoteric doesn't actually have the original esoteric function. It is much the same as when you create images with television or MTV: you are pretending to create images, but the real function is to rob you of your imagination. In a similar way, when we give out American foreign aid, the conscious agenda is to help other people, but the unconscious agenda is to create a structure of relationship that subtly brings forth dominance and control and celebrates our own American imperial superiority. So the gift becomes a way of controlling the receiver. In this sense, any form of appropriation has the quality of literalization—of giving you the letter but robbing you of the spirit. It appears to give but actually takes away the possibility of your having the real experience.

Now I am no Luddite; I write my books with a Macintosh Powerbook and I have a phone, fax, and VCR. So, yes, I do recognize that there are some technologies that are user friendly—such as the telephone or radio— but that there are others such as television and virtual reality that are not so biologically friendly and have highly toxic side effects. No technology is neutral. As McLuhan said, "the medium is the message." Television is not simply a means of communication but more of an unconscious architecture in which we live. We shape and adapt our lives to this architecture as we make our way through and around it. What the saint was for medieval culture, the celebrity is for ours. The celebrity is a performance of the culture. To the degree that the membrane of one's identity has been eroded by the celebrity's presence in living room and bedroom, that personage becomes part of our new electronic symbiotic consciousness. So some individuals will become obsessed with one celebrity or another. Like a medieval saint, or hysteric, depending on your point of view, who can take on the stigmata of Christ in meditation on his image, the obsessed subject of the media takes on the life of the celebrity, and to prove his ownership, seeks to take that life.

People unconsciously pick up on the culture of a technology and try to express the invisible environment in various ways, whether it is through paranoia or mystical visions or religious cosmologies of one sort or another. In the 1950s, when television was constellating the new invisible environment, the science fiction movies of the time were full of images from *The Invasion of the Body Snatchers* or *It Came from Outer Space*. As networks of satellites and transmission towers went into place, feelings of cultural invasion and extraterrestrial abduction began to appear. The abduction mythos of Adamov in the 1950s has now become a general pop phenomenon with Whitney Streiber's book and movie *Communion* and Dr. John Mack's bestseller *Abduction*. Because we are a technological and intensely materialistic culture, the return of the astral plane into our field of awareness tends to constellate itself in literalist stories of abduction. When one slips from waking mind into the hypnagogic state of early sleep, sense perceptions are imagistically transformed. So the sense of our beating heart becomes the footsteps of someone else in the room, or the weight of our hands on our chest is transformed into a monster sitting on our chest, a succubus. Since males always have an erection in the rapid-eye-movement dreaming state, the imagistic transform is that the little dark men have come into the bedroom and are performing genetic experiments and extracting semen from the sleeping body. If one steps back to consider all the books and films about abduction and all the new bestsellers about angels, then one can appreciate that postmodern humanity is being culturally reconfronted with the astral plane, with its array of angels and demons. Since we technological materialists don't know what to make of multiple dimensions and parallel worlds, we concretize our intuitions and have the demons coming at us in solid metallic flying saucers.

But all these parables of extraterrestrial invasion and genetic experiments on sleeping humans are really a paranoid narrative that renders visible the invisible environment. The body *is* being snatched and invaded. And, at the same time, the body of the planet, the integrity of the biosphere, is also being invaded and becoming threadbare. So from ozone holes in the atmosphere to auric holes in the human body from psychedelic drugs and parasitizing technologies, old Homo sapiens is in for it. Rama's stabilization of the physical plane that we have taken for granted has come to its end, and now cultural intrusion in the form of genetic engineering and reproductive technologies is replacing natural selection. We are at a new catastrophe bifurcation in human evolution, one in which we have to reconfront the demonic and the astral plane and learn again how to tell the difference between the spiritual and the psychic. For us materialistic Americans and Europeans, spiritual discrimination does not come easy, and we all too easily fall victim to the demonic as it becomes expressed in New Age cults, psychic religions, channeling, or "new edge" technologies and drugs; but what they all have in common is a sense of glamour, galactic inflation, and a Luciferic rush.

The 1990s seem to be a rerun of the 1960s. Marx said that history tends to repeat itself, but that the first time is tragedy, the second time is farce. I guess Hegel is now standing Marx on his head, so that the 1960s was farce and the 1990s will be the tragedy. This time we don't just have hippies moving into communes and tripping on acid, we have the deconstruction of the human body, the electronification of humanity. I have argued in my previous books that evil is often the annunciation of the next level of order, so I guess before we can evolve into noetic polities we are going to experience the meltdown of the individualistic man of the Renaissance and the Enlightenment into collectives of noise. The modern discotheque is a sign of the times. People are packed in by the hundreds, and there is no space for solitude, reflective thought, or sensitive touching; there is not even anything resembling music; there is only industrial house music and slam-dancing as the decadent evolutionary bodies collide and shatter in drugged states of consciousness sliding with downers into the basins of attraction of demonic noise.

Welcome back to the astral plane. Mystics, shamans, and my old ancestral Celtic animists once knew how to make their way through the astral plane quickly and move up into the world of spiritual understanding. They understood the danger of being captured by the fairies and warned that one should never eat the food of witches or fairies. No such luck for this latest generation of humanity, nursed on amphetamines and MTV and graduated into the dopamine rush of virtual reality; now their neuroreceptors are gone and schizophrenia has become not an individual illness but an entire culture.

I see this condition as a tragedy and not a farce because in all the great spiritual traditions of the world, there is the recognition that when we have become enlightened, the transformation occurs in the physical body. As I noted before, in the spiritual evolution of consciousness there are three stages of transformation: *illumination, initiation,* and *enlightenment.* Illumination has its locus of action in the etheric body. This is the familiar condition of the awakening of kundalini, the opening of the third eye, and the discovery of the whole system of chakras in the etheric body. What the yogis do not talk about, however, is that the immediate result of illumination is the illumination of one's darkness. One's instinctive self becomes activated, one's preverbal mind, and especially the very first thought one had in coming out of the mother's body becomes intensely energized. There is an occult relationship between the mother and the experience of birth and the Tantric *shakti* and the experience of yogic rebirth. This period of illumination is a very difficult and rocky time of confrontation with the shadow, with the preconscious and unconscious as companions to the first experience of the superconscious or *samadhi.*

If one is able to stumble one's way through this stage, then the next stage is initiation. The locus of activity for initiation is in the astral body. This sequence of experiences is sort of like a foundation giving you "a matching grant." For each of the subtle bodies, a disembodied colleague is sent to serve as a helper in the spiritual work. So for the etheric body, a jinn is sent. I am taking this term from the *Koran* and Sufism in particular. We get our word genie from this term, jinn. We humans are made of earth, but these elementals are made of fire. The jinn is the colleague of the shaman and works close to the physical plane on the etheric plane. The jinn is good at weather changes or ensouling machines or weapons to achieve magical results. Race car drivers or jet pilots sometimes stumble unconsciously into this realm when they superstitiously ensoul their machines and then do absolutely amazing feats that no ordinary driver or pilot can equal.

The colleague that emerges in the field of our astral body is what Jung called the contrasexual anima-animus. I prefer to call this being Tara. Since I am male, I will only speak from my own experience and consider this spiritual guide as Tara. At some point in his contemplative practice, a man stops projecting his desires onto women in the outside world and begins to have, let us say, an active love life with an epiphany of the feminine in the psychic realm. This interior figure, such as Dante's Beatrice, is an exalted teacher who instructs men in the mysteries of life. At the level of the conscious ego, this being is completely beyond the ego's command and control. She is in charge and determines when and just how deep the relationship is to be. Eventually, after years of meditation and contemplative practice, the psychic experience arises in which the man moves to the other side of the river that divides the astral from the mental plane and there, at that shore of other worlds, has sacred intercourse with Tara. This is the *hieros gamos* of the ancients, or the Yab-Yum *maithuna* statue of Tibetan Tantrism.

This interior feminine modality of consciousness is, however, not a single being, but rather a dual one and often appears in the man's psychic life in both the modality of, let us say, Kuan Yin, the universal mother of compassion, and Tara, the individual initiatic consort and guide to spiritual development. In Christian terms, one can think of this divine emanation as the two Marys—Mary the universal mother, and Mary Magdalene the initiatic consort. In Hinduism, this dyadic modality is expressed as the cosmic *shakti,* the creative force of the universe, and the individual tantric *shakti,* the initiatic consort to one's yogic practice. So, for example, Sri Aurobindo will speak of the mother or the cosmic *shakti,* and at other times of the mother of the ashram and his individual consort in the manifestation of the supramental, Mira Alfassa Morrissey Richard.

The colleague, or matching grant, for the mental body, the *vijnanamayakosa* of the yogis, is what I choose to call the Seraph. This being, unlike the eternal feminine form of Tara, does not appear in a human body. This being is an angelic one whose consciousness is not polarized between crotch and crown, genitals and brain, but is completely holographic—it is a creature of a thousand eyes. The eyes seem like facets of a crystal and the creature seems made more out of music and mathematics than flesh. The music of Bach and the Cathedral of Chartres seem to be metaphors that approach this form of universal life. This being is so transcendent to the biological realm in which we take our human life that, at least from my limited experience, it can only be experienced in states of yogic *samadhi* in which the heart has stopped beating and one moves into extremely subtle microsections of fractal time.

As each of these beings are brought forth and take up their symbiotic life in the corresponding energy sheath of our subtle bodies, a moiré pattern is created, an overlapping of elemental, psychic, and angelic energies that creates "the holy grail." Into this vessel of our expanded, symbiotic incarnation emerges the colleague of our highest body, the *anandamayakosa,* and this being is called the Purushottama by Aurobindo or the "indwelling-Christ" by David Spangler.

The Divine Comedy is also a description of this process of initiation. But rather than presenting a jinn as a colleague for the etheric body, Dante presents Virgil, a human being no longer confined to the world of the flesh. Tara is Beatrice; the Seraph is the "Angel Sphere" of Canto 28; and the vision of the face of Christ is the consummation of Canto 32, lines 85-88.

> Riguarda omai ne la faccia che a Cristo
> più si somiglia, ché la sua chiaressa
> sola ti piò disporre a veder Cristo.

(Look now upon the face that is most like
the face of Christ, for only through its brightness
can you prepare your vision to see Him.)[9]

As for the final stage of enlightenment, it is pretty hard for me to talk about it since I haven't got that far, but more than one religious tradition insists that the locus of its activity is the physical body. To prevent enlightenment, therefore, it is helpful to mess up one's body with drugs and toxic technologies, for these tend to keep one entrapped in the astral plane. Two of the clearest signs of this form of astral entrapment are addiction to states of being high and psychic forms of inflation in which one becomes a self-elected guru or a self-proclaimed messianic figure. Illumination is about "I," but enlightenment is about "we." The great wisdom traditions of the universal religions all insist that the passage from stage two to three involves humility, a "Dark Night of the Soul," a passage through a "Cloud of Unknowing," or, in the words from T. S. Eliot's *Four Quartets,* "a condition of absolute simplicity costing no less than everything."[10] Just about the worst thing you can do is to become addicted to ecstatic highs through drugs, or run around on the lecture circuit as a Mushroom Mullah proclaiming the American consumer's approach to enlightenment: "take this and eat, for this is the body and blood of the new covenant." Since the devil is the ape of God and is always out of timing—energizing and celebrating what has been passed over in spiritual evolution—this form of American theme park mysticism is a tourist trap. It is a spiritual version of Disney's EPCOT—for those who do not wish to go to the real Europe there is the shopping mall boutique in which France is reduced to a restaurant and a tourist gift shop.

In the process of enlightenment, the astral plane, that glorious world of imaginative perception and deception, is consumed in a light that dissolves all imagery and mediated forms of knowing. You can find a description of this in the prophecies of St. John the Divine in Revelation 2:1:1: "And I saw a new heaven and a new earth: for the first heaven and the first earth were passed away; and there was no more sea."

The sea is the traditional, archetypal image for the psychic realm, for the collective unconscious—the watery realm that mediates between the Earth's crust and the sky. When the new heaven comes down, the Earth is transformed, and so the very nature of physical matter is transformed. In this condition of enlightened matter and the human body, the intermediate and imperfect realm of the psychic is no longer needed. The metaphor that

John chooses for this is the sea disappearing, as if the sun had come closer to Earth and the sea were burned away.

In the book of Revelation, when the Christ appears at the end of historical time, the New Jerusalem descends out of the sky. In egotistical forms of inflation, humanity tries to ascend and "conquer space," so the mirror opposite of this New Jerusalem is the Tower of Babel. Babel, you will recall, ended in scientific forms of specialization in which no specialist could understand the other's jargon—which seems to be a good parable for our time, in which the quantum physicist cannot speak to the molecular biologist. So the paradox of science is that its maximum development and extension into a culture leads to a condition of cultural entropy in which no cultural connections are possible. The New Jerusalem descends out of its own transcendent power, and as it comes to meet humanity, there is the marriage of the Christ and humanity. In this consummation of evolution, the astral is totally taken up, absorbed, burned out, and eliminated. Now just think about it—that would pretty much put every psychic channel and cult out of business, for the astral plane is the stock and trade for every medium, acid head, pink pyramid Arcturan, or Ascended High Master doing business today.

It is a truism of history, of course, that when something is about to disappear, it has its most brilliant sunset. So humanity is now flushing out its tanks and all this astral goo is out there in public where we can take a good look at it. We are at a catastrophe bifurcation in human evolution, at one of these initiations in which we have to reconfront Ravana and learn how to distinguish the demonic from the spiritual. And that is not easy for a materialistic culture, for we have long ago put away the yogic knowledge that would enable us to discriminate between channeling and intuition, psychedelic illumination and spiritual enlightenment. The battle of Rama and Hanuman against Ravana is being fought all over again. As we move toward the end of the millennium, we are witnessing this explosion of the collective unconscious in new forms of astrality that are coming out of electronic technologies, virtual reality, and the new "brain food" of neu-roreceptor drugs. So the *Ramayana* is an ancient text that, in the turn of the historical spiral, offers us an insight into our posthistoric world.

11

THE *UPANISHADS* AND THE *BHAGAVAD GITA*: THE EMERGENCE AND ARTICULATION OF THE HIGHER SELF

As an adaptation to an ecology, literature behaves ecologically in more ways than one. Like a forest moving through the stages of succession to climax, literature unfolds through three stages: formative, dominant, and climactic. The formative work enters into a new ecological niche of consciousness through the work of solitary and shamanic pioneers; the dominant work stabilizes the mentality through the work of an institutional elite; and the climactic work consummates and finishes the mentality for all time through the work of an individualistic genius.

A formative work introduces the elements of folk experience and presents the material that the culture will work with and elaborate through its developing institutions; a dominant work develops folk materials into priestcraft and high art, and a climactic work raises the elements to a universal level of culture that transcends its local origins and, in its way, finishes or consummates the elements of experience that had been presented in the original folk vision. The Gilgamesh epic, for example, is so universal an expression of the human confrontation with death that it speaks to our culture as deeply as it spoke to the world of the second millennium B.C.E. Within the terms of the experience of the male as a symbol of the vanishing modality of time, it finishes and completes the Mesopotamian vision of the dying male and the enduring goddess and rings out across time with a transcultural universality that echoes throughout other cultures, from the Greek *Oedipus Rex* to the German *Faust* to the American *Moby Dick*.

In the civilization of ancient India, the *Rig Veda* is the formative work, the *Upanishads* is the dominant work, and the *Bhagavad Gita* is the climactic work.[1] The formative, the *Rig Veda,* presents the primitive ritual of the sacrifice and the transformation of body and mind that will later be elaborated through Brahmanic priestcraft into temples, institutions, castes, as well as caste-escaping solitary yogis symbolically turning butter into ghee, semen into *soma.* The *Upanishads,* the dominant work, articulates for the millennia the basic psychology of the states of consciousness experienced in the waking mind, the dreaming mind, the mind of dreamless sleep, and the foundational consciousness underneath all these states—the universal mind of Atman, experienced unconsciously in dreamless sleep but recovered superconsciously through the *samadhi* of yogic meditation. The climactic work, the *Bhagavad Gita,* consummates and finishes for all time the basic Indian vision of the psychology of egoic historical time and divine eternity; it raises the notion of the sacrifice in the *Rig Veda* to another level and takes the image of the two birds that occurs in both the *Rig Veda* and the *Upanishads* and transforms it into a philosophy of *prakkriti* and *purusha,* nature and spirit. The *Gita* presents a psychology of individuation that moves beyond the Vedic pantheistic dissolution in the all of the dawn, or the Vedantic negation of perception in "all is Maya." In the dialogue between the Lord Krishna and the warrior Arjuna, the intensely conscious and highly individuated self discovers the validity of acting in history by offering up the fruits of action to the universal God. The *Gita* rises out of its historical time and place to become a work of universal human culture, and its power to inspire other cultures continues to this day, through Emerson and Thoreau to Steiner, Yeats, Aurobindo, Gandhi, Christopher Isherwood, and Aldous Huxley. The work continues to live with us with much more power than either the *Rig Veda* or the *Upanishads*—great as these works are. Formative and dominant works articulate and support their native cultures, but climactic works are transcultural and are themselves formative of a new global canon for a new planetary culture, and that is precisely why I as a contemporary writer use them as foundational texts for a new transcultural shift in consciousness in which we move from religion and nationalism to a radically new postreligious spirituality that Aurobindo prophetically identified as "the Manifestation of the Supramental."[2]

To appreciate this literary process of development within a cultural ecology, consider the metaphor of the two birds. Here is its first formulation in the *Rig Veda*: "Two birds, friends joined together, clutch the same tree. One of them eats the sweet fruit; the other looks on without eating."[3]

What the prehistoric *rish*is discovered was the structure of the nervous system. We now prefer to call this dyadic division of consciousness the central nervous system and the autonomic nervous system, but the wall between them is beginning to be seen as a permeable membrane, as research in biofeedback shows unconscious processes are accessible to consciousness. For the ancient *rish*is, consciousness was divided between perception and a nonsensory witness to perception. For these practitioners of yogic meditation, it was possible to separate interpretation from perception. One does not have to interpret an impulse as pain to scream out; one can simply observe it as neural activity. Fakirs or howling dervishes, of course, develop this capacity to a high art so they can impale themselves impassively. A more common experience for the rest of us might be when we feel that ice is "burning" and hot is "cold." Once when I had my eyes closed while shampooing my hair in the shower, I touched the hot water faucet and it felt intensely cold. When sight was not there to help out in the act of interpretation, I could discover how the interpretation of perception is a constructivist act. If the faucet is hot, then I want to jump back and yell in pain; but if it is merely cold and not going to burn my skin, then I don't need to worry. But perhaps the burning and blistering of the skin is also an interpretation, and if I learn how to separate perception from interpretation, I may be able to become a fakir or a yogi impassively watching his pain. I can't do this, and I remember how terrorized I was as a child of seven when the nuns told me stories about the torture of St. Lawrence. The Romans tortured him by frying him alive on a griddle, and half way through, the saint turned to his tormenters and remarked: "I'm done on this side, friends, you can now turn me over." Until then, I had always thought I wanted to become a saint, but when I heard that story I knew that sanctity was beyond anything I could understand or attain. The thought that anybody could fry a human being like a pancake was so inconceivable that it simply destroyed childhood by introducing worlds of evil and good beyond my innocent experience.

Here is how this image of the two birds of the nervous system is picked up and developed in the *Upanishads*: "There are two birds, two sweet friends, who dwell on the self-same tree. The one eats the fruits thereof, and the other looks on in silence."[4]

The *Upanishads* is a watershed in the evolution of consciousness. Instead of being ethnocentric and dividing all global history between B.C. and A.D., we really should divide it between before *Upanishads* and after *Upanishads* — B.U. and A.U. — because the sophisticated psychology of consciousness in the *Upanishads* represents a quantum leap forward in human development. In the *Rig Veda* there is a complex and obscure symbolic code that elliptically refers to states of experience for those who have already had the experiences, but in the *Upanishads* there are radical yogi psychologists who insist that one can be a Brahmanical priest and throw butter on the fire until the cows come home but still never become truly enlightened. In the *Mundaka Upanishad*, the yogi makes light of the priest:

7. Such rituals are unsafe rafts for crossing
    the sea of samsara, of birth and death.
    Doomed to shipwreck are those who try to cross
    the sea of samsara on those poor rafts.

8. Ignorant of their ignorance, yet wise
    in their own esteem, these deluded men
    Proud of their vain learning go round and round
    Like the blind led by the blind.[5]

And in the *Svetasvatara Upanishad*, there are no obscure references to magical practices, but very straightforward instructions on exactly how to practice yoga to gain enlightenment. "With upright body, head, and neck lead the mind and its powers into thy heart; and the OM of Brahman will then be thy boat with which to cross the rivers of fear. And when the body is in silent steadiness, breathe rhythmically through the nostrils with a peaceful ebbing and flowing of breath."[6]

The yogis of the *Upanishads* mapped consciousness into four states of being. There is the normal waking mind, the dreaming mind, the mind of dreamless sleep in which the soul unconsciously returns to Brahman, and the supraconscious state of concentration of *samadhi* in which one watches the mind pass through all the stages. The mind that we have unconsciously in dreamless sleep is recovered consciously in the *samadhi* of yogic mediation. When there is no object of perception — as in the waking state — and when there is no surrogate object of psychic or dream perception, when there is just pure consciousness in which being with the lower-case "b" returns and is saturated with universal Being with a capital "B," then enlightenment floods in. Here is the *Mandukya Upanishad*'s way of expressing this:

1. AUM stands for the supreme Reality.
   It is a symbol for what was, what is,
   And what shall be. AUM represents also
   What lies beyond past, present, and future.

2. Brahman is all, and the Self is Brahman.
   The Self has four states of consciousness.

3. The first is Vaishvanara, in which
   One lives with all the senses turned outward,
   Aware of only the external world.

4. Taijasa is the name of the second,
   The dreaming state in which, with the senses
   Turned inward, one enacts the impressions
   Of past deeds and present desires.

5. The third state is called Prajna, of deep sleep,
   In which one neither dreams nor desires.
   There is no mind in Prajna, there is no
   Separateness; but the sleeper is not
   Conscious of this. Let him become conscious
   In Prajna and it will open the door
   To the state of abiding joy.[7]

Waking mind, dreaming mind, and dreamless sleep are states of consciousness that are recapitulated in the states of being: mineral, vegetal, and animal. Rocks have the universal consciousness of dreamless sleep; they echo with the music of the spheres and in their heavy metal forms still ring with the vibration of the stellar supernova that formed our solar system. Plants do not echo with the music of the dead and vanished binary star that formed us, but with the star, our sun, that is still with us. They respond to light and live awash in a dreamy state of the collective consciousness: the forest and not the tree, the ecology and not merely the single organism. Animals, by contrast, move and are not rooted in the soil; they have individuated minds that have a targeted, highly focused waking consciousness, one intent on objects, on food. Higher animals, such as chimpanzees, have developed this objective level of awareness up to a primitive sense of self. The task of humans is to unite all these levels of consciousness—the mineral consciousness of dreamless sleep, the vegetal consciousness of dreaming mind, and the animal consciousness of the waking mind—into the pure light of superconsciousness in *samadhi*.

The yogic technique used by the teachers of the *Upanishads* was based on sound, the sound of the seed-mantra AUM, or Om as it is also transliterated. "Ah" is the sound of inhalation, the act of the conscious, waking mind. "Uh" is the sound of the suspended, interior activity of the dreaming mind. "Mmm" is the sound of delight as the mind returns to Brahman in the universal state of dreamless sleep. When all three sounds are joined in the single mantra of AUM, then the three minds also are joined in the higher state of yogic *samadhi*.

The mind of dreamless sleep is the mineral mind. The psychic, dreaming mind is the mind of plants; it consists of a dreaming, emotional reactivity and sensitivity without necessarily the ability to have motion or targeted consciousness. But with the animal, we have the emergence of a neural phase-space in which all of the signals that are coming in from different senses, coming in at different times, have to have a stable delay-space in which they can be cross-referenced. This field of cross-referencing can be called an ego. If one signal is coming in a half a second out of sync with another, then there has to be a delay-space in which the signals linger to become coordinated, and that moiré pattern in which the multiple channels of different senses—smell, sound, and sight—become coordinated is the emergent property or condition of the ego. So the ego is an evolutionary achievement of the animal consciousness and has a characteristic of target consciousness—of field and goal and purpose. *You* are hunting for *that*. You are a fox chasing a hare, and as you focus on it, you tend to forget everything else. You are not a stationary tree rooted in the soul of the forest interacting with the sun and the atmosphere. And you are not the rock of the sacred mountain interacting with and responding to the vibrational music of the stars. As an animal hot in pursuit of another, you have your own agenda, and that egoic, focused agenda is, from one point of view, a wonderful evolutionary achievement. It is not, I would claim, a psychopathology; it is actually an evolutionary emergent state. The ego only becomes psycho-pathological when we take it out of context to alienate a being from Being. If we lose the receptivity of the plant to the sun, and if we lose the sensitivity of the mineral kingdom to the galaxy, in which the crystalline lattice of the molecules of the sacred mountain are singing the ninety-nine names of God in resonance with Andromeda, then we get the isolated ego, alienated from Being and screaming in pain with the fear of death. If we lose a sense of the interconnectedness that underlies the extensive field of the delay-space of the ego, then, yes, we do have a psychopathology that the Buddhists seek to overcome by eliminating the sense of self, the ego. When the animal ego eliminates the elemental consciousness of immensity, as well as the psychic sensitivity to the "we" rather than the "I," then it becomes demonic. Then we get the kind of Luciferian inflation that we see in the character of Ravana in the *Ramayana,* or of Satan in Milton's *Paradise Lost.*

So the project of the *Upanishads* is to teach us how to yoke—the literal meaning of *yoga*—the individual development of ego and mind to the universal mind, to have Atman and Brahman become one. The first stage of this is, of course, the saturation in universal Brahmanic consciousness in which the ego simply disappears. Time and the world are stopped with the stilling of the breath and the heartbeat. But the *Bhagavad Gita,* developing out of this whole Vedic tradition, tries to go beyond the rejection of the world as illusion, as *maya,* to create a dynamical synthesis of the various traditions of Sankhya psychology and yogic practice and bring them together in a yoga of action in the world—a *karma yoga* that develops a sacralization of the personality. The ego embedded in the historical conditions of societal con-flict and battle is not to escape into a state of world-denying detachment, but to live in its time and offer the fruits of action to Krishna. This is the new idea of the sacrifice, the new psychological sublimation of the ancient idea of sacrifice presented in the *Rig Veda.* Attachment to achievement and accumulation is to be avoided by going beyond the ego to the *purusha,* the spirit that observes the natural processes of *prakriti.* The two birds of the *Rig Veda* and *Upanishads* are philosophically generalized into the two cosmic principles of spirit and nature, *purusha* and *prakriti.* But rather than celebrat-ing an inner Atman that is an aloof and disdaining witness to the vain illusions and deceptions of history, the *Bhagavad Gita* celebrates an individ-uated *purusha,* a divination of individuation, and this interior divinity is the *purushottama.*[8] This is the part of the self that is the interface between Atman and Brahman but is nevertheless a celebration and affirmation of individuation and Being. In the vision of the *Gita,* being isn't in conflict with Being. William Blake's way of describing this affirmative mode of perception would be to say that eternity is in love with the productions of time.

So the *Bhagavad Gita* presents us with a yoga through which we can achieve the resolution of individual existence and cosmic process. Gilgamesh is not able to become the sage Utnapishtim, but Arjuna is able to move beyond his heroic, extroverted self to have the vision of divinity. The *Gita* tells us specifically how to find a quiet place, how to sit, how to watch the breath, how to practice mediation to achieve enlightenment. In yoga, we sit at the edge of our breath the way we would sit at the edge of the ocean. The ordinary person can go to the seashore, watch the waves of the ocean come in and out, and feel a kind of universal peace, but the yogi can sit at the shore of his own breath, watching inhalation come and go, watching thoughts pass like clouds through the vast sky of his nonthinking mind. Thoughts come and go, but the yogi knows that his big mind is the sky and not the clouds of discrete thoughts.

We will also come across this yoga of breath next when we consider the *Tao Te Ching.* Chapter 10 of the *Tao Te Ching* asks, "In concentrating your breath and making it soft — can you make it like that of a child?"[9] The Bible can tell us, in Matthew 6:22, that "the eye is the light of the body, and if thine eye be single, thy whole body shall be full of light," but says "if"; it doesn't give us specific instructions on how to achieve the opening of the third eye and illumination. Unfortunately for all of us in Christendom, illumination became identified with crazy heretics and Gnostics who claimed to have secret knowledge. The Gnostics were first denounced by Bishop Irenaeus in the second century; as the church gained social power, heretics of all sorts were killed in such pogroms as the Albigensian Crusade and, later, in the Inquisition, and the persecution of witches in particular and women in general. Anyone who ever claimed to have had an individual and direct experience of the divine was considered a heretical threat to the church and was tortured and burned at the stake. So Christianity lost the specific yogic knowledge of how to progress from illumination through initiation to enlightenment. The yogic techniques were only alive in other traditions, such as the Jewish Cabala, the Sufi mystery schools, the yogic ashrams, the Tibetan Tantric and Zen Buddhist traditions, and Taoist alchemy.

This loss is the tragedy of the West and is why in the New Age movement of the 1960s and 1970s, we had to travel all over the world to recover this lost esoteric knowledge. This cultural project was, of course, not the first effort in this direction, for at the turn of the century, the

Theosophical movement was hard at work to bring yogic knowledge into the general culture of our Western scientific civilization.

In defense of orthodoxy, one can say that two of the dangers of Gnosticism are an astral entrapment and an intense denial of the material world. Gnostics are prey to psychic inflation and a self-elected guruhood in which magic generates a sense of the sorcerer's power that can bring about a loss of heart, a loss of compassion. Notice that in Carlos Castenada's popular books about the Yaqui sorcerer Don Juan, that Don Juan is always talking about being located in a hostile universe in which he has to wage a battle of competing energies against inorganic beings.[10] This is not Dante's vision of "the love that moves the sun and others stars." In 2 Corinthians, St. Paul, struggling to find an opening for Christianity between Roman imperial persecution and Near Eastern Gnostic psychosis, says that if one becomes like a sounding brass but has not love then one has lost the Christ. So the battle between Gnosticism and orthodoxy developed into a battle between Gnostic escape from the world through special knowing and the Christian emphasis on love and society that, ironically, ended in Inquisitorial cruelty and political tyranny. The tragedy of the West is that both sides were wrong, and so we all lost.

But the genius of the *Bhagavad Gita* is that it doesn't separate gnosis from the world, and that is the unique excellence of the text. It is very much about *bakhti* and karma yoga , the paths of devotion and being in the world, even in the most difficult circumstances imaginable — of being right in the middle of a battlefield. In a stroke of literary genius, the anonymous author of the *Gita* inserted his yogic transformation of the individual and history, time and eternity, Arjuna and Krishna, right into the primary epic of his culture, the great battle poem of the *Mahabharata.* So the *Gita* is a climactic text for Vedic culture; it takes all the themes that were introduced and developed in the *Rig Veda* and the *Upanishads* and raises them up to such a new level that it completes and consummates them. The *Gita* becomes not simply an Indian literary work but an expression of a universal human culture. In this sense, the *Bhagavad Gita,* as a climactic Indian text becomes for us now, a formative text for our planetary culture.

In our global development, we have moved from the ancient arithmetic mentality to the classical geometrical mentality to the modernist dynamical mentality and now finally to the new chaos dynamical mentality, a mentality that is based on the new sciences of complexity, on the new art forms that cross one genre with another, and on the new multidisciplinary sciences such as Lovelock's geophysiology that give us a biospheric vision our new planetary cultural ecology. Each of these historical mentalities has expressed itself in a great, climactic text that rose above its historical limitations to become a universal work of art. The Gilgamesh epic, the *Bhagavad Gita,* and the *Tao Te Ching* are therefore not simply ancient texts that are the intellectual property of scholars and academic specialists; they are last wills and testaments through which the ancients bequeathed to us the wealth that belongs to all of us, not simply to the scholars of ancient languages in the academy. If we come forward and claim these ancient texts as our own, then paradoxically the past of the sages that never really had its time to manifest as a civilization creates a visionary future that our present industrial society is not capable of becoming on its own. All of this is not about them; it is about us.

THE ROAD
NOT TAKEN:
CHAOS DYNAMICS
AND THE COSMIC
FEMININE IN THE
TAO TE CHING

Throughout this study of literature and the evolution of consciousness, I have used the metaphor of the catastrophe bifurcation and said that humanity is experiencing a catastrophe bifurcation in the emergence of a new global civilization. "Catastrophe" is a word that English has taken from Greek; it means "to turn over." When we turn over material in a compost heap, we create a catastrophe for the anaerobic bacteria in the rotting garbage as we suddenly flood them with oxygen and sunlight. The chaos dynamists say that there are three kinds of catastrophes: subtle, explosive, and "out of the blue." The mathematicians' use of these poetic metaphors makes me feel as if it is quite all right for me to return the favor and use their idea of a catastrophe bifurcation as a poetic metaphor for a cultural transformation of history. Since I have been arguing all along that literature and mathematics have been inseparably linked throughout history in the arithmetic, geometric, dynamical, and now chaos dynamical mentalities, this collaboration between metaphor and math is quite appropriate. Since I am a cultural historian and not a prophet, I have no idea whether this catastrophe will be subtle, explosive, or out of the blue. I tend to think that our process of global cultural transformation is so complex a dynamic that it will be all three at once. The economic shift is subtle, the cultural shift is explosive, and the spiritual one is out of the blue.

To perceive our unique historical condition in time in this shift from an international culture of economically competing and warring industrial nation-states to a biospheric ecology of noetic polities, we need to look at other times in history during which humanity experienced systemic transformations of culture. Each of the earlier transformations has a certain descriptive power, but each is limited because all of them seem to be descriptive; it seems as if we are experiencing a great coda and recapitulation of human evolution. Because genetic engineering and the newly emerging nanotechnologies allow us to tinker with evolution by natural selection, we can say that our contemporary cultural transformation is greater than the one that took place during the industrial revolution and is more like the hominization of the primates, when we stepped out of nature into culture for the first time. Because our new global systems of electronic communication seem to be so constitutive of our new informational culture, we can also look back to the Renaissance, with its shift from medievalism to modernism, to see it as a metaphor for our historical situation. But what is unique to our time, and what makes these earlier examples of cultural transformation inadequate as models of our time, is the change in the rate of change itself. The hominization of the primates took place over millions of years, and even those comparatively rapid transformations such as the Renaissance and the industrial revolution took place over more than a century. The rate of change for our contemporary cultural transformation is so rapid and so intense that it is occurring within the space of an individual's lifetime—which is another way of saying that the individual life and consciousness is now constitutive of the dynamic of the planetary transformation. Our consciousness is now actually part of the phase-space of the new noetic polity; in fact, this is why I choose to use such new terms as noetic or musical polities. The quantum physicists have told us that this intimate relationship between mind and matter is true for the microcosm of elementary particles, so we should suspect that it is even more dynamically perceivable for the macrocosm of our global cultural situation.

If the individual consciousness is part of the complex dynamical system of our new biospheric cultural ecology, then we need to develop a healthier appreciation of consciousness and not simply look to descriptions of technology as if they were descriptions of culture. Historians, for the most part, simply do not do this, but continually limit their descriptions to technological terms such as the Stone Age, the Bronze Age, the Iron Age, the "plutonium age." If I seem weird as a cultural historian, and disturbingly unprofessional to my academic colleagues in the universities, it is because I do not restrict myself to technological and economic descriptions and reach out for models of consciousness in art, religion, and more highly developed explorations of consciousness in the world's mystical traditions. My fascination with mysticism as a model of consciousness has gotten me into a lot of trouble in the normal worlds of journalistic and academic criticism, but I think that if our culture in general were to adopt the "eliminativism" of the neurophilosophy of Patricia and Paul Churchland and the nonexplanations of consciousness of Dan Dennett,[1] then we all would get into much more trouble as the noetic polity of our planetary culture went into collapse. Our failure of imagination in the effort to understand consciousness would generate, not simply an economic depression, but a cultural dark age, in fact, an evolutionary collapse. The most immediate and external expression of this collapse would be "the war of all against all" that Rudolf Steiner predicted could be a possible end for the twentieth century. This condition would be one in which global systems of organized crime—the Medellín cartel, the Italian Mafia, the Russian Mafia, and the Chinese Mafia—interlock with nuclear terrorist attacks and ethnic and national warfare to produce a cultural condition of entropy that could not be brought under the control of any national system of governance. The American president would not be able to go on television to give a speech in which he told reality to stop and begin to behave in a civilized manner.

Because the transformation of culture is now an event that takes place within the time frame of an individual human life, our consciousness of culture is actually part of the dynamical system of the cultural transformation. The chaos dynamists have taught us about the "butterfly effect," of how the flapping of a butterfly's wings in Mexico can generate a blizzard in Moscow. In the cascade of accumulating events, an individual event can generate an enormous difference in the complex dynamical system. One single bifurcation can lead to an entirely new evolutionary chreod.[2] If individual consciousness is now constitutive of our global complex of nature and culture, amplified as it now is by electronic networks, then the individual consciousness can be far more dynamically effective now than it has been before in history. Now more than ever, we need to appreciate the linkage of consciousness and culture. And one very good place to look to gain an appreciation of the effect of consciousness on the transformation of culture is to that period of global change that the German philosopher Karl Jaspers called the first axial period of world civilization, the sixth century B.C.E.

In this great coda and recapitulation of human history, we are now turning on the spiral of time and the first axial period that expressed a spiritual evolution of humanity all across the world — from Pythagoras and the Greeks to the Hebrew prophets to Buddha in India and Lao Tzu in China — is closer to us now than it was to our great-grandfathers who lived in the era of the European empires and the technological expansion of the West. The esoteric teachings of the conquered peoples — yoga, Zen, Sufism, Taoism, and Native American spirituality — are being retrieved by the children of the technological overlords. There are now literally thousands of teachers and spiritual leaders moving across cultural boundaries.

In the first axial period, the civilizational movement that had begun in the fourth millennium B.C.E. reached its end and crystallized in militaristic terror. Assyrian militarism and collectivization through terror was what civilization at that time was all about. Militarism and the suppression of the feminine brought forth a new dark age culture of violence. And yet, right in the heart of that culture of militarist violence came the global emanation of all the initiatic dispensations, including Pythagoras, the Hebrew prophets, Buddha and Kapila, and the unknown author of the *Bhagavad Gita* in India, and Lao Tzu and Confucius in China. This first axial period expressed a cultural shift from militaristic empires to moral civilizations. And now, once again, we are in a period of militaristic violence — in Bosnia, Somalia, Rwanda, Afghanistan, Armenia, Chechnya — and because of fundamentalist and nationalist hysterias everywhere, we are quite possibly moving toward a form of global cultural entropy. If we attempt to stabilize our condition by seeking to go back to the familiar world of the nation-state, the race, the fundamentalist religion, or the tribe, we will end up increasing violence in a planetary Bosnia in which each of these social forms of identity seeks supremacy over the other. The only way out is up, but to understand the openings of this higher dimension, we need to have just the kind of insight that the visionary philosophers of the first axial period provided for their time.

The *Tao Te Ching* is a major document of this cultural shift of the axial period. The anarchic Taoism of Lao Tzu held out a vision of culture to humanity, but humanity voted no. Taoism is the road not taken. The ancient

Chinese chose the other road in the fork—the road of hierarchy and order, of Confucian propriety crystallized into an imperial civil service, and of a geometrization of the world space in which the Chinese were at the center of the universe and inferior foreigners were at the periphery. The flow of the Tao and the anarchic wisdom of Taoism went underground to surface again in isolated springs of Chan and Zen Buddhism.

I see the *Tao Te Ching* as a once and future vision of possibilities, as a metaphor for where we are once again as we enter a second axial period, and in the catastrophe bifurcation of the present, reconfront the fork in the road to wonder about the road not taken long ago. To appreciate the historical context of Lao Tzu, known as "the Old One of Long Ears," consider the following poem from the *Book of Songs*—which was supposedly edited by Confucius. The poems are, of course, much older than Confucius's edition, and the date assigned to this poem by its translator is 685 B.C.E. The poem gives us a sense of where the culture was then in terms of the nature of the community and the relationship between masculine and feminine in the articulation of nature.

Ceaseless flows that beck,
Far stretch the southern hills.
May you be sturdy as the bamboo,
May you flourish like the pine.
May elder brother and younger brother
Always love one another,
Never do evil to one another.
To give continuance to foremothers and forefathers,
We build a house, many hundred cubits of wall;
To the south and east its doors.
Here shall we live, here rest,
Here laugh, here talk.
We bind the frames, creak, creak;
We hammer the mud, tap, tap,
That it may be a place where wind and rain cannot enter,
Nor birds and rats get in,
But where our lord may dwell.
As the halberd, even so plumed,
As an arrow, even so sharp,
As a bird, even so soaring,
As wings, even so flying,

Are the halls to which our lord ascends.
Well leveled is the courtyard,
Firm are the pillars,
Cheerful are the rooms by day,
softly glowing by night,
A place where our lord can be at peace.
Below, the rush mats; over them, the bamboo mats.
Comfortably he sleeps,
He sleeps and wakes
And interprets his dreams.
'Your lucky dreams, what were they?'
'They were of black bears and brown,
Of serpents and snakes.'
The diviner thus interprets it:
'Black bears and brown
Mean men-children.
Snakes and serpents
Mean girl children.'

So he bears a son,
And puts him to sleep upon a bed,
Clothes him in robes
Gives him a jade scepter to play with.
The child's howling is very lusty.
In red greaves shall he flare,
Be lord and king of house and home.
Then he bears a daughter,
And puts her upon the ground,
Clothes her in swaddling clothes,
Gives her a loom-whorl to play with.
For her no decorations, no emblems;
Her only care the wine and food
and how to give no trouble to father and mother.[3]

Lao Tzu's celebration of "the mysterious female" is in direct opposition to the dominant culture of his time. The world around Lao Tzu is the patriarchal world of warriorship, of hierarchy and geometrical order. In the Mandarin model of the world space, there is respect for the ancestors, for the fathers, and for the women — mothers, wives, concubines, daughters —

who all know and keep their place. The settlement is square. From early Anyang to the later Forbidden City of Beijing, the human settlement is square and is a crystallization of the four quarters. In this geometrization of the world space, life is fixed in rigid custom and the imperial civil servant is its avatar.

The Tao, like light, seems to be both wave and particle, and Lao Tzu and Confucius archetypally express its complementarity. Confucius saw the Tao as immanental in human relationships; he strove to embody the Tao in the modes of justice and propriety. For a time, he even served as a chief of police, and for the last fourteen years of his life he traveled all over China, trying to establish a society of justice and decorum; but in spite of his efforts China slid down into civil war and chaos.[4] Lao Tzu is the mirror opposite of this call to the world of civic duty; his Tao is the long wave and not the discrete particle. Small wonder that he left the court and the centers of princely power and took to the hills. In our century, this archetypal opposition is like the difference between the revolutionary nationalists Mahatma Gandhi and Sri Aurobindo: one moves into revolutionary politics but cannot avert a civil war, the other moves into exile and the politics of human evolution. Legend has it that as Lao Tzu left the kingdom, the border guard demanded that he leave something behind, so the old anarchic sage took brush in hand and left him—and us—with the poems of the *Tao Te Ching*. So opposite to patriarchal, warrior society is Lao Tzu that he seems to reach back into the world that existed before civilization, before patriarchy and the militaristic organization of society. The anarchic—which in Greek means of the original—Taoism of Lao Tzu expresses what in anthropology would be called a nativistic movement.

Nativistic movements are revitalization movements that seek to take a culture back to its roots in a mythically recreated past. When a traditional culture is at the edge of extinction, then a mystery school springs up that seeks to go back to the ways of the ancestors as a way of avoiding the decadence of the moderns. Think of the Ghost Dance of the American Plains Indians in the nineteenth century. Think of the insurrection of the Métis in Canada led by the messianic figure Louis Riel, of the revolt of the Mahdi against the English in the Anglo-Egyptian Sudan, or of Patrick Pearse, the leader of the 1916 Easter Rising of the Irish against the English. Think of Jomo Kenyatta in Kenya and Malcolm X in New York.

The nativistic movement is a universal phenomenon. When a traditional culture is at the edge of extinction, and when a new technological civilization is consolidating its conquest and dominance, then the last light of the old flares up. Most often the nativistic leader is the divided man who in his own parentage feels the intense conflict between the dominant culture of the father and the ancient culture of the mother. Malcolm X, the fair-skinned Black man with red hair, said that he hated the White rapist's blood that flowed in his veins. One can trace this archetypal pattern all the way back to Moses in the Bible or Quetzalcoatl in Mexico. Recall the famous picture of Gandhi in top hat and morning coat—when the English had him caught in their culture—to understand the passion with which he traded his British clothes for an Indian loin cloth. Think of Aurobindo, the Cambridge University graduate, the man British Intelligence identified as the most dangerous revolutionary in India, and then consider the passion with which he throws it all aside to return to his native Mother India. Lao Tzu is one of this visionary company of men who seek to revitalize an ancient and ignored culture.

The leader of a nativistic movement is someone who is torn apart by the "cognitive dissonance," the contradictions of his simultaneous belonging to two worlds. The nativistic leader is one who rejects the technological, dominating masculine culture of the overlords to identify with the culture of the downtrodden, the culture of the raped mother. Often, in his own family life, the nativistic leader experiences the cultural clash as embodied in his parental relationships. The archetypal situation would be one in which the alien father enters as the warrior, conquers the local culture, kills the men, and rapes the women. From this violent union, a child is born who does not know who he is or which culture he should affirm. But while the father is busy with empire and conquest, the son is raised by the mother, and she whispers to him subversive tales of the old ways, the old culture. And so as an adolescent feeling the first stirrings of his own emotional and sexual force, he vows to win back the body of the mother from its domination by the cruel father. Thus, Patrick Pearse as a boy gets down on his knees and vows to free Mother Ireland from the domination of the English. Patrick Pearse changed his name to Padraic in the spirit of the Gaelic Revival, but Pearse's father was English, and Padraic's baptismal name was Patrick Henry Pearse. There were several Quetzalcoatls in Mexico, some mythic, others legendary, but the last of the Quetzalcoatls was a prophetic leader named Ca Acatl Topiltzin. This Quetzalcoatl probably had a Toltec father and a Teotihuacan mother. I have written about this legendary figure in my book *Blue Jade from the Morning Star*.[5] I suppose I have written two books on nativistic movements, one on Quetzalcoatl, the other on the insurrection in Dublin in 1916,[6] because the collision of two worlds, of two religions, fascinates me since my mother was Roman Catholic and of southern Irish ancestry, and my father was Presbyterian and of northern Irish ancestry. The Lindisfarne Association, in its own way, is a highly refined version of a nativistic movement; it attempts to counter technological domination through a resacralization of science brought about by an energizing of the old esoteric mysteries. Having learned the ways of the overlords at MIT, and having succeeded in their world on their terms, I took a radical turn in the 1960s and abandoned that technological definition of culture to seek out the ways of the ancestors. Against a global backdrop of religious warfare, I worked to bring all the esoteric yogic practices of the world's universal religions together in a spiritual fellowship of artists, scientists, and contemplatives. Of course, having the benefit of history, and seeing the delusions of messianic grandeur expressed in people such as Padraic Pearse and Louis Riel, I had enough of my father's good Protestant common sense to avoid both the revolutionary delusions of politics and the paranoid delusions of religion to seek out the way of the writer who moves to the edge as a way of avoiding the basin of attraction of the center. I read Lao Tzu's *Tao Te Ching* when I was sixteen, and the archetypal pattern of the sage who abandons the capital to take to the hills and write poetry and practice yoga was absolutely entrancing to me. It was another confirmation of James Joyce's vision of "silence, exile, and cunning" as a way of creating a conscience higher than Roman Catholicism or Irish nationalism through art.

So for me the *Tao Te Ching* is more than an ancient archival document, a quaint scholarly antique. It is a work that determined the formation of my life. As a work that captures the whole genius of the axial period, it captures the whole sense of mystery through which culture is influenced and inspired by the impulses from another realm. One cannot explain the axial period of Pythagoras and Lao Tzu in a simple system of cultural trade and transmission. One has to think of this global cultural transformation more in the way that Doris Lessing describes it in her novel *Briefing for a Descent into Hell.*[7] This is a story about souls in the spiritual world before birth organizing a rescue mission in which several people determine to take incarnations in various cultures as a way of countering a great evolutionary crisis. No one culture owns or is to dominate the transformation. So the New Age movement of my time is not owned by Findhorn or Auroville, by Steiner or Aurobindo, or Anybodynanda. Followers always try to own the transformation. So the anthroposophists lock on to Steiner, or Satprem, a follower of Aurobindo and secretary to the Mother, literalizes the metaphor of the cells, deifies the Mother, and, essentially, canonizes himself. The substitution of cult for culture is the mistake all followers make, but it is a mistake that anarchic Lao Tzu did not make. He did not found a religion and build temples to himself. He celebrated a process and did not try to sell a product. A Foucault pendulum has a distinct point, but its phase-space is vastly larger than its point. Looking at the prophet and ignoring the phase-space of cultural transformation is stupid because that system of idolatry just drags us down into a civic religion. We end up back in the world of the temple, the palace, the imperial civil service, and, eventually, back into the conquering armies of empire. What we have in the case of the nativistic leader is someone who feels the cognitive dissonance of the conflicting cultures, but identifies with the dominated feminine rather than the dominating masculine, who identifies with the subtle rather than the objectively obvious, with the weak rather than the mighty, with the past rather than the present. So I see Lao Tzu as a nativistic leader who is seeking to go back to a more ancient Taoist culture. Lao Tzu did not invent Taoism, and he was called "the Old One" not so much because he himself was old, but because he is an invocation and recovery of the ancient culture of the ancestors, of the Old Ones. The *I Ching* is more ancient than the *Tao Te Ching*. There are clear indications that the idea of the Tao and the alchemical process that proclaims that "Reversal is the movement of the Tao," as well as the hieroglyph of yin and yang are all traditional materials that antedate Lao Tzu.

So Lao Tzu is clearly not creating a new religion. He is attempting to go back and hold on to ancient wisdom, and the worldview he is trying to recover is the exact mirror opposite of everything that is ascendant in his time. If one wants to understand Lao Tzu, one has only to hold the text up to a mirror and ask oneself, what is the mirror opposite of what Lao Tzu puts forth. Reality for the civilization of his time meant hard masculine action, accumulation of wealth, and possession of vast territories in big states; reality was the weapon, war, the territorial conquest and expansion of a supremely empowered ego personified in the figure of the emperor. Now, negate all those values, deconstruct each one of these objective realities, and you get the anarchic subtlety of Lao Tzu. Rather than the celebration of the spear and the sword, we find in the *Tao Te Ching* the celebration of the prehistoric vulva as the primordial icon of the cosmos:

Chapter 6:

The valley spirit never dies;
We call it the mysterious female.
The gates of the mysterious female —

These we call the roots of Heaven and Earth.
Subtle yet everlasting! It seems to exist.
In being used, it is not exhausted.[8]

The phallus, by contrast, in being used is exhausted. It dramatically
expands, triples its size, trumpets forth its seed, and then collapses into
exhaustion as it withdraws back into its humble state. Cock or king, organ
or empire, it's much the same thing.

Now, if we recall the writings of Marija Gimbutas on "the Civilization
of the Goddess," we will remember that the world's first universal religion,
from Iberia to Siberia, was the religion of the Great Goddess. This religion
of the great mother was spread everywhere, even into the New World. I
remember how surprised I was when I was in Tiahuanaco in Bolivia and one
of the Quechua Indians at the site was selling a little piece of hand-carved
stone that he called Patcha Mama. Two figures were joined at the hips into
the rock that held them in common; one woman was the matron with fully
developed breasts, the other was the maiden with small and budding breasts.
James Mellaart, the excavator of Çatal Hüyük, found an almost identical
small figure from Neolithic Anatolia, dating from 6500 B.C.E. This archetypal
couple of the matron and the maiden is older than the patriarchal couple of
dad and mom, Zeus and Hera. These images of the eternal feminine—
Goethe's *ewige Weibliche*—are part of the most ancient tradition of humanity's
first universal religion. Lao Tzu's project is, therefore, the expression of a
nativistic movement that seeks to recover the values of this lost culture.

The gates of the female are obviously the vulva, and the valley is, of
course, another kind of vulva. As I have mentioned before, our English word
"cunt" is really an ancient sacred word that is connected to a cosmology. You
can still see it in Spanish: *cuñeta* means ditch, and so the archaic notion of the
feminine is this fertile ditch of Mother Earth. Priests and ministers will tell
us that "cunt" is "a bad word," but anyone who has seen the artist Judy
Chicago's famous installation of the dinner party knows that the cunt is a
wisecrack.

Chapter 28:

When you know the male yet hold on to the female,
You'll be the ravine of the country.
When you are the ravine of the country,
Your constant virtue will not leave.

And when your constant virtue doesn't leave,
You return to the state of the infant.[9]

It is hard, in our language, to translate these ancient ideas. Although Lao Tzu is speaking about the cosmic feminine, Henricks, in his transition, uses the word "virtue." But virtue comes from the Latin word for man, *vir*, and so millennia of patriarchal association cling to this classical term; it carries ideas of manly virtue, nobility, the intrinsic male seminal essence. So even our very notion of virtue carries with it several thousand years of patriarchal cosmology. Since Lao Tzu is trying to deconstruct the whole complex of warrior values, translation becomes supremely difficult.

Chapter 76:

When people are born, they are supple and soft;
When they die, they end up stretched out firm and rigid;
When the ten thousand things of grasses and trees are alive,
they're supple and pliant.[10]

In the processual worldview of Tao, we encounter the mirror opposite of the geometrical worldview in which all things are fixed into their proper place in an abstract, mental space. Objects located within this world space, are hard, fixed, and crystalline, but the Tao is subtle, soft, and feminine. The cosmic process of the Great Mother can embrace opposites; it is a dynamical and inclusive movement in which "reversal is the movement of Tao." Objects that are fixed within an abstractly idealized world space can be thought to have single causes, but in a processual world view, whether it is Lao Tzu's or Whitehead's, simple location and single causes are naive simplifications. What Lao Tzu is celebrating is what has finally come round again now in our second axial period as we move from linear systems of causation to chaos dynamics and what, at the Santa Fe Institute, is called "the new sciences of complexity."

The primary metaphor for the object in all its obviousness is the erect phallus, and the primary metaphor for the subtlety of the Tao is the ravine, the vagina, the form whose very nature comes from its emptiness.

When they are dead, they are withered and dried out.
Therefore we say that the firm and rigid are companions of death,
While the supple, the soft, the weak and the delicate are
companions of life[11]

Here we encounter the archetype of the rigid phallus versus the soft vulva.

> If a soldier is rigid, he won't win;
> If a tree is rigid, it will come to its end.
> Rigidity and power occupy the inferior position;
> Suppleness, softness, weakness and delicateness occupy the superior position.[12]

When all of these images — of flow, of process, of softness and subtlety, of reversal in which that which is completely empty holds the essence of life — are added up, then what we see is an anarchic vision of a culture that is the antithesis of everything we would understand as the State. Confucius affirms *li* (propriety), the virtue of each person and object in its place in the geometrical worldview. But propriety can all too easily become simply property as women are tamed and domesticated into mothers, wives, concubines, and obedient daughters. Eventually, if they are not killed at birth as unwanted daughters, they become objects of display whose bound and mutilated feet are not allowed to contact the powerful ground of Mother Earth. Through the power of literacy — the technology that split humanity between literate and illiterate — the bureaucrats of the imperial civil service would wed writing and militarism to create the hierarchy of the State.

Lao Tzu's anarchic vision may seem impossible and utopian, but what is being presented is really a vision of the prehistoric matristic village. If one reads Marija Gimbutas's *Civilization of the Goddess,* and looks at her excavations of those prehistoric villages that were not fortresses but agricultural villages, one can see that the way of life that she describes as the Old Europe of 6000 B.C.E. is basically what Lao Tzu is trying to recover in 600 B.C.E.

Chapter 80:

> Let the states be small and people few —
> Bring it about that there are weapons for "tens" and "hundreds,"
>   yet no one use them;
> Have the people regard death gravely and put migrating far from
>   their minds
> Though they might have boats and carriages, no one will ride them;
> Though they might have armor and spears, no one will display them.
> Have the people return to knotting cords and using them.

They will relish their food,
Regard their clothing as beautiful,
Delight in their customs,
And feel safe and secure in their homes.
Neighboring states might overlook one another,
And the sounds of chickens and dogs might be overheard,
Yet the people will arrive at old age and death with no comings
and goings between them.[13]

This is not a vision of capital-intensive economies of scale and state transport systems but rather of autonomous individual villages saturated with a sense of the larger process of circularity of the Tao. And what is empowering the release of possessions and possessiveness is the practice of a yoga that enables the completely autonomous individual to connect directly with the Tao. Now here is where translations really become important. Some of the yogic practices that Lao Tzu describes are very clearly knowledge that only an initiate could have. Only an initiate practitioner of these yogic techniques would recognize what the metaphors are describing. When one looks at Stephen Mitchell's translation of the *Tao Te Ching*,[14] one sees a politically correct, New Age text, one that says "she" instead of "he." Mitchell is trying to show that New Age sensitive males are not as bad as their NFL-watching, beer-drinking contemporaries. But the difficulty is that Mitchell translates the text into his contemporary subculture. So what we get is Marin County rather than ancient China.

Consider Mitchell's translation of chapter 10:

Can you coax your mind from its wandering
and keep to the original oneness?
Can you let your body become
supple as a newborn child's?
Can you cleanse your inner vision
until you see nothing but the light?
Can you love people and lead them
without imposing your will?
Can you deal with the most vital matters
by letting events take their course?
Can you step back from your own mind
and thus understand all things?

Giving birth and nourishing,
having without possessing
Acting with no exception
Leading and not trying to control:
this is the supreme virtue.[15]

Robert Henricks's *Te-Tao Ching* seems much closer to the Chinese worldview, and so if we are trying to excavate the evolution of conscious-ness—to tell the human story from one end to the other—then getting a feeling for the archaic Chinese mind is critical to understanding the unfold-ing of one mentality into another. If modern translations make the text sound too much like our time, then they make it impossible to get a sense of what another mentality might have been like.

To prove to you that I am not being too hard on Mitchell, let me give you the same poem, chapter 10, as it is translated by Henricks. The first line—"In nourishing the soul and embracing the One—can you do it without letting them leave?"—means can you practice yoga so that the soul and the subtle bodies are not actually leaving the body and thus putting you into a kind of comatose death-state, but instead can you practice observing your state of consciousness so that you experience a conscious death. The stop-ping of the heart in meditation and the suspension of the breath is an advanced yogic practice.

In concentrating your breath and making it soft—can you make it like that of a child?[16]

In contrast to Henricks, Mitchell turns the image of the baby's breath into a sweet, California metaphor for having a skin soft as a baby's:

Can you let your body become supple as a newborn child's?[17]

The text is not talking about baby skin and a California getting in touch with one's inner child; it is talking about an esoteric yogic breathing tech-nique. To be specific, there is one yogic technique in which one says "hong" upon inhalation, and "sau" upon exhalation. (In some other Indian dialects, this is written as *ham-sa*.) One sits at the edge of one's breath, and watches the waves come in and out—the thoughts like clouds in the sky coming and going—and eventually, breath, thoughts, and heartbeat go away, and one passes into a state of immersion in the Tao. As one begins to sit at the edge of one's own breath, the breath gets softer and softer, like a baby's breath, and eventually it disappears totally. When the breath disappears, then the heart stops also and one's mode of consciousness shifts from waking mind into *samadhi*. Of course, this is an advanced practice, so it doesn't happen right away. It takes some years of faithful, committed practice. But when it happens, "the gates of heaven open," as Lao Tzu describes it in Henricks's translation of this same chapter 10.

> In opening and closing the gates of Heaven—can you play the part of the female?

Lao Tzu is using "the gates of heaven" as a metaphor and icon of the vulva, of the cosmic feminine, of what in yoga would be called the *shakti;* but the gates are also symbols of the chakras and the subtle body system. When one sensitizes oneself through the practice of yoga, then one shifts one's consciousness from the conventional feeling of the muscular, meat body to these other swirls of energy. Then one begins to move through the gates of heaven, then one feels *tan tien* or *Hara* in Japanese Zen—the center below the navel. So Lao Tzu, here in the poem of chapter 10, is metaphorically describing a particular yogic practice:

> In cultivating and cleaning your profound mirror—can you do it so that it has no blemish?"

Lao Tzu's image of cleaning one's profound mirror is one that passed over from Taoism into Zen Buddhism. In his book *Religion and Nothingness,* [18] the great Buddhist philosopher and Zen practitioner, Keiji Nishitani—whom I met in Kyoto shortly before his death—discusses this metaphor of Dogen's (the founder of the Soto Zen lineage) of the profound mirror inside the mind and how through Zen meditation one must polish the mirror so that it is without blemish. Another image that Nishitani uses is a silver bowl filled with snow. There is a famous tale of koan practice in which the Zen master looks at his student and asks him, "Have you had your breakfast?" The student answers yes, and then the master responds by saying, "Then clean your bowl." Koan language is a highly metaphoric code in which practitioners signal back and forth to one another in the highly stylized culture of the Zen monastery. What this language means, when translated into our sensibility, is this: The Zen master, being an advanced initiate, can see the aura of the subtle bodies of his students in the meditation hall, the Zendo. He sees that one of his students has achieved an advanced level of attainment, so he asks him, metaphorically, if he has had his breakfast, and in this case the breakfast is of light rather than miso soup. The student responds in the affirmative, but with such a sense of attachment to his own achievement that it indicates there is still a lingering sense of pride of accomplishment, so the master counsels him immediately to avoid the dangers of inflation by cleaning his bowl, his vessel. The goal is a state of unity in enlightenment in which there is no lingering sense of the self that can say, "Wow! I've just had an enlightenment experience." The chosen image of this union of vessel and light is snow in a silver bowl. Henricks's translation preserves the clarity of reference to meditational practices:

> In loving the people and giving life to the state — can you do it
>   without using knowledge?
> In opening and closing the gates of Heaven — can you play the
>   part of the female?

Can you become passive? Can you get out of your own way? Can you give birth without trying to own the child? All the metaphors chosen are expressions of the feminine. Henricks's translation concludes:

> Give birth to them and nourish them.
> Give birth to them but don't try to own them;
> Help them to grow but don't rule them.
> That is called Profound Virtue.

"Virtue" is not *le mot juste*, but we don't have a word for it; presumably, the word should be something like *femina*. All in all, when one tries to reach across time to enter into the spirit of the *Tao Te Ching*, it is necessary to read more than one translation. The translation that inspired me when I was a teenager was the verse translations of R. B. Blackney, which I still prefer to Mitchell's, but Henricks's is very good and does enable one to recognize the esoteric practices. Each translator has his own agenda, and so if he is a White sensitive New Age male from Marin County who has done some Zen, then what you are going to get is a White sensitive male's New Age *Tao Te Ching* that will make it sound as if it were written in northern California in 1994. Superficially, Mitchell's version may seem more poetic, and his edition may be more popular, but Henricks's is superior. It expresses the strength of a

Sinologist who has studied recently discovered ancient texts that antedate
the canonical text of the *Tao Te Ching* and has undertaken the labor of an
entirely new translation. But unlike scholars of religion who translate
esoteric texts without any feeling or knowledge of the experiences they
present in their translations, Henricks has preserved the allusions to yogic
practices. This combination of rigorous scholarship and gentle sensitivity is
appropriate to the text and fitting expression of "the mysterious female."

To bring all of this to a close, I choose to end this discussion of
literature and the evolution of consciousness with Henricks's *Te-Tao Ching*
because it presents us with the fork in the road that is relevant to our future
evolution of consciousness. The Taoist vision takes us back to the prehistoric
feminine and points to a posthistoric feminine we are only now beginning to
appreciate. In this celebration of the feminine, this recovery of the first
universal religion of humanity, this celebration of anarchic decentralization
and dispersed villages, we glimpse the possibilities of a world that is an
alternative to the giantism of transnational cyberpunk corporations and
monstrous cities such as Tokyo, Mexico, Los Angeles, and São Paulo. Like
the metaindustrial villages I wrote about almost a generation ago in *Darkness
and Scattered Light*,[19] these villages cannot come into being without a certain
yogic knowledge of coming into Being. Lao Tzu's villages can be dispersed
because they are saturated with the experience of the Tao. Obviously if we
don't have this sense of the Tao then what we do have is what Karl Marx
called the idiocy of rural life. Without the yoga, the village doesn't work.
With the yoga, the unique individual is an exemplar of the Universal. Right
now we are at a crossroads and do not know whether the distributive lattice
of electronic information will be controlled by transnational corporations
that produce a global MTV culture or by individuals dissolving the mediations of the state to generate the immediacy of cultural communion and
solitary meditation. It's a choice between the culture of media or the culture
of meditation.

At our second axial period, we turn on the spiral of history and
confront the archetypes of Lao Tzu and Confucius once again. We have a
choice between two types of global management—Taoist or Mandarin
Confucian. In the first axial age, humanity opted for violence and rigid order
and chose to articulate the geometrization of the world space. It moved with
all its power into the geometrical mentality with its hierarchical civilizations
run by warriors and priests. With writing as the dominant means of communication, perhaps there was not much chance of achieving the decentralized, anarchic vision of Lao Tzu. The question that confronts us now is

whether or not our new global means of communication can give us a second chance for something better. The world of NAFTA and GATT that energizes the gigantic transnational corporations also energizes the peasant insurrections of Chiapas, so we had better come up with something better pretty quick.

The Confucian model of society is one we all can understand because it was the hierarchical, geometrical model that took over civilization everywhere, from the nobles of China to the knights and priests of medieval Europe. When these two cultures—decentralized and centralized—conflicted in the West, they struggled over the destiny of Christendom. The Taoist vision was that of the Celtic church, a culture in which there were no cities only monasteries. The Roman church with its hierarchical papacy and college of cardinals triumphed, and the rest is the dreary history of the suppression of women, the Inquisition, and the witch burnings.

These battles have occurred over and over again in history, but what is fascinating for our time is that now we have a chance to understand what Lao Tzu was trying to put forth. Now we can have a completely contemporary understanding of chaos dynamics, the new sciences of complexity, and a world of process in which reversal is the movement of Tao. Or we can have a monocrop world in which gigantic corporations control the media, patent genes, produce new animals, and through medibusiness monopolize fertility and the technologies of human reproduction. In this world there would no longer be a feminine, in the sense of a womb and vulva that gives birth to the human; there would only be the laboratory in which the human body is an archaic biological content within a larger enveloping technological structure.

An understanding of decentralization in the Tao can only work if individuals live in a supersaturated solution in which they all have access to an interior yoga through which they can connect with the cosmos. If they have to get their culture from the conglomerates of the entertainment industry, then such global collectivization will generate a thousand different versions of the peasant revolts of Chiapas.

All the ancient texts that I have used to explore our modern world are once and future poems of possibility. Once they are seen all together in the imagination of the reader, then they can become a hypertext description of our contemporary evolution of consciousness. The project for our time is not one of simply moving from one elitist mathematical mentality into another—say from Newtonian mechanics to chaos dynamics—but of moving from one culture into another. This new culture involves the recovery of the feminine; the deconstruction of patriarchy; and the deconstruction of capital-intensive economies of scale run by military-athletic-entertainment-industrial complexes with their shadow economies of drugs, arms traffic, and crime. The Taoist project remains the same as it was in the first axial period, and we are again at a catastrophe bifurcation in which humanity has a clear choice to adopt the mandarinism of big science or the yogic anarchism of Lao Tzu. If we recover *anarché* as the original, then the anarchic form of empowerment should be one in which the unique individual, through the immediacy of his or her own breath, can connect to the universal Tao and the Zen of their original nature. Over two thousand years ago, humanity chose the militarist and hierarchical path at the fork in the road. Now here we are again, and I, of course, hope that the road not taken 2,000 years ago will be the road we take this time for this axial shift of the year 2000.

Notes

Foreword

1. Sri Aurobindo, *The Supramental Manifestation and Other Writings* (Pondicherry, India: Sri Aurobindo Trust, 1989).

2. Conversation with Marshall McLuhan at the Coach House, St. Michael's College, the University of Toronto, in the winter of 1972.

3. The first campus of the Lindisfarne Association was on eleven acres on the shore of Fishcove in Southampton, New York. This activity ran from 1973 to 1977. The second campus was the four buildings of the Holy Communion Church at the corners of Sixth Avenue and Twentieth Street in Manhattan. (This facility is now the discotheque Limelight.) This program of "Lindisfarne-in-Manhattan" lasted from 1976 to 1979. In 1979, the Lindisfarne Association moved to Crestone, Colorado, to establish a mountain retreat and a summer conference center. In the autumn of each year, a Lindisfarne symposium has been offered at the Cathedral of St. John the Divine in New York.

Chapter 1

1. James Joyce, *Finnegans Wake* (New York: Viking Compass, 1959), p. 52.

2. Marshall McLuhan, *Understanding Media: The Extensions of Man* (New York: McGraw Hill, 1965), p. 45.

3. See Marija Gimbutas, "The Sacred Script, Chapter 8 in *"The Civilization of the Goddess* (San Francisco: HarperCollins, 1991), pp. 307-323.

4. Because the word "matriarchy" suggests a centralized state ruled by a queen or matriarch, many scholars now prefer the more general term "matristic." A matristic society may have authority in the hands of a ruling mother, but military power is in the hands of the mother's brother. Matristic, as a term, allows for many different cultural balances between custom and government, authority and force.

5. Eörs Szathmary and John Maynard Smith, "The Major Evolutionary Transitions," *Nature*, March 16, 1995, p. 227.

6. Ken Wilber, *Sex, Ecology, Spirituality: The Spirit of Evolution* (Boston and London: Shambala, 1995).

7. The English edition is Jean Gebser, *The Ever-Present Origin*, trans. Noel Barstad with Algis Mickunas (Athens, Ohio: Ohio University Press, 1991). There is a German paperback selection, Jean Gebser, *Ausgewählte Texte* (München: Goldmann Verlag, 1987). Gebser's complete works are published in a boxed, eight-volume edition: Jean Gebser, *Gesamtausgabe* (Schaffhausen, Switzerland: Novalis Verlag, 1986).

Chapter 2

1. Lynn Margulis, *Symbiosis in Cell Evolution* (San Francisco: Freeman, 1980).

2. Freeman Dyson, *Origins of Life* (Cambridge University Press: 1985), pp. 11-16.

3. See Lynn Margulis and Ricardo Guerrero, "Two Plus Three Equal One: Individuals Emerge from Bacterial Communities," in William Irwin Thompson, ed., *GAIA 2: Emergence, the New Science of Becoming* (Hudson, NY: Lindisfarne Press, 1991), pp. 50-68

4. See William Irwin Thompson, ed., *GAIA, A Way of Knowing: Political Implications of the New Biology* (Great Barrington, MA: Lindisfarne Press, 1987).

5. Stuart A. Kauffman, *The Origins of Order: Self-Organization and Selection in Evolution* (New York, Oxford University Press, 1993). For the general reader there is now Stuart Kauffman, *At Home in the Universe: The Search for the Laws of Self Organization and Complexity* (NY: Oxford University Press, 1995).

6. See Francisco Varela, Evan Thompson, and Eleanor Rosch, *The Embodied Mind: Cognitive Science and Human Experience* (Cambridge, MA: MIT Press, 1991).

7. G. Spencer-Brown, *Laws of Form* (New York: E.P. Dutton, 1979), p. 1.

8. See Tito Serafini, Timothy E. Kennedy, et al., "The Netrins Define a Family of Axon Outgrowth," in *Cell*, 78, No. 3, (August 12, 1994), pp. 409-424.

9. See Roger Penrose, *Shadows of the Mind: A Search for the Missing Science of Consciousness* (New York: Oxford University Press, 1994), pp. 357-377.

10. Humberto Maturana, "Everything is Said by an Observer" in *Gaia, A Way of Knowing*, ed. William Irwin Thompson (Great Barrington, MA: Lindisfarne Press, 1987), pp. 65-82.

11. Penrose, *Shadows of the Mind*, p. 359.

12. See Lynn Margulis and Dorion Sagan, *What is Life?* (New York: Simon and Schuster, 1995).

13. H. R. Maturana and Francisco J. Varela, *Autopoiesis and Cognition: The Realization of the Living* (Boston, MA: Boston University Studies in the Philosophy of Science, Reidel, 1980). The first edition was published in Spanish in Santiago, Chile, in 1972.

14. See Sandra Blakeslee, "How the Brain Might Work: A New Theory of Consciousness," *The New York Times*, Tuesday, March 21, 1995, pp. B7-10.

15. Gerald Edelman, *The Remembered Present* (New York: Basic Books, 1990). See part 2, chapter 3.

16. Varela, Thompson, and Rosch, *Embodied Mind*.

17. See Edelman, *Remembered Present*; Daniel Dennett, *Consciousness Explained* (Boston, MA: Little, Brown, 1992).

18. Marcel Proust, *A La Recherche du Temps Perdu* (Paris: Robert Laffont, Editions Bouquins, 1987), p. 57. "The sight of the little madeleine had not recalled anything to me before I had tasted it."

19. Ibid., p. 59. ". . . the shapes—and that of the little shell of pastry, so richly sensual under its folds so severe and devout—"

20. Ibid., p. 57. "She sent to look for one of those short and plump cakes called little madeleines that seem to have been moulded in a scallop shell."

21. D. Michael Stoddart, *The Scented Ape: The Biology and Culture of Human Odour* (Cambridge University Press, 1990).

Chapter 3

1. See Ludwik Fleck, *The Genesis and Development of a Scientific Fact* (Chicago: University of Chicago Press, 1978).

2. See Plato, *The Last Days of Socrates, The Apology*, trans. Harold Tarrant (London: Penguin Classics, 1993), p. 55.

3. George Stade, *Partisan Review*, 1974, pp. 136-143.

4. For an explanation of the multidimensional 3-sphere, and to understand how a sphere is a cross-section of a 3-sphere, see Mark A. Peterson's "Dante and the 3-sphere," *American Journal of Physics*, 47 (12), Dec. 1979, pp. 1031-1035.

5. Misia Landau, *Narratives and Human Evolution* (New Haven, CT: Yale University Press, 1991), p. x.

6. Ibid., p. 6.

7. Richard Leakey and Roger Lewin, *Origins* (New York: E.P. Dutton, 1977), p. 126.

8. Ibid., p. 127.

9. Ibid., pp. 183-184. In their new book, *Origins Reconsidered* (New York: Doubleday, 1992), which appeared eight months after the talk on which this chapter is based was given, Leakey and Lewin indicate that they, too, have become sensitive to the imaginative quality of their scientific narratives. "This was the dominant fantasy—and I use the word advisedly—that held sway in anthropology for a long time, not least because it seemed to be a plausible account." See p. 68.

10. Elaine Morgan, *The Descent of Woman* (New York: Bantam, 1973).

11. Leakey and Lewin, *Origins*, p. 34.

12. Donald Johanson and Maitland Edey, *Lucy: The Beginnings of Humankind* (New York: Penguin Books, 1981), p. 310; see also Donald Johanson and James Shreeve, *Lucy's Child: The Discovery of a Human Ancestor* (New York: Viking, 1989).

13. Johanson and Edey, *Lucy*, p. 380.

14. In their subsequent volume, *Origins Reconsidered* (New York: Doubleday, 1992), Leakey and Lewin maintain the worldview expressed in *Origins:* "What can we say of the mental machinery of humans, three times greater than that in the large primates? Once again, there seems to be an obvious explanation: technology." See p. 249.

15. Dan Dennet, *Consciousness Explained* (Boston: Little, Brown, 1991), p. 101.

16. Fleck, *Genesis and Development.*

17. Admittedly, "Lucy" was a spectacular find, but the newest creation of Australopithecus ramidus is founded on a tooth. See T. D. White's cover article in *Nature,* September 22, 1994, pp. 306-313.

18. Johanson and Edey, *Lucy,* p. 289.

19. C. Owen Lovejoy, "The Origin of Man," *Science,* January 23, 1981, pp. 341-350.

20. Donna Harraway, *Primate Visions* (London: Routledge, 1989).

21. See Adrienne Zihlman's review of *The Last Ape: Pygmy Chimpanzee Behavior and Ecology* by Takayoshi Kano in *Nature,* October 29, 1992, p. 786.

22. Adrienne Zihlman, "Women as Shapers of Human Adaptation," in ed. Frances Dahlberg, *Woman the Gatherer* (New Haven, CT: Yale University Press, 1981), pp. 89, 93.

23. Donna Harraway, *Primate Visions.*

24. Evelyn Fox Keller, *A Feeling for the Organism* (New York: Freeman, 1982).

25. Mary Catherine Bateson, *Composing a Life* (New York: Morrow, 1991).

26. See Patricia Waugh, *Metafiction* (New York: Methuen, 1984), p. 22.

Chapter 4

1. Zecharia Sitchin, *The 12th Planet* (Santa Fe, NM: Bear and Co., 1991).

2. See Stanislav Grof, *Beyond the Brain: Birth, Death, and Transcendence in Psychotherapy* (Albany: State University Press of New York, 1985), p. 217.

3. Liam Hudson and Bernadine Jacot, *The Way Men Think: Intellect, Intimacy, and the Erotic Imagination* (New Haven, CT: Yale University Press, 1991).

4. William Irwin Thompson, *The American Replacement of Nature* (New York: Doubleday/Currency Books, 1991).

5. Sitchin, *12th Planet,* p.126.

6. Marija Gimbutas, *The Civilization of the Goddess* (San Francisco, CA: HarperCollins, 1991), p. 241.

7. Sitchin, *12th Planet,* p. 262.

8. Ibid., p. 126.

9. Mark Johnson and George Lakoff, *Metaphors We Live By* (Chicago, IL: University of Chicago Press, 1980).

10. Rudolf Steiner, *Cosmic Memory: Prehistory of Earth and Man* (West Nyack, NY: Steiner Publications, 1959), p. 128.

11. See Gerhard Wehr, *Rudolf Steiner: leben, erkenntnis, kulturimpuls* (München: Kösel Verlag, 1987), p. 143.

12. See Arthur Zajonc, *Catching the Light* (New York: Bantam, 1993).

13. Steiner, *Cosmic Memory*, p. 89.

14. Charles Darwin, *The Descent of Man and Selection in Relation to Sex* (Princeton, NJ: Princeton University Press, 1981), p. 207.

15. Rudolf Steiner, *An Outline of Occult Science* (Spring Valley, NY: Anthroposophic Press, 1972).

16. Sitchin, *12th Planet*, p. 130.

17. J. Alan Hobson, *The Dreaming Brain* (Cambridge, MA: Harvard University Press, 1988).

18. See Rudolf Steiner, *How to Know Higher Worlds*, trans. Christopher Bamford (Hudson, NY: Anthroposophic Press, 1994)

19. See Dante, *Paradiso*, canto 28.ll.70-73.

20. "Everything begins in mysticism and ends in politics." See Charles Peguy, Oeuvres en prose (Paris: Bibliotheque de la Pleiade, 1961), "Notre Jeunesse," p. 518.

Chapter 5

1. Marcel Griaule, *Conversations with Ogotemmeli: An Introduction to Dogon Religious Ideas* (London: Oxford University Press, 1965), p. 17.

2. For a fascinating discussion of the woman and artifacts of Dolni Vestonice, see Walter A. Fairserus, Jr, *The Threshold of Civilization: an Experiment in Prehistory* (New York: Scribners, 1975), pp. 85-112. See also Joan Halifax, *The Wounded Healer* (New York: Continuum Books, 1976).

3. Olga Soffer, Pamela Vandiver, Martin Oliva, and Ludik Seitl, "Case of the Exploding Figurines," *Archaeology*, January/February 1993, pp. 36-39.

4. Ibid.

5. For the February 1968 issue of *Scientific American*, the artist Jack Kunz did a drawing in which the symmetry of these Paleolithic figurines was understood as two cones joined at their base. The equator of the two cones thus corresponded with the pregnant stomach of the Great Mother. This drawing, which was not explained further in the text of the cover article, was presented as an accompaniment to Andre Leroi-Gourhan's essay "The Evolution of Paleolithic

Art." See also Andre Leroi-Gourhan, *Treasures of Prehistoric Art* (New York: Abrams, 1967).

6. See William J. Broad, "The Core of the Earth May be a Gigantic Crystal Made of Iron," *The New York Times*, Tuesday, April 4, 1995, p. B7.

7. Antonio de Nicolas, *Meditations through the Rg Veda* (Boulder and London: Shambala Books, 1978), p. 56. See also Ernest McClain, *The Myth of Invariance: The Origin of the Gods, Mathematics and Music from the Rg Veda to Plato* (New York, Nicholas Hays, 1976).

8. Marija Gimbutas, *The Civilization of the Goddess* (San Francisco, CA: HarperCollins, 1991), p. 262.

9. See Wendy Doniger O'Flaherty, *Women, Androgynes, and Other Mythical Beasts* (University of Chicago Press, 1980), p. 18.

10. See James Mellaart, *Earliest Civilizations of the Near East* (New York: McGraw Hill, 1965), p. 112. See also William Irwin Thompson, *The Time Falling Bodies Take to Light* (New York: St. Martin's Press, 1981, 1996), p. 148.

11. Gimbutas, *Civilization of the Goddess*, p. 249: "Best represented in Neolithic southeast Europe is 'The Sorrowful Ancient,' a figure sitting quietly on a chair with hands on knees or supporting his chin. Sculptures of this type representing the quiet, mature, or aged god, have been found in various cultural groups between the 7th and 4th millennia B.C.E. such a sculpture of a male god was found together with a female figurine in the Cernavoda cemetery of the Hamangia culture in Romania near the Black Sea. Both are seated, wearing masks. The male sits in a chair, elbows resting on his knees, head supported with his hands, reminiscent of Rodin's 'Thinker.' Since he was buried together with a female goddess who probably represented the old Earth Mother, we may guess that this sorrowful male god represents dying vegetation. (See figure 7-42.) This is analogous to the historically known flax-god Linos, who spends winter as a seed, is born in spring, dies in summer, and returns to earth again."

12. Anne Baring and Jules Cashford, *The Myth of the Goddess: Evolution of an Image* (New York: Viking/Penguin Books, 1991), pp. 155, 161.

Chapter 6

1. Marija Gimbutas, *The Civilization of the Goddess* (San Francisco, CA: HarperCollins, 1991), p. 308.

2. See Jacques Derrida, *Of Grammatology* (Baltimore: Johns Hopkins University Press, 1974), p. 56: "I would wish rather to suggest that the alleged derivativeness of writing, however real and massive, was possible only on one condition:

that the 'original,' 'natural,' etc. language had never existed, never been intact and untouched by writing, that it had always been a writing."

3. William Irwin Thompson, "Civilization and Alienation in Ancient Sumer," in *The Time Falling Bodies Take to Light: Mythology, Sexuality, and the Origins of Culture* (New York: St. Martin's Press, 1981), pp. 159-208.

4. Humberto Maturana and Francisco Varela, "The Natural Drift of Living Beings," in *The Tree of Knowledge: the Biological Roots of Human Understanding* (Boston, MA: New Science Library, Shambala, 1987), pp. 93-117.

5. Jean Gebser, *Everpresent Origin* (Columbus: Ohio State University Press, 1989).

6. Elaine Morgan, *The Descent of Woman* (New York: Bantam, 1973).

7. The translation of this poem is to be found in Diane Wolkstein and Samuel Noah Kramer, *Inanna: Queen of Heaven* (New York: HarperCollins, 1983).

8. Zecharia Sitchin, *The 12th Planet* (Santa Fe, NM: Bear and Co., 1989).

9. William Irwin Thompson, *Blue Jade from the Morning Star: An Essay and a Cycle of Poems about Quetzalcoatl* (Great Barrington, MA: Lindisfarne Press, 1983).

10. See *The Exaltation of Inanna*, William W. Hallo and J. A. Van Dijk, (New Haven, CT: Yale University Press, 1968).

11. Homer, *Iliad*, book 21.ll.64-135.

12. Miguel Asin Palacios, *Islam and the Divine Comedy* (London: Frank Cass and Co., 1968).

13. See George Thomson, *Aeschylus and Athens* (London: Lawrence and Wishart, 1973), pp. 155-163.

14. See R. T. Rundle Clark, *Myth and Symbol in Ancient Egypt* (London: Thames and Hudson, 1978), pp. 195-208.

15. Plato, *Timaeus and Critias*, trans. Desmond Lee (London: Penguin Books, 1977), p. 58.

16. Mark A. Peterson, "Dante and the 3-sphere," *American Journal of Physics*, 47, no. 12, December 1979, pp. 1031-1035.

17. Herman Melville, *Moby Dick* (New York: Modern Library, 1958; 1982), p. 236.

18. Donella H. Meadows, Dennis Meadows, Jørgens Randers, William Behren III, *The Limits to Growth: A Report of the Club of Rome's Project on the Predicament of Mankind* (New York: 1972).

19. William Irwin Thompson, *Imaginary Landscape: Making Worlds of Myth and Science* (New York: St. Martin's Press, 1989).

20. See N. Katherine Hayles review of Michael Joyce's *Of Two Minds: Hypertext Pedagogy and Poetics* (Ann Arbor, MI: University of Michigan Press, 1995) in *Scientific American* 274, no. 1, January 1996, pp. 104-105.

Chapter 7

1. See R. T. Rundle Clark, *Myth and Symbol in Ancient Egypt* (London: Thames and Hudson, 1978), pp. 195-208.

2. Stuart Kauffman, *At Home in the Universe* (New York: Oxford University Press, 1995).

3. William Blake, "The Human Abstract" in *The Portable Blake*, ed. Alfred Kazin (New York: Viking Press, 1946), p. 113.

4. W. B. Yeats, *The Collected Poems* (New York: Collier, Macmillan, 1989), p. 187.

5. David Ulansey, *The Mithraic Mysteries* (New York: Oxford University Press, 1989).

6. Martin Bernal, *Black Athena: The Afroasiatic Roots of Classical Civilization* (London: Free Association Books, 1987), p. 275.

7. William Irwin Thompson, *Imaginary Landscape: Making Worlds of Myth and Science* (New York: St. Martin's Press, 1989), pp. 3-42.

8. See Bernal, *Black Athena*, p. 117: "Plutarch spelled out in detail the general image of Egyptian religion that appears to have been common among cultivated Greeks, at least since the 4th century B.C.E. According to this, the zoolatry and apparent superstition of Egyptian religion were merely an allegorical veneer for the masses; the priests, and/or those who had been initiated, knew that in reality the zoolatry and fantastic myths concealed deep abstractions and a profound understanding of the universe."

9. Clysta Kinstler, *The Moon Under Her Feet* (San Francisco, CA: HarperCollins, 1991). See also Susan Haskins, *Mary Magdalen: Myth and Metaphor* (New York: Riverhead Books, 1993).

10. See *The Epic of Gilgamesh*, trans. Maureen Gallery Kovacs (Palo Alto, CA: Stanford University Press, 1989).

11. The story can be found in Samuel Noah Kramer, *The Sumerians, Their History, Culture, and Character* (University of Chicago Press, 1963), p. 198. My discussion can be found in *The Time Falling Bodies Take to Light: Mythology, Sexuality, and the Origins of Culture* (New York: St. Martin's Press, 1981, 1996), p. 181.

12. Kramer, *The Sumerians*, p. 203.

Chapter 8

1. *The Rig Veda*, trans. Wendy Doniger O'Flaherty (London: Penguin Classics, 1981), p. 245.

2. There is strong debate among scholars as to the identity of the plant called *soma* in the *Rig Veda*. Some scholars identify it as ephedra, others as the

mushroom Amrita muscaria. See Asko Parpola, *Deciphering the Indus Script* (New York: Cambridge University Press, 1994), p. 149 and Terence Mc-Kenna, *Food of the Gods* (New York: Bantam Books, 1992), pp. 97-121.

3. Sri Aurobindo, *The Secret of the Veda* (Pondicherry, India: Sri Aurobindo Trust, 1971); Antonio T. de Nicolas, *Meditations through the Rig Veda* (Boulder, CO, and London: Shambala Books, 1978); Doniger O'Flaherty, *Rig Veda*.

4. See George Gheverghese Jospeh, *The Crest of the Peacock: Non-European Roots of Mathematics* (London: I. B. Tauris, 1991), pp. 6, 108.

5. See Charles Penglase, *Greek Myths and Mesopotamia* (London: Routledge, 1994).

6. Michel Serres, *Les Origines de la géométrie* (Paris, Flammarion, 1993), p. 92.

7. Aurobindo, *Secret of the Veda*, p. 364.

8. de Nicolas, *Meditations*, p. 193.

9. See Heinrich Zimmer, *Myths and Symbols in Indian Art and Civilization* (Princeton, NJ: Princeton University Press, Bollingen Books, 1972). See also Asko Parpola, *Decyphering the Indus Script* (New York: Cambridge University Press, 1994), pp. 188, 250. Parpola argues that the Proto-Shiva's posture may go back to Sumerian seals in which a bull god is pictured seated with lower legs folded in toward the groin. Presumably, this icon of the bull is the theromorphic image of the god Enki. In the elaboration of this image from Sumer to Mohenjo Daro, the bull imagery is shifted to horns on the head, and the folded knees, with the hands extended to the knees in a yogic mudra, seem to indicate the development of some form of yogic practice. Needless to say, all interpretations of this iconography are highly speculative.

10. Ernest McClain, *The Myth of Invariance: The Origin of the Gods, Mathematics and Music from the Rig Veda to Plato* (New York: Nicholas Hays, 1976).

11. de Nicolas, *Meditations*, p. 63.

12. Shawn Eyer, "Psychedelic Effects and the Eleusinian Mysteries," in David Fielder, ed., *Alexandria: The Journal of the Western Cosmological Traditions*, vol. 2, (Grand Rapids, MI: Phanes Press, 1993), pp. 65-93.

13. Plato, *Timaeus and Critias*, trans. Desmond Lee (London: Penguin Classics, 1971), p. 29.

14. *The Book of Songs*, trans. Arthur Walley (Boston: Houghton Mifflin, 1937), pp. 283-284.

Chapter 9

1. "But if we allow things to take their course, we shall face the war of all against all at the end of the twentieth century." See *The End of the Millennium and Beyond*

from the Work of Rudolf Steiner, compiled and edited by Richard Seddon (London: Temple Lodge Publishing, 1993), p. 20.

2. See Rudolf Steiner, *The Spiritual Hierarchies and their Reflection in the Physical World* (Spring Valley, NY: Anthroposophic Press, 1970).

3. Michael Murphy, *The Future of the Body: Explorations into the Further Evolution of Human Nature* (Los Angeles, CA: Jeremy Tarcher, 1993).

4. See R. B. Onians, *The Origins of European Thought about the Body, the Mind, the Soul, the World, Time, and Fate* (New York: Cambridge University Press, 1951; 1988), p. 109.

Chapter 10

1. *The Ramayana of Valmiki*, three vols. trans. Robert Goldman and Sheldon Pollack, (Princeton, NJ: Princeton University Press, 1984), is a translation for scholars of comparative literature. The *Ramayana*, as retold by William Buck (Berkeley, CA: University of California Press, 1976) is for the general reader.

2. See Heinrich Zimmer, *Philosophies of India* (Princeton, NJ: Princeton University Press, Bollingen Series, 1951), p. 142.

3. Paul Davies, *Other Worlds: Space, Superspace, and the Quantum Universe* (New York: Touchstone Books, Simon and Schuster, 1980), p. 11.

4. There is a hardbound reissue of the Flash Gordon comics. See Alex Raymond, *Flash Gordon* vol. 1, *Mongo, the Planet of Doom* (Princeton, WI: Kitchen Sink Press, 1990).

5. *King René's Book of Love*, ed. F. Unterkircher (New York: George Braziller, 1980)

6. See Henri Corbin, *Spiritual Body and Celestial Earth: From Mazdean Iran to Shi'ite Iran* (Princeton, NJ: Princeton University Press, Bollingen Editions, 1977), pp. 73, 81: "The historian Tabari (ninth century) has preserved for us some of the earliest information available about a mysterious region, which his description enables us to identify as the 'Earth of the Emerald Cities.'. . . So, to become aware of it is to see the world of the Soul, to see all things as they are in the Earth of Hurqalya, the Earth of the emerald cities, it is the *visio smaragdina*, which is the surrection and the resurrection of the world of the Soul."

7. For an analysis of the cosmology of the fairy tale of *Rapunzel*, see my "Rapunzel: Cosmology Lost," chapter 1 in *Imaginary Landscape; Making Worlds of Myth and Science* (New York: St. Martin's Press, 1989), pp. 1-43.

8. D. Michael Stoddart, *The Scented Ape: The Biology and Culture of Human Odour* (New York: Cambridge University Press, 1990).

9. *The Divine Comedy of Dante Alighieri,* trans. Allen Mandelbaum (New York: Bantam Classics, 1984), p. 291.

10. T. S. Eliot, Collected Poems 1909-1962 (London: Faber and Faber, 1986), pp. 222-223.

Chapter 11

1. *The Song of God: Bhagavad Gita,* trans. Swami Prabhavananda and Christopher Isherwood; introduction by Aldous Huxley (New York: Mentor Books, New American Library, 1944; 1972).

2. Sri Aurobindo, *The Supramental Manifestation and Other Writings* (Pondicherry, India: Sri Aurobindo Ashram Trust, 1972).

3. *Rig Veda,* trans. Wendy Doniger O'Flaherty (London, Penguin Classics, 1981), verse 20, p. 78.

4. *The Upanishads,* trans. Juan Mascaro (London: Penguin Classics, London, 1965), p. 80.

5. *The Upanishads,* trans. Eknath Easwaran (Tomales, CA: Nilgiri Press, 1987), p. 111.

6. *The Upanishads,* trans. Juan Mascaro (London: Penguin Classics, 1965), p. 88.

7. *The Upanishads,* trans. Eknath Easwaran (Tomales, CA: Nilgiri Press, 1987), p. 60.

8. See Sri Aurobindo, *Essays on the Gita* (Pondicherry, India: Sri Aurobindo Ashram Trust, 1970), p. 279.

9. *Lao-Tzu, Te-Tao Ching,* trans. Robert G. Henricks (New York: Ballantine Books, 1989), p. 62. *Tao Te Ching* is the most familiar word order for the title, but in Robert G. Hendricks' new translation based on the recently discovered Ma-wang-tui texts, the word order is changed to *Te-Tao Ching.*

10. See Carlos Castaneda, *The Art of Dreaming* (New York: HarperCollins, 1993), p. 169.

Chapter 12

1. See Daniel Dennett, *Consciousness Explained* (Boston: Little, Brown, 1991); see also P. S. Churchland, *Neurophilosophy: Toward a Unified Science of Mind/Brain* (Cambridge, MA: MIT Press, A Bradford Book, 1986).

2. "Chreod" is a term introduced by the biologist C. H. Waddington; it means an evolutionary path of development, especially a new one that opens up after bifurcation. See Erich Jantsch, *The Self-Organizing Universe* (Oxford and New York: Pergamon Press, 1980), p. 57.

3. *The Book of Songs,* trans. Arthur Waley (Boston: Houghton Mifflin, 1937), pp. 283-284.

4. See *The Essential Confucius,* trans. Thomas Cleary (San Francisco, CA: HarperCollins, 1992), p. 11.

5. William Irwin Thompson, *Blue Jade from the Morning Star: An Essay and a Cycle of Poems on Quetzalcoatl* (Hudson, NY: Lindisfarne Press, 1983).

6. William Irwin Thompson, *The Imagination of an Insurrection: Dublin, Easter 1916* (New York: Oxford University Press, 1967; Hudson, NY: Lindisfarne Press, 1982).

7. Doris Lessing, *Briefing for a Descent into Hell* (London and New York: Viking, 1971).

8. Robert G. Henricks, *Te-Tao Ching,* p. 58.

9. Ibid., p. 80.

10. Ibid., p. 47.

11. Ibid.

12. Ibid.

13. Ibid., p. 36.

14. Stephen Mitchell, *Tao Te Ching: A New English Version* (New York: HarperCollins, 1992).

15. Ibid., p. 10.

16. Henricks, *Te-Tao Ching,* p. 62.

17. Mitchell, Tao Te Ching, p. 10.

18. See Keiji Nishitani, *Religion and Nothingness* (Berkeley, CA: University of California Press, 1982).

19. William Irwin Thompson, *Darkness and Scattered Light: Four Talks on the Future* (New York: Doubleday/Anchor Books, 1978).

INDEX

About the Author

WILLIAM IRWIN THOMPSON was born in Chicago in 1938, grew up in Los Angeles, graduated from Los Angeles High School and Pomona College, and took his doctorate at Cornell University in 1966. He has taught at Cornell, MIT, and York University in Toronto. His interdisciplinary interests are indicated by the fact that he has served as visiting professor of religion at Syracuse University, visiting professor of political science at the University of Hawaii at Manoa, and visiting professor of Celtic studies at the University of Toronto. Thompson became nationally known as an essayist due to his best-selling book on contemporary affairs, *At the Edge of History,* which was nominated for the National Book Award in 1972. He received the Oslo International Poetry Festival Award in 1986 for his novel *Islands Out of Time* and his book of poetry *Blue Jade from the Morning Star.* As a cultural historian and philosopher, he is most widely known for *The Time Falling Bodies Take to Light: Mythology, Sexuality and the Origins of Culture* and *Imaginary Landscape: Making Worlds of Myth and Science.* In 1972 Dr. Thompson founded the Lindisfarne Association, a fellowship of artists, scientists, and contemplatives that is headquartered at the Cathedral of St. John the Divine in New York City, but he also maintains a retreat and conference center in Crestone, Colorado.